I'M OFF THEN

Losing and Finding Myself
on the Camino de Santiago

Hape Kerkeling

Translated from the German by Shelley Frisch

Free Press

New York London Toronto Sydney

*f*P

Free Press
A Division of Simon & Schuster, Inc.
1230 Avenue of the Americas
New York, NY 10020

First Free Press trade paperback edition June 2009

FREE PRESS and colophon are trademarks of Simon & Schuster, Inc.

For information about special discounts for bulk purchases,
please contact Simon & Schuster Special Sales at 1-866-506-1949
or business@simonandschuster.com.

The Simon & Schuster Speakers Bureau can bring authors to your live event.
For more information or to book an event, contact the Simon & Schuster Speakers
Bureau at 1-866-248-3049 or visit our website at www.simonspeakers.com.

Map © Eckehard Radehose/Piper Verlag GmbH
All photographs courtesy of the author
Book design by Ellen R. Sasahara

Manufactured in the United States of America

1   3   5   7   9   10   8   6   4   2

Library of Congress Cataloging-in-Publication Data

Kerkeling, Hape.
[Ich bin dann mal weg. English]
I'm off then : losing and finding myself on the Camino de Santiago /
Hape Kerkeling ; translated from the German by Shelley Frisch.
p. cm.
Originally published: München : Malik, © 2006, with German title
Ich bin dann mal weg : meine Reise auf dem Jakobsweg.
1. Santiago de Compostela (Spain)—Description and travel. 2. Spain, Northern—
Description and travel. 3. Spain, Northern—History, Local. 4. Kerkeling,
Hape—Travel—Spain—Santiago de Compostela. 5. Germans—Travel—Spain—
Santiago de Compostela. 6. Kerkeling, Hape—Diaries. 7. Spiritual journals—
Spain—Santiago de Compostela. 8. Spiritual biography—Spain—Santiago
de Compostela. 9. Spiritual biography—Germany. I. Title.

DP402.S23K47 2009
914.6'11—dc22

2008051464

ISBN 978-1-4165-5387-8

*I dedicate this book
to my beloved grandma Bertha, and . . .*

Contents

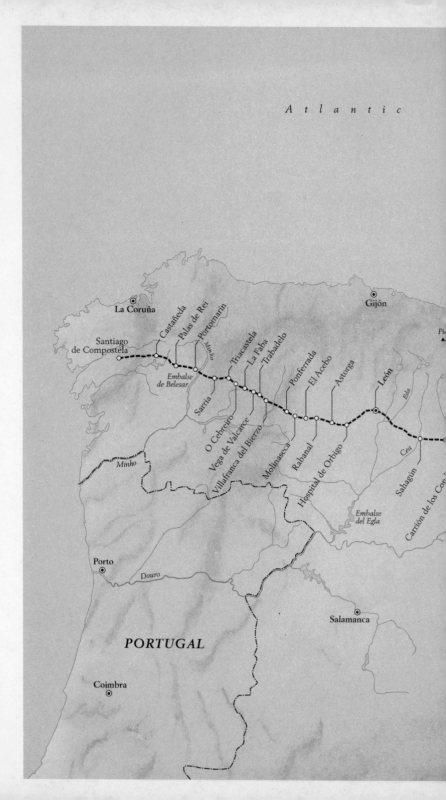

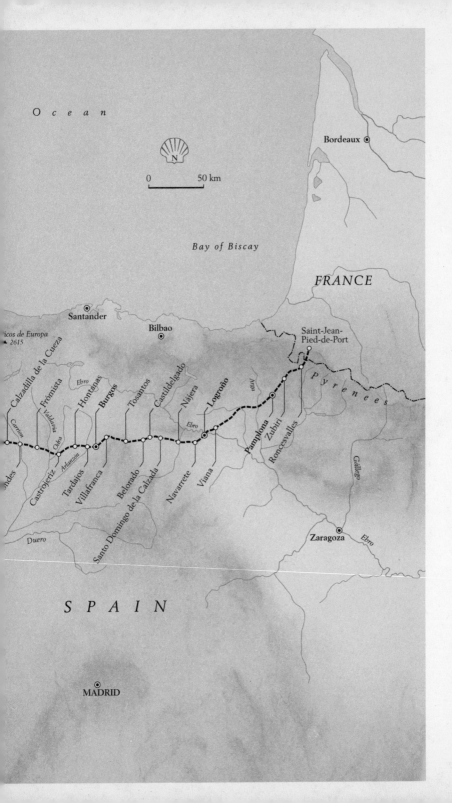

I'M OFF THEN

The Camino poses a single question to each of us: "Who are you?"

✠ ✠ ✠ ✠ ✠ ✠ ✠ ✠ ✠ ✠ ✠ ✠ ✠ ✠

June 9, 2001

Saint-Jean-Pied-de-Port

I'm off then!" I didn't tell my friends much more than that before I started out—just that I was going to hike through Spain. My friend Isabel had only this to say: "Have you lost your mind?"

I'd decided to go on a pilgrimage.

My grandma Bertha always knew something like this would happen: "If we don't watch out, our Hans Peter is going to fly the coop someday!"

I guess that's why she always fed me so well.

I could be lying on my favorite red couch right now, comfortably sipping a hot chocolate and savoring a luscious piece of cheesecake, but instead I'm shivering in some café at the foot of the Pyrenees in a tiny medieval town called Saint-Jean-Pied-de-Port. An enchanting postcard idyll, minus the sun.

Unable to make a complete break with civilization, I sit down right by the main road. Although I've never even heard of this place before, there seems to be an unbelievable amount of traffic whizzing down the road.

On the rickety bistro table lies my nearly blank diary, which seems to have as hearty an appetite as I. I've never felt the need to capture my life in words before—but since this morning I've had the urge to record every detail of my unfolding adventure in my little orange notebook.

So here begins my pilgrimage to Santiago de Compostela.

The journey will take me along the Camino Francés, one of the official European Cultural Routes. I'll be trekking over the Pyrenees, across the Basque country, the Navarre and Rioja regions, Castile and León, and Galicia, and after about five hundred miles I will stand right in front of the Cathedral of Santiago de Compostela. According to legend, this is the location of the grave of Saint James, the great missionary for the Iberian people.

Just thinking about the long trek makes me want to take a long nap.

And here's the amazing part: I'll hike it! The entire length. *I will hike*. I have to read that again to believe it. I won't be alone, of course: I'll be toting my twenty-four-and-a-quarter-pound, fire-engine red backpack. That way, if I keel over along the route—and there is a real chance of that happening—at least they can see me from the sky.

At home I don't even take the stairs to the second floor, yet sstarting tomorrow I'll have to cover between 12 and 18 miles a day to reach my destination in about 35 days. The couch potato takes to the road! It's a good thing none of my friends knows exactly what I'm up to. If I have to call the whole thing off by tomorrow afternoon it won't be too embarrassing.

This morning I took my first wary peek at the start of the official Camino de Santiago. Uphill from the city gate, on the other side of the turrets and walls of Saint-Jean, is the entrance to the Spanish Pyrenees, and the first segment of the Camino Francés is marked by a steep cobblestone path.

My route begins in Saint-Jean-Pied-de-Port.

I see a gentleman of around seventy who has difficulty walking, yet is evidently quite determined to undertake this pilgrim's marathon. I watch him in disbelief for a good five minutes until he slowly disappears into the morning fog.

My guidebook—I chose a wafer-thin one, since I'll have to lug it with me over the snowcapped peaks of the Pyrenees—says that for centuries, people have undertaken the journey to Saint James when they have no other way of going on with their lives—figuratively or literally.

Since I have just dealt with sudden hearing loss and surgery to remove my gallbladder—two ailments that I think are perfectly suited to a comedian—it's high time for me to readjust my own thinking. It's time for a pilgrimage.

I paid the price for ignoring the inner voice that had been hollering "TAKE A BREAK!" for months. When I forged ahead with my work, my body took revenge and shut down my hearing. An eerie experience! I was so furious at my own folly that my gallbladder exploded, and the next thing I knew, I was back in the emergency room with the symptoms of a heart attack.

I finally paid attention and drifted into the travel section of a well-stocked bookstore in Düsseldorf, looking for a suitable destination with one thought in mind: I've got to get away! It was high time for a time-out.

The first book I happened upon was Bert Teklenborg's *The Joy of the Camino de Santiago*.

What an outrageous title! Eating chocolate can be a joyful experience—or maybe drinking whiskey—but can a *route* bring you joy? Even so, I bought this presumptuously titled book. And devoured it in a single night.

The way to Santiago de Compostela is one of the three great Christian pilgrims' trails—the others are the Via Francigena from Canterbury to Rome and the pilgrimage to Jerusalem from anywhere.

According to legend, the Santiago trail was used by the Celts in pre-Christian times as a path of initiation. Veins of electromagnetic power in the earth and lines of energy (called ley lines) are said to be aligned with the Milky Way along the entire trail, all the way to Santiago de Compostela (which may mean "field of stars"), and even beyond that to Finisterre at the Atlantic coast in Spain (then considered "the end of the world"). The Catholic Church kindheartedly forgives the sins of people who complete a pilgrimage to Santiago. But that's not my primary incentive; I'm drawn to the idea that the pilgrimage will help me find my way to God and thus to myself. That's certainly worth a try.

I spend the next few days in a near trance, scoping out my itinerary and buying a backpack, a sleeping bag, a sleeping pad, and a pilgrim's passport, but once I'm on the flight to Bordeaux, I emerge from my daze and hear myself say out loud: "Am I nuts?"

It's been two decades since I first visited Bordeaux. Perhaps I've been in a bad mood ever since? I arrived there for the second time, only to discover that it is just as ugly and gray as it was when I visited at sixteen. I decided to spend the night at the Atlantic Hotel, a stately neoclassical building across the street from the train station. This is meant to be a consolation for the coming five weeks of dilapidated dormitories filled with snoring Americans and belching Frenchmen and no decent sanitary facilities.

It turns out I would have been better off in a dormitory. I was greeted with a friendly smile, shown to a drab little hole-in-the-wall, and quoted an exorbitant price. Instead of a window, the room offered harsh blue fluorescent lighting. I didn't complain, but I could feel my nonexistent gallbladder acting up!

If Bordeaux had been nicer, I might not have continued on.

But there is nothing to keep me in the room, since the last guy to sleep here had the good sense to empty out the minibar. So, out I go, back to the train station.

In the gigantic main hall, I marshal my high school French to issue this halfway decent sentence: "Mademoiselle, one ticket from Bordeaux to Saint-Jean-Pied-de-Port, one way, second class, please." The charming lady behind the counter beams at me.

"À quelle heure, monsieur?"—Ah, yes; at what time do I want to travel? That's a good question.

"At about seven A.M." I decide on the spot, which is how I do things.

"What was the name of that place again?"

Great! None of the maps I studied listed a train connection to Saint-Jean-Pied-de-Port—so there must not be one! I mumble the name again while she pores over enormous timetables from past centuries with a quizzical look on her face, then announces, to my complete surprise, "Monsieur, there is no such place in France."

I am as flummoxed as if she'd just claimed that God is dead.

"Waaait a minute," I say, "the place does exist, but maybe the railroad doesn't go there. Surely there's an interstate bus or something of that sort." The lady politely stands her ground: "No, no, the place does not exist. Believe me." Naturally I don't. There's a principle at stake here!

Who could seriously doubt the existence of Saint-Jean-Pied-de-Port?

After an excruciating couple of minutes, she discovers that the place exists after all! And there's even a convenient set of connections. I feel as if I'd wished this place into existence. Maybe I'll have the same good luck with God?

I leave the train station with my ticket in hand, wondering what I'm actually doing here, whether any of this makes sense. I look up, only to see a huge billboard advertising the latest technological gadget with the catchphrase "Do you know who you really are?" My answer is quick and clear-cut: *"Non, pas du tout!"*

I decide to give that some thought once I'm back in my hotel room. I leaf listlessly through a tattered city guide to Bordeaux to find out what I missed last week, and come across another version of the same ad campaign. This one declares, "Welcome to Reality!" Touché!

My room hasn't sprouted any windows since I left. My cell phone charger doesn't fit into the French outlet, and as a matter of fact I would like to go back home already—or should I go on? I opt for going on. Then I fall asleep.

When I arrive this morning, Saint-Jean is already packed with pilgrims of all ages and nationalities. The city evidently reaps a handsome profit from pilgrim business. Rustic walking sticks and scallop-shell pendants—the pilgrims' insignia—are sold on every corner. There are kitschy statues of saints, pilgrims' lunch platters—think French fries with meat course—and hiking guides in every conceivable modern language. I opt for a simple walking stick, although it seems much too long, much too heavy, and much too unwieldy.

On the way to the local pilgrims' hostel I turn over in my mind how to say *stamp* in French. In Spanish it's *sello*—that's written in the pilgrim's passport, the *credencial del peregrino*. In the entryway the word finally occurs to me: *Timbre! Naturellement*. I've got my sentence formulated in my head: *J'ai besoin d'un timbre*. Then I hear the elderly gentleman at the table speaking Oxford English while stamping the passports of a young four-man band from Idaho and assigning them beds one through four. It turns out he's British and spends his summer vacations here in this little office, endorsing pilgrims' passports and assigning bed numbers. And he seems to be enjoying it. My own enjoyment drains away the moment I realize that I am about to be allotted bed number five in an ice-cold, twenty-man dormitory, right next to the high-spirited country quartet from Idaho. Sure enough, they have their dreadfully heavy instruments in tow: three guitars and some sort of flute.

When my turn comes, the nice man asks me: "What's your profession, sir?" I mull over some possible responses, then loudly announce, "Artist!" The man looks at me dubiously. This question didn't come up with the musicians. The billboard said, "Do you know who you really are?" Evidently I don't. Though my little white sunhat does make me look like Elmer Fudd.

Before he gets around to assigning me bed number five, I flee with my first official stamp in hand, although I have yet to trek a single foot. To make up for the previous night in Bordeaux, I'm going to stay at the Hôtel des Pyrénées, the best address in town! The *albergue* (pilgrims' hostel) here is a bit too—shall we say—chummy for my liking. Sometimes it's pretty obvious that I'm from Düsseldorf, Germany's premier status-conscious city.

So the Catholic Church has it on record that I began my pilgrimage here. At the end, in Santiago, there'll be a fabulous gilt-edged certificate in Latin—the *compostela*—signed by Secretarius Capitularis. And all my sins, which, as the Catholic Church sees it, are many, will be forgiven. I feel as though I've stepped into a clergy sitcom.

The stamps are issued only in official *albergues,* churches, and monasteries along the route. If you travel by car or train, you can't get your hands on a pilgrim's certificate, because the places that issue stamps can be reached only by foot or bicycle. You can claim to be a true pilgrim only if you have completed at least the last 62 miles before you get to Santiago de Compostela on foot, or the last 124 miles by bicycle or horse. Most people choose to trek the entire Camino Francés, the traditional pilgrim's route. You don't have to be Catholic to get a pilgrim's passport. Though I was raised Catholic, I would describe myself as a kind of Buddhist with a Christian veneer, though that sounds more complicated than it is. You just have to embark on a spiritual quest—and that is what I am doing.

While I sit in the bistro sipping away at my café au lait, I consider my expectations for the pilgrimage. I could set off with this question in my head: Is there a God? Or a Yahweh, Shiva, Ganesha, Brahma, Zeus, Ram, Vishnu, Wotan, Manitu, Buddha, Allah, Krishna, Jehovah, etc.?

Since my earliest childhood I have devoted a good deal of thought to this question. As an eight-year-old, I enjoyed going to communion instruction, and I recall to this day exactly what was taught there. I felt the same way later in confession training, religious instruction, and confirmation classes. I never had to be coaxed into going (no one would have pushed me anyway, since I'm not from a strict Catholic family). My interest in all things religious ran high throughout my high school years.

While other children had to be dragged to mass kicking and screaming, I really enjoyed it, though I kept these feelings to myself. Of course, our parish priest's sermons didn't bowl me over, but they couldn't squelch my keen interest. There wasn't a single spiritual course that left me cold; every type of worldview fascinated me. For a while I seriously toyed with the idea of becoming a theologian or converting so I could become a Lutheran minister. As a child I hadn't the slightest doubt about the existence of God, but as a supposedly enlightened adult I have to consider the question again.

What will happen if at the end of the journey the answer comes back: No, sorry, He doesn't exist. There is NOTHING. Believe me, monsieur!

Could I live with that? With Nothingness? Wouldn't life on this funny little planet seem altogether pointless? I would imagine that everyone wants to find God . . . or at least know whether He does, or did, or will exist . . . or something.

Maybe the better question would be: Who is God?

Or where, or why?

This is how scientists go about it.

I'll start with a hypothesis: There is a God!

Since it would be pointless to fritter away my limited time seeking something that ultimately might not even be there, I'll go ahead and assert that it is! I just don't know where. And should there turn out to be a creator, He will be pleased as punch that I never doubted His, or Her, or Its existence.

In the worst-case scenario, the answer would be: "There is a God and at the same time there isn't one; you may not understand that, but once again, I'm sorry—those are the facts, monsieur!"

I could live with that, because it would be a kind of compromise. Some Hindus, by the way, subscribe to this seemingly illogical view.

So: Who is looking for God here, anyway?

I am! Hans Peter Wilhelm Kerkeling, thirty-six years old, Sagittarius, Taurus Ascendant, German, European, adoptive Rhinelander, Westphalian, artist, smoker, dragon (in the Chinese zodiac), swimmer, motorist, utilities customer, TV viewer, comedian, bicyclist, author, voter, fellow citizen, reader, listener, and monsieur.

Apparently I don't have a very clear idea of who I am, so how am I supposed to figure out who God is? Maybe I should start with the smaller of these questions: Who am I?

At first I had no interest in confronting that issue, but since I am being called upon to do so by a constant stream of advertisements, I guess I have no other choice. The first step will be to discover myself; then I'll take it from there. Maybe I'll get lucky, and discover God here. Of course, it's possible that he lives right around the corner from me in Germany, and I could have saved myself lots of trouble.

In my oxygen-deprived French cell last night, I got three hours of sleep, tops, which probably explains this muddled train of thought. Today I'll get to bed early; tomorrow I want to be up and out by 6 A.M.

If there is a God, at least He has a sense of humor. Here I am, sitting with a café au lait on a potato-shaped planet racing at top speed through the universe. Not that I notice it, but it's a fault.

Insight of the day: Start by figuring out who I am.

June 10, 2001

Roncesvalles

I'm so tired, I can barely hold my pen.

This morning I left my luxurious hotel shortly before seven and headed for Roncesvalles in Spain. Breakfast wasn't served until eight, so instead I treated myself to a power granola bar. (I brought along three of them from Germany for emergencies.) I filled my one-quart plastic water bottle only halfway, because every additional ounce makes my backpack heavier.

The second I set foot on the official pilgrims' route it starts pouring, and I quickly realize in this raw, damp air that my overpriced rain jacket lets in both the rain and the cold. Not a single other pilgrim is en route in this thick fog.

I was planning to get off to a nice slow start today so I could get used to the weight on my shoulders and my new walking stick. Fat chance! In this weather you walk to get somewhere as fast as you can. The stupid pilgrim's walking stick keeps getting tangled between my feet, and every time I stumble just the tiniest bit, my backpack pitches forward, making it hard for a pudgy guy like me to stay on his feet. You can't get a reasonable pace going like that. Either I race ahead breathlessly, or I move at a crawl.

In the rain and fog I can't tell whether the scenery here is beautiful or not. The photograph in my full-color guidebook shows an enchanting panorama of a snow-covered mountain, topped by a spectacular sunset. The book declares this region one of the most magical in Europe, one that I must see. I'm told there are lush grasslands under steep rock formations, and sheep who enjoy the unconditional right of way. Maybe so; I'll never know.

I stumble uphill on a three-hour trek, stoically working my way through the fog to the Pass of Roncesvalles at 3,468 feet, and trying to ignore my backpack, which clearly wants to pull me back downhill.

At some point, I just can't go on. It occurs to me that if I collapse now, even my bright red backpack, reflectors and all, would do me no good. In this mountain fog I would be unde-tectable from above. This exceedingly tragic thought sends me into gales of laughter, which is, after all, the best medicine. But laughing wears me out even more. Reason prevails, and I decide once and for all that I will resign myself humbly to my fate and stop walking.

I sit down on a rock at the side of the road in the pouring rain, to enjoy the invisible panorama of the Pyrenees. A glance to my right tells me that I will not make the steep ascent, since my wad-dling pace suggests that the peak is probably hours away. A glance to my left reveals that I won't be any more likely to handle the approximately three-hour descent. This qualifies as a bona fide emergency, entitling me to a granola bar and a cigarette. The sod-den tobacco has taken on a distinctive tang. The rain no longer bothers me; everything is dripping wet anyway—including, by the way, everything in my "guaranteed waterproof" backpack. I sit on the rock, puffing away and laughing.

I stayed there for maybe fifteen minutes when suddenly, out of nowhere, a small blue minivan appears to my left in the fog. I spring into action and force it to stop, gleefully waving my walking stick. It isn't about to get by me and my reflecting backpack on this narrow little street anyway. The creaky three-wheeled car comes to a stop. The passenger door is opened from the inside and a bright red farmer's face greets me with a friendly smile.

"So, where are you headed in this lousy weather?" a voice rings out to me in an earthy French dialect.

"Up!" I reply, because for the life of me, I can't remember the French word for "summit." With a hint of a welcoming gesture and a muttered word, the farmer invites me into the car. Without unbuckling my backpack, I sit down next to the man, who is wearing his workman's overalls and smoking a Gauloise. My nose is practically plastered to the windshield. Even so, I can't help but catch a whiff of the stench emanating from the back. I turn around, and a gigantic ram's head bleats at me from the cargo area. A second animal nonchalantly pushes his rear end up into my face. We're heading toward the summit at full tilt.

"How far is it until . . . up?" I ask, to break the ice.

"Not much farther. Two miles, maybe?" he replies, while offering me a dry cigarette, which I light quickly.

"Then I was nearly up already," I sigh in relief.

"Are you one of those pilgrims?"

"Yup!" I answer, and think: There. Now I've said it. I'm a pilgrim!

"Don't you think you're in over your head?" he asks skeptically.

Yes, I'm in over my head, but I'm not about to admit it in the presence of two stinking sheep.

As the car wends its way up the steep slope, the bleating ram retches and vomits a stream of green sputum. The driver shoots me a jovial grin, as though this were a major accomplishment. I can't come up with anything to say but "Isn't he feeling well?"

The farmer sets my mind at ease: "He always does that! He doesn't like to ride in the car."

My driver lets me out on a hillock leading to a muddy forest path. The rain is coming down in buckets, the fog is as thick as can be, and the temperature is bone-chilling. He turns toward me, jolly as ever, the cigarette butt dangling from his lip, and announces: "You're already past the hard part! The summit isn't far away." I give him a heartfelt thank-you, and can't resist wishing the ram a speedy recovery. The car zooms away, and through the fog I make out signposts. Taking a breather has restored my spirits, and I'm ready to resume my hike to Spain. When I reach for my water bottle I realize that it must have slipped out of my backpack while I was in the car. It's raining cats and dogs, and I'm dying of thirst.

After countless additional little ascents—the air is already getting a bit thinner up here so I stop more often—I make it to the famous Fontaine de Roland, right near the Spanish border, where Knight Roland fought so bravely but futilely against the Basques—or was it the Moors? This fountain is steeped in history: Charlemagne himself is said to have drunk from it, but I'm not in the mood for historical niceties—I'm dehydrated. Paraphrasing Brecht's famous saying: "First comes food, then morality," I'd say that first comes drinking, then culture. I hobble to the fountain as quickly as I can, my backpack perversely swaying up and down, tugging harder than ever at my poor shoulders. I press the stylish golden faucet of the Fontaine de Roland and—nothing! No water!

I try it several more times, but the fountain seems to have dried up.

Torrents of water to my left and torrents to my right, red, mucky, and muddy. But no water in the fountain.

My guidebook tells me that this is the only well with drinking water on this entire section of the trail, that Roland, the Paladin of Charlemagne, was brutally murdered by the Saracens—so it was the Saracens!—and that in bad weather it takes at least four and a half hours of hiking to get to my destination. Fantastic! Can't someone send over a plumber?

I hear the sound of a motor approaching, and out of the fog, from the mountain slope above the fountain, a small fire engine veers into sight.

This is no hallucination! Two jolly firemen get out and slowly make their way toward me through the fog. *"C'est tout bien, monsieur?"* It's nice of them to ask how I'm doing. My answer rolls right off my tongue (anyone this thirsty gains an instant command of French): "I'm fine, but the faucet of the historic Fontaine de Roland is broken. It's hard to believe, but there's no water in it!" In a split second they come up with a solution. They don't get the faucet to work, but in a joint show of strength, they yank a hose out of the ground behind the fountain and let me guzzle from it!

After I drink at least half a gallon, the guys repair the damage—neatly rendering the well unusable once again. I can't help asking, "What in heaven's name are you doing up here in this awful weather?"

The burlier of the two explains with a smile: "Nothing at all. My buddy started feeling sick. Yesterday we had a big firemen's ball in Saint-Jean-Pied-de-Port, and he drank too much. Now we have to stop every ten minutes so he can throw up." And as quickly as the firemen had appeared, they vanished behind the wall of fog.

Humans and animals seem to have a tough time of it here, but for some mysterious reason, it winds up working to my advantage. I am grateful for the second time today.

The firemen were French, which means that I am not yet in Spain, and that the greater part of my journey still lies before me. With a spring in my step, I forge ahead through the forest, which is getting denser by the moment, and over my imaginary mountains. The sky simply will not clear up.

After three additional hours of hiking I'm still facing a good two hours on my feet. The rain is coming down harder and I'm growing weaker. By now I've slowed down so much that within the past half hour a dozen pilgrims have passed me. Where did they all pop up from? For hours I haven't seen anyone, and now all these sodden people are trudging by without as much as a hello.

Finally the trail heads downhill again. My heart beats faster. The descent on the mud-and-scree path through the beech forest is at most eight inches wide but so steep that my left knee begins to throb and then to hurt like hell. Nothing helps. I groan out loud just to stand the pain, and I don't care if anyone hears it in this god-forsaken wilderness. I am feeling immensely sorry for myself.

Thank God I bought this walking stick during my little tourist spending spree. It did nothing but hold me down on the way up, but now it is holding me up on the way down. Without it I would not be able to brace myself on this mudslide. I can't wallow in self-pity. I dragged myself up here, and now I will drag myself right back down. Of course, I have to be in Roncesvalles before sundown or it'll be pitch black, and I'll be in trouble up to my eyeballs. Up to now I haven't come across any boundary stone, so I must still be in France. Spain, can't you meet me halfway?

The pain in my knee is getting unbearable, and I'm close to

tears! My clever little guidebook reassures me that every pilgrim will cry at least once along the way.

But not on my very first day! Another ten minutes and I'll keel over! And then—miracle of miracles—just when I'm about to burst into tears, I emerge from the thick woods into a clearing and see the monastery walls of Roncesvalles. I feel like a medieval leper accepting a crust of bread from a good Samaritan. I did it. Sixteen miles on foot across the Pyrenees! Not counting my little jaunt with the rams, that is.

The massive Roncesvalles Monastery, the official *albergue,* looks like Sleeping Beauty's castle, way too grand for this humble hamlet, and seemingly on the verge of swallowing it up. After a brief tour through the monastery, in which I stick to the ground floor, since I wouldn't be able to manage the height of a curb at this point, it turns out that the dormitories, the toilets, and the showers do not live up to the grandeur of the monastery's exterior. It is awfully cold and dirty. There are about fifty pilgrims camping in the main hall, with their soaking clothing spread out on the damp stone floor. Sweaty, bone tired, and contented people are draped in every corner. I must look just like them.

When I collect my first real pilgrim's stamp, the stocky Basque senior citizen behind the desk asks me, "How come you want only a pilgrim's stamp; don't you need a bed?"

My Spanish—in contrast to my French—is not too shabby. Spanish was one of my two major subjects in high school, and I still love this language. So I reply breezily: "No, I don't need a bed; I'll sleep at a hotel." The man rises up from his desk in a rage, bangs his fist on the table, and snaps at me: "What's wrong with you? That's some new trend! Pilgrims need to sleep in an *albergue* to share their experiences with other pilgrims; they can't isolate themselves in a hotel!"

I look at the bed monitor in disbelief and say, "I am happy to share my experiences, but I have no interest in sharing athlete's foot." Then I turn on my heel and go. Instead of sitting around griping, this guy might think about wiping down the shower stalls. I wouldn't sleep in this monastery if my life depended on it. I am enduring the hike of my life, and I can't add insult to injury by sleeping in this *refugio*. Admittedly, you can't expect too much from a place that bills itself as a "refuge."

I hobble to the other side of the village's only street.

I decide to stay at the little boarding house directly across from the monastery. It is reasonably priced and in good shape, and the warm room they give me has a bathtub. The first thing I do is spread out my wet belongings on the floor and over the heater. Every step I take sends terrible pains shooting through my knee. I hope I won't have to quit my journey after the very first segment. At least I don't feel the pain when I'm not moving. Unfortunately, the only free room is on the second floor. It takes me forever to get upstairs, and to be on the safe side I eat something downstairs as soon as I arrive (calamari in its own ink) so I won't have to climb down and up again. My (misguided) travel guide says there's a grocery store here—but there isn't. I have no idea how I'll be getting food and drink tomorrow. Even if there were a grocery store somewhere, there's a chance I won't be able to make it down to the ground floor in the morning.

So this is what I accomplished today. By hook or by crook, I made it up to a summit. My body, especially my lower limbs, is sending me another clear message. It has taken the form of a single dull pain. Maybe my quest for meaning is like my search for the summit in the fog—I may not be able to see anything, but it's there! I'm glad to be in Spain, and tomorrow I'll continue on. I feel as though I traveled through a foggy birth canal to get to Roncesvalles. It was a difficult birth, but mother and child are doing well, and the umbilical cord is cut! I will simply ignore my aching bones.

Insight of the day: Although I cannot see the summit through the fog, it's there!

June 11, 2001

Zubiri

This morning the pain in my knee is as good as gone. I can move my knee without wincing! After a decent breakfast in the restaurant I got going at about 10 A.M., heading toward Zubiri. According to my travel guide, which lists distances between stop-off points, today's trek will take only six and a half hours. The trail once again leads across the mountains.

Since my hiking boots are still soaking wet, I have no choice but to start walking in my flip-flops, which I originally bought on the advice of the very German tourist books I consulted, to avoid direct foot contact with unclean shower stalls. My heavy Canadian boots are hanging on my backpack to dry.

How would I have made out without my Canadian boots?

The beginning of the trail is easy and lovely to walk. On top of that, it now feels like the middle of the summer. I feel as though I'm getting yesterday's damp cold air out of my system. The trail takes me through beautiful forests full of butterflies and lizards, but unfortunately there is no sign of other pilgrims.

Finally I can also enjoy the mountain panorama, which resembles the Alps. Too bad the signposts marking the route are so unpredictable. You have to look carefully for the hand-painted yellow arrows on the street, on trees, fences, or stones in order to stay on the right trail. Even so, I get the feeling not that I'm flip-flopping my way to Santiago but that Santiago is striding right toward me!

The first Basque villages I pass through are absolutely beautiful. The Basque country as a whole strikes me as a huge enchanted forest. The houses are fanciful, and the architecture reminds me of Cochem on the Moselle River or the Timmendorf beach houses at the Baltic Sea. And I wonder how the ETA, the Basque nationalist separatist organization, can plant bombs in an enchanted forest.

On a beautiful path running along the mountain range, I see twelve enormous birds of prey circling right over me. I count them up several times, then hasten to capture this majestic sight with my disposable camera. I have no idea whether there are eagles in the Pyrenees, and my know-it-all travel guide doesn't mention them, but these birds certainly look like eagles. I hope they're not vultures that see me as rich pickings. It's a good thing that I don't know my ornithology; I decide to call them eagles.

After the third mountain path with an absolutely indescribable view, my knees begin to throb like crazy.

Once again I am plagued by doubts as to whether I, a pudgy

A touch of Moselle River and Baltic Sea in the Basque country

couch potato, am really in good enough shape to cross the Pyrenees in flip-flops. Hiking eighteen miles a day is no walk in the park. Tormented by recurrent throbbing and stabbing pains in my knee, I am forced to reduce my pace, particularly because I am shuffling along in flip-flops instead of in proper footwear. Every once in a while I pass by a Basque farmer staring at me in amusement, knowing full well that the beach is more than a hundred miles away.

I finally arrive in a town that consists of little more than a small bar. I treat myself to some food and drink and stash away some bananas, water, and bread for later.

Revived, I forge ahead, and even after a good half hour I am pleasantly surprised by the spring in my step. But something is missing. A sound! I'm not hearing the scraping of my walking stick on the asphalt. That's just great! I left it in the bar. I double back to get it. The downhill sections are impossible without my stick, and in some crazy way I actually miss that thing.

The scorching heat quickly saps my strength, and I'm about to throw in the towel—or should I say walking stick? What am I doing here? Am I out of my mind? If my doctor only knew how I am overdoing it! I should just take myself, flip-flops and all, down to the sea.

But I adjust my attitude and cheer myself on: "Keep on going, fatso! You're going to make it."

I come upon an old hamlet and find, in the shadow of a big tree, an enormous wooden cattle trough with a steady flow of fresh, ice-cold spring water splashing into it. I stick my head into the water and feel decades younger. After making sure that there is not a soul around, I slip out of my clothes and bathe my whole body. Good thing I have my flip-flops on! My swollen ankles and knees slowly shrink back to their normal size.

Naturally, two pilgrims pick this very moment to appear. They are German ladies of a certain age, who appear to be retired high school teachers. Luckily, their water bottles are filled to the top, which means that they can manage without my bathwater. They sit down next to me looking somewhat miffed, but eventually they can't help grinning at the sight of me. I act as though I'm French, and hop out of the trough with a *"Ça va?"* The ladies continue on, and I help myself to a cigarette and a banana with bread. I pour some of the bathing water into my water bottle, which I am now watching like a hawk. It is just as important as the walking stick.

It wouldn't be so bad to leave behind my backpack, which weighs a full twenty-four and a quarter pounds. Twenty-four and a quarter pounds! Not that there is very much in it. A pair

In this wooden cattle trough, the "Frenchman"
sat and called out "Ça va?" to the ladies.

of long pants (I have my shorts on today), two long-sleeved shirts, two T-shirts, my porous poncho, one sweater, two pairs of underwear and socks, one toiletries bag, a tube of portable laundry detergent—since every day is wash day for me—Band-Aids for blisters, antiseptic spray, suntan lotion, my cell phone, a camping mat, a sleeping bag, a towel, a rather thick book, my damp travel guide, and my power granola bar for emergencies. All that—plus my drinking water—adds up to twenty-four and a quarter pounds.

By now the sun has dried off my hiking boots, so I'm ready to go, and I set off for Puerto de Erro, which is 2,625 feet above sea level. For two and a half hours, the path runs uphill. My body is not amused, but the pain is bearable. Here and there I take a little break and smoke a cigarette.

My travel guide explicitly warns me about the steep descent to

Zubiri, which is not for novices. But the two German grandmas are ahead of me, and I figure that if they can make it, I can too. I'm an easygoing guy.

When I catch up to them just before the top of the pass, both are clutching their knees and groaning in pain. The two other people I meet in the course of the day, a middle-aged Dutch man and an athletic French woman, are also suffering from pains in their knees.

This descent, which continues for an additional two and a half hours, is sheer hiking hell! Who cares that the weather is nice? The trail down through the forest is devilishly difficult. I twist my ankle six times, the last time so badly that I'm certain I'll wind up with a torn ligament. The only way to make any forward movement without a walking stick would be to take a nosedive. I can hardly bend my knees. The torment is unending! I can't see the trail; everything looks like a ravine straight out of Karl May's *Travel Adventures in Kurdistan*. I start to doubt that this is still the official pilgrims' trail. It's more like a dried-up waterfall. I have no choice but to approach all this climbing as an exercise in meditation. Just concentrate on the next step, and don't look ahead, or else I'll fall flat on my face before I even get to the tough part.

These muddy paths are full of big rocks, so turning around while you're walking can be hair-raising. Don't do it! Keep your eyes straight ahead. If you do want to turn around, pause first.

I am really getting to know my body, and I have to say that it is cooperating quite nicely—in two regards. If I don't push it to the limit, but talk sweetly to it, the way I would to a sick horse, and don't rush it along, it'll do what I want. This is how I make it all the way to Zubiri, which you reach by crossing a medieval pilgrims' bridge over the Río Aga, popularly called *puente de la rabia* ("bridge of rabies").

When I arrive at the *albergue,* I am greeted by the sound of music from the Idaho four-man band. They are sitting on the playground right under a clothesline full of laundry. There would be no way to complete this trek on foot with small children. I won't bother to describe the *refugio;* suffice it to say that I will once again be spending the night in a nice little hotel. By happy coincidence, the innkeeper is the cousin of the pharmacist, so I'm able to get analgesic gel and elastic kneepads. As bad luck would have it, though, my room is up on the fourth floor, and there's no elevator. Someone is evidently out to get me. I hope I'll be able to continue on to Pamplona tomorrow.

Tonight I'm going to eat calamari in its own ink again. Sensational! It does look a bit revolting, but it seems to be the national dish here, even though the sea is several hundred miles away. I guess if I can hike in flip-flops, they can also eat squid.

Insight of the day: Don't turn around! Ever onward!

June 12, 2001

Pamplona

I could have predicted as much: nothing is working, least of all my legs. Last night the pain was so bad that it was practically impossible to fall asleep. At nine this morning I tried to get up, and both legs, from the soles of my feet right up to my thighs, were stiff and everything was hurting: soles, heels, knees, shins, muscles.

Somehow I managed to work my way down to the breakfast room on the ground floor. And yet, even though I'm stuffing my face more than I ever have in my life, when I caught my reflection in the hotel's hallway mirror, I saw less fat.

After breakfast, I tied up my heavy bundle and tackled the pilgrim's route, which offered me a wonderfully steep ascent. After less than a mile, I'd had it. My body needs to rest up for a day, ideally in Pamplona, which is eighteen miles down the road. There is no train or bus connection, so today this pilgrim becomes a hitchhiker.

This street is not meant for stray, limping pilgrims; it's extremely dangerous. I get into position with my thumb raised, but I am barely able to stay on my feet. Now and then, a car races by me like a bat out of hell. Most passengers greet my attempt to hitchhike with a shake of the head, or even by giving me the finger. The whole thing seems doomed to failure.

No sooner do I light a cigarette than a small white Peugeot appears in the distance. So I put out my thumb, take off my sunglasses, and smile! The last time I did this was in Greece, when I was eighteen. It didn't work then, either.

The car comes closer, and I make out at least three people and lots of luggage. So I put my thumb back down; not even my red backpack would have room there. And yet the car slows and comes to a stop. The license plate tells me they're French: a middle-aged gentleman and two middle-aged ladies.

"*Où est-ce que vous allez, monsieur?*" Where do you want to go?

"To Pamplona!" I say. Please, God, let them be driving to Pamplona!

"*Montez*—get in. You can't keep walking, the way you're feeling!" the man says, to my surprise, and I ask, "How do you know?"

The lady in the backseat smiles at me and says, "You're wearing a kneepad! When a pilgrim cannot continue on his own, he ought to be helped out, don't you think? That's a good deed."

I agree wholeheartedly, and squeeze into the backseat next to the lady, where it turns out my backpack and I fit quite nicely. The distinguished gentleman continues driving, while remarking to me, "You are lucky we are French!" I look at him in confusion and ask why, hoping that these otherwise pleasant retirees are not planning to make racist remarks. "You know," he continues, "the Spanish flatly refuse to pick up pilgrims. They feel that anyone who doesn't complete the route on his own steam doesn't complete it at all."

I immediately feel guilty about accepting the ride, but my foot hurts, and maybe some good will come out of our encounter.

The three of them are from Toulouse. We start a lively conversation. My French is not too shabby, as my travel companions confirm. The lady in the front seems rather dejected, so I ask, "Where are you headed?"

"To Logroño," she replies tersely. "It's also on the Camino."

The lady next to me, who is in her midfifties, is more approachable. "The husband of our friend in the front was hiking from Toulouse to Logroño on the Camino de Santiago, just like you. Shortly before he got to Logroño, he drank contaminated water from a fountain, and nearly died of it. We're going to visit him in the clinic, and we hope he'll be released in a week."

For a moment I'm speechless. The poor guy had walked nearly three hundred miles, and then this! I'm going to drink nothing but bottled mineral water.

It doesn't take us long to get to Pamplona. These folks are nice enough to drive me directly into the center of town, where I find a vacancy at a small hotel called San Nicolás. The window of my third floor room looks out onto a dark airshaft and has acoustics like a cathedral. Somewhere in the building a baby screams his guts out. But this concert sets me back only seventeen marks a night, so who am I to complain? It's clean, centrally located, and an official *albergue*.

Later I hobble off to have a look at the grand capital of the Navarre region, which was once a Roman settlement. Every step is painful, so I soon opt for a seated view on the Plaza del Castillo. I see several pilgrims limping through the town. The Camino seems to take its toll on everyone, but apparently young people and Germans suffer the most. Luckily, the famous Pamplona "running of the bulls" is still weeks away, so no one will be required to run for his life.

Since I haven't a clue what to do with myself on my free day, I just sit and watch people go by on the main square. And since you can virtually never go wrong by eating, I order a plate of tuna with pepper and some mineral water. As the tray comes closer, I catch a whiff of rancid oil. When the waiter puts the food down, I see that the meal looks even worse than its stench had led me to suspect. I am looking at the crowning achievement of rotten cuisine. The fish is gray, I can't find even a hint of pepper, and the oil—sure enough—is rancid. There's no need to take a taste to figure that out. I drink up the mineral water, jump to my feet, and scoot away as fast as I can. Without paying! I've never done that before. The pilgrim as pilferer. Of course, I drank up the bottle of water, compliments of the house. The last thing I need now is gastritis.

But I'm also grouchy today, which I attribute to the pains in my knee, and I feel a bit lonesome. Naturally, I could call home, but if I do that, I'm likely to end the journey on the spot.

Still, I have no desire whatsoever to join up with other pilgrims.

Pamplona, where I became a pilferer

Most of them appear to be ultra-Catholic, and so sure of themselves that I wonder why they're on a pilgrimage in the first place. They will be the same people when they complete their journey as they are now—assuming they make it all the way to Santiago.

I would like to steer clear of any preconceived notions and see what new experiences each new day brings. This journey ought to transform me in some way.

I keep running into the middle-aged Dutch fellow named John and the athletic French woman in her midforties. Both always call out a friendly hello and I can see that they would welcome a longer conversation, but I exchange just a few words with them. That's plenty, as far as I'm concerned, unless I sense some sort of connection—and I don't!

Since I've started my walk, I have the sense that my ingrained habits are loosening. Somewhat like my backpack, I am soaking things in. I used to push aside so many of my thoughts, figuring I had no time for them; now I let them take me where they will.

As I walk along the trail, I think about how my career took off and the lucky twists of fate that made my dream come true when I was between the ages of fifteen and twenty.

Even as a child, I just knew that one day I would be in the limelight. Things really got going in 1981. I said to myself, If you want to become a comedian, you need material! So I started jotting down notes.

Every once in a while I read some of my motley absurdities to friends, who invariably gave me quizzical looks and asked, "You think that's funny?" I kept on going, because I did think it was funny—very funny, in fact! My family was somewhat taken aback but let me do what I wanted.

One afternoon I was having coffee and cake at my godmother Anna's house, and she plunked down the latest issue of the German TV guide *Hör Zu* in front of me: "So you want to be on TV? They're doing a talent search." I saw a picture of Carolin Reiber and under it a straightforward question and an invitation: "Are you talented? Get in touch with me!"

Great, I figured. My friends may not laugh at my jokes, but those jokes are sure to knock Carolin Reiber's socks off. Although the contest deadline had been a week earlier, Aunt Anna set me straight: "So what? Just write a different date on the letter! Who reads postmarks anyway?" She was right.

I blathered my endless supply of sketches onto a cassette and, after listening to it several times, decided that it would be best to provide background material for the sketches. So I added another cassette with a five-minute explanation of each sketch.

Four weeks later, I received an invitation for two to a broadcast in Berlin.

"Congratulations! You and five other contestants have been selected from a pool of over six hundred submissions to display your talent in Berlin!" Great! It was probably my (unintentionally) comic supplementary cassette that had tipped the scales. My father and I set out for Berlin. I was sixteen at the time.

As bad luck would have it, our departure date coincided with my first day of school after summer vacation, and in theory I was supposed to be sitting in geography class, not at the airport in Düsseldorf. But my father thought this special occasion was worth missing the first two days of school for.

As we sat at the gate, waiting for our flight to be called, my high school principal—who was also my history teacher—sauntered in. The timing could not have been worse. Of course, he saw me right away and rushed toward me, stating the undeniable truth: "You're flying to Berlin on the first day of school!"

My father took over and spun an outlandish tale about an aunt who had died in Berlin. He pointed out how sad this whole thing was, and how attached to her I was. Herr Dr. Koch looked solemn and left us to our mourning.

Once we were in the airplane, I took my father to task, insisting that telling the truth would have worked out better. When I arrived in Berlin, I had to fasten a four-inch paper daisy to my lapel so I'd be recognized by the editor picking me up at the airport. It declared: "I read *Hör Zu!*" How else would the staff from *Hör Zu* recognize me? So, shortly before I got off the plane, I pinned on the giant daisy. When my principal said good-bye to me, he couldn't take his eyes off the flower.

The contest took place in a hall at the Berlin Convention Center, with lots of people walking by. The jury was a group of top-notch experts. When it was my turn to perform, I did exactly what I'd tried out at family celebrations and school functions, and before I knew it, my humor had struck a chord in the crowd of the convention visitors as well. At the end of the contest, I was declared a winner in every category.

After that I bombarded every broadcasting company with my cassettes. And one station actually got back to me. Lutz Hahn, who worked at Saarland Broadcasting, helped me revise and improve all the material for my sketches. Twenty-five scripts were taped in Saarbrücken and later broadcast, which brought me a big fat check. Working for Saarland Broadcasting was fun and fabulous. Without Lutz Hahn's support and personal encouragement, I never would have made it on the air.

The Saarland Broadcasting tapes caught the eye of West German Broadcasting, and Georg Bungster, the commissioning editor, invited me to participate in a little series of WGB radio productions. It's amazing that these two men stuck their necks out for me, a seventeen-year-old snot-nosed kid, and let me make recordings for them. I am eternally grateful! Then Dieter Pröttel invited me and "Nicki" (whose name was Doris at the time) to be on his "Talent Show." The only thing I got out of it was the realization that radio was not my medium—television is.

Shortly before my eighteenth birthday, I wrote more of my infamous letters, this time to Bavarian Broadcasting and all the other TV stations for which I had yet to work, enclosing an updated sample cassette.

I was showered with nasty rejections. Only a single reply, from Bavarian Broadcasting, was very polite. It was a kind and lengthy rejection letter. But because it was the last in a long series of rejections, I replied with an insolent note, whereupon this woman called me up at home to say: "You know, if you are really as talented as you say you are, then sign up for the first Passau Cabaret Contest. They'll be awarding a new prize for up-and-coming cabarettists, the Executioner's Hatchet! But first you need to learn some manners, and my only bit of advice is this: Never write anyone this kind of letter again."

Of course, I was already picturing myself onstage, shiny trophy in hand. So I got in touch with the people at the renowned jazz and cabaret stage there, the Scharfrichterhaus (Executioner's House). I may not be a political cabarettist, but my texts are certainly mordant.

The rejection letter from Passau was quick in coming. It contained a friendly explanation that this contest was for cabarettists from southern Germany, Austria, and Switzerland, and added that my material lacked conviction, since it was not political in nature.

Okay, so that was that! But my buddy Achim Hagemann and I had also applied to the West German Commercial Television Springboard Theater. We had developed a musical sketch revue for a theater in Cologne owned by West German Commercial Television.

The two of us again applied, with the help of a cassette that we recorded in my bedroom. Its questionable quality did not stop us from getting an invitation for an audition. We were in! Every seat in the little theater was filled. A hundred twenty German TV hopefuls stared tensely at the professionally floodlit stage. There were tap dancers, singers, comedians, ventriloquists, magicians, and acrobats.

The manager, Ingrid Jehn, struck a haughty pose and explained to us in her Saxon dialect, which sounded oddly pleasant coming from her, how very hard it would be to make it to the top, and that she was able to take only three of the more than one hundred people present, because the rest of the available spots had already gone to others—including to the future winner of the forthcoming contest for the coveted Executioner's Hatchet.

When she finished her impressive monologue, her glance fell on me: "You! You have such an honest face! You start." Achim and I made our way onto the stage. He headed for the piano, and I went to the microphone. Achim played for dear life, and I gave it all I had.

We weren't even nervous. The innocence of youth! The crowd of competitors watched impassively from their plush armchairs.

None of our songs swept them off their feet, and not one of our jokes brought a smile to their lips. Achim and I stayed cool, calm, and collected, but our act was a fiasco. I got my first little snicker when I tried desperately to yank the microphone out of the stand. I wanted to move around the stage and not just stand in place.

Never had I encountered a microphone stand like this. How would I get the microphone out? I tugged at it until it popped off and banged into my tooth. It split apart—not the mike, unfortunately, but my right incisor, a piece of which flew into the roaring crowd in a high arc.

We were rewarded with enthusiastic laughter and wild applause. Everything an artist could wish for. That bit with the tooth would be great in Vegas!

Horrified, I ran across the stage, shouting: "My toof, my toof, has anyone seen my toof?" They roared with laughter. Maybe I was a born comedian after all. The only one who helped me look was my man at the piano, Achim. The tooth was gone! Frau Jehn was clearly unimpressed by our outrageous presentation. She gave us a limp handshake and said coolly, "We'll be in touch with you!" My false tooth—a right incisor—is my permanent souvenir of this performance.

Three days before the contest in Passau, I got a telephone call from the director of the Scharfrichterhaus. One of the cabarettists, he explained, had fallen ill, thus opening up a space for one more participant. Thirteen contestants would be a good number for the cabaret. Might I still be interested? Only the hotel costs would be covered. I jumped at the chance, and pleaded with my grandma to help me. She gave me the money I would need for the trip and a hundred marks on top of that.

Thirteen participants prepared to take the stage in snow-covered Passau. I was number thirteen. The pub theater was filled to the rafters, and the air was redolent with smoke and wheat beer: a classic Bavarian scenario. This was my first time on a real stage.

In the jury sat the director of the theater, Sigrid Hardt, theater critic for the Munich newspaper *Abendzeitung;* the editor of Bavarian Broadcasting, who didn't think I had a shred of talent; Ottfried Fischer, who was already a big celebrity in Bavaria; and some other important guy.

Two Austrians in black turtleneck sweaters and corduroy slacks were up first. They had already been awarded several prizes, including the prestigious Salzburger Stier (Salzburg Bull). A torrent of verbal acrobatics poured out onto the stage. They were brilliant, inspired, and passionate. No doubt about it—I was looking at the winners! I didn't stand a chance, and there was no second place here!

The punch lines were razor sharp, and we were doubled over with laughter. It was so impressive that I started contemplating not going on at all. All that nice money from my grandma out the window! How would I ever explain to her that I didn't even get onstage? So I told myself: It's an honor just to be here!

The applause for the two guys from Salzburg was endless; they were already being celebrated as the winners. The eleven acts that followed ranged from middling to bumbling, from reasonably nice to catastrophic. The evening began to drag.

Number twelve was a Bavarian cleaning lady. None of her punch lines caught fire, and she kept losing her place in her monologue, which she hadn't quite memorized. The high spirits of the early evening had died off after the first act, and she put the final nail in the coffin. The audience gave her an icy reception, and she slunk off the stage without any applause. It was a tough break! My heart went out to her.

Then it was time for number thirteen. I was so nervous I could hardly breathe. The emcee introduced me apologetically: "He's young, so we figured, why not?"

I tried to act as though I'd gotten a glowing introduction and sat down with my manuscripts at my wobbly wooden table, clinging to it for dear life. After the first few words, I got the sense I was going strong! After the first couple of minutes, the audience was in stitches, and clapping like crazy. Ottfried Fischer was laughing so hard, and pounding his massive fists on the table, that I couldn't hear myself speak. My moment onstage was a triumph. The people were shouting, screaming, and going berserk—they even rose to their feet! I had survived my trial by fire, and even if I didn't win that day, I would surely come in second! Deep within me, I knew, of course, that the Austrians were better, more professional, more mature, and more polished. When I left the stage, the two Salzburg guys were standing there, and they patted me on the back: "Looks as though we're not getting the prize this time around! The people out there love you!"

The jury deliberated well into the night and obviously had a hard time reaching a consensus. Then Otto Fischer announced the result just before midnight: "We didn't have an easy time of it, but we think this prize ought to go to the artist who is likely to have the most promising career ahead of him." That would be the Austrians. Be a good loser, I thought to myself. Then I heard my name, and a flurry of flashbulbs followed. "How's your tooth?" a woman in the crowd called out.

Ingrid Jehn, who was there on behalf of West German Commercial Television Theater, offered her congratulations and told me that I could now look forward to a four-week guest stint at her theater. The editor of Bavarian Broadcasting recorded my performance for the radio, and it was on the air in Bavaria the following day. The gigantic silver hatchet was pressed into my hands, and the *Abendzeitung* ran a piece in the arts and entertainment section the next day called "The Angel with the Evil Eye."

When I came home with the hatchet, my grandma was proud and happy. From there things progressed quickly and steadily. For a whole month I performed at the Springboard Theater, fabulously moderated by Ingolf Lück, and my performances were broadcast in the early-evening hours, just before prime time. It was great.

And then I got a call from a lady at Bremen Broadcasting. "Hello, my name is Reckmeyer. Am I speaking to the 'angel with the evil eye'? Surely you know who I am."

Her name didn't ring a bell.

"You wrote me a letter a few years ago saying you wanted to take over the role of Dicki Hoppenstedt on the Loriot TV series."

How embarrassing! Sure enough, I had a vague memory of having cranked out a letter to that effect when I was twelve years old. A lady replied: "Unfortunately, we can't cast you at this time, but we've put your name into our files."

I still have that letter. I remember thinking, At least this rejection doesn't dash my hopes once and for all!

Frau Reckmeyer made me a nice offer.

"We'd like you to make an appearance on a Bremen TV show for teens."

Great! I was going to appear live on a local Bremen TV station! I said yes, and headed off to Bremen. On the train I read in a newspaper that it was not a local broadcast at all but a national program on Channel One, set to air at 8:15, and my fellow performers included the singers Nena and Depeche Mode. Uh-oh. My knees were knocking by the time I arrived at the TV station in Bremen.

Birgit Reckmeyer turned out to be a friendly and very cool individual. And she had tacked the letter I had written to her in 1977 in my childish scrawl to her office wall.

This was the first time I'd ever been inside a really big television studio, and I was overwhelmed. Mike Leckebusch, the emcee directing the broadcast, went to great lengths to initiate me, a pimply nineeen-year-old, into the world of TV.

I arrived on the dot of four that afternoon for my first rehearsal. In the studio some snotty American woman with two dancers was rehearsing a song she hoped to make a summer hit. This gum-chewing woman got on my nerves; she practiced and practiced and practiced, but kept getting the steps wrong. The dancers rolled their eyes while she interrupted the taping umpteen times with a silly giggle, which drastically cut into my own rehearsal time.

The woman called herself Madonna, and her song was "Holiday." I sat next to the stage and stared crossly at her performance. Then the director went ballistic and told her to get her act together. She kept pulling her chewing gum out of her mouth and sucking on it whenever she got nervous. It was clear she'd never amount to anything! I was looking forward to Nena, who was slated to rehearse right after me. When Madonna took a break, my rehearsal got squeezed in. In the meantime, Nena came into the studio with her band.

I was awestruck. Madonna, who was lounging around with her dancers in the seating area, was also quite impressed. Nena had just had a number one hit in the United States, and she peeked in at my rehearsal and grinned from ear to ear, which I decided to take as a good omen! The director liked what I'd done and thought I ought to stick to a single rehearsal or else my sketch might not seem quite as fresh in the broadcast. I was a pro, and tonight I'd show that Madonna what show business was all about.

I was nineteen, I was young, I was near broke, and the pay was pathetic.

My spot on the broadcast went over really well, and the very same evening Bremen Broadcasting offered me my own show on Channel One. At the age of nineteen, after I'd been plugging away for a mere four years, I'd reached the goal that had seemed so elusive. I couldn't believe my good luck.

When I got home the next day, my grandma had an even more amazing surprise in store for me.

"Who do you think called up this morning? You'll never guess!" My grandma tried to heighten the suspense: "You'll never get it in a million years!" She had me there. "It was Otto!" she revealed.

"Huh? Who's Otto?"

"Otto Waalkes—you know who that is! He wants to get together with you!"

Otto Waalkes was the king of German comedians. In a tizzy, I called up Rüssel Räckords in Hamburg and talked to a guy who worked with Otto. He invited me to a comedy festival at the LOGO club in Hamburg, organized by Otto.

"Otto saw you on TV, and now he'd like to see you perform live! Feel like coming?"

What kind of a question was that? They'd reserved a plane ticket to Hamburg, booked me a room at the Intercontinental Hotel, and were paying me on top of it.

The evening of the performance, the LOGO was full to bursting. My comedian counterparts in Hamburg, who were all older than I, took me for a country bumpkin and ignored me, but I peeked through the curtain and saw Otto sitting right there in the audience. My pulse started racing. The audience was on fire, because the first comedians had done a superb job onstage.

Appearing before an audience like this was sure to be fabulous, and I couldn't wait to do my act. Shortly before I went on, I asked a stagehand to position my table just to the right of the big column in the middle of the stage; otherwise the audience would not be able to see me perform.

When I went onstage, I was greeted with a big round of applause, but I panicked when I realized that my table was planted directly behind that monstrous column. Hardly anyone could get a good look at me, certainly not while I was sitting.

If that happened to me today, I would simply push the heavy table wherever I'd like it to be, throwing in a few choice comments. But back then the thought didn't even cross my mind. So I sat down, disappeared into the woodwork, and began. Two-thirds of the people couldn't see me at all, and even those who could see and hear me were not laughing. I was the party pooper of the evening. I was supposed to fill twenty minutes of programming, but after ten minutes without so much as a chuckle, people started to look at their watches. What was I to do? I decided to get to the end as quickly as I could. I left the stage to a polite ripple of applause, feeling like a beaten dog. The stagehand asked whether I was finished. He was referring to the act. I said yes, and meant myself.

The plan was for me to join Otto at his table. What an embarrassment! No way could I look him in the eye. Still, I couldn't back out. With my head held high, I strode through the audience to his table.

Otto was sitting there in high spirits, with five friends who all looked at me as though I'd just single-handedly blown our country's chance to win the World Cup. Otto jumped to his feet, took my arm, and pulled me toward the exit. His wife, Manou, followed. Once we were outside, he said hello and told me that he was happy to be meeting me at long last. Otto and Manou were easygoing and amiable. Otto, who was raring to go, suggested, "How about we get a drink somewhere? I'm glad we're out of that place. The atmosphere in there was just awful."

Great, and who was responsible for that? Me. I blurted out an apology of sorts, "I'm sorry that I made such a mess of my performance. I'm not sure why; somehow nothing seemed to go right today." Otto looked baffled. "What are you talking about?" His wife was just as incredulous.

"Well, you know—no one laughed. It could hardly have gone worse!"

Otto laughed. "So? That doesn't mean anything. I thought you were great!" His wife agreed: "That was really funny!"

My God, they were being nice, telling me a whopper of a white lie, probably figuring that if they didn't, I'd jump off the Hamburg TV tower within the half hour.

Otto saw that I really was unhappy about my performance, and explained to me, "The others got a rise out of the audience because what they do reminds them of what I do. The audience gets that, and laughs. Sometimes people even copy my routines. People haven't caught on to the kind of thing you do. It's unconventional. They'll have to get used to you. Give them time. In two years they'll be rolling in the aisles!" I didn't buy what he was saying, but I could see that the king of the German comedians was being sincere.

Otto was in top form, and we had a grand time that evening. Manou kindly invited me to spend the night at their house, then headed home.

"Feel like checking out some stars?" Otto asked. "Come on, we'll go stargazing. I love that!"

So he took me to a lavish celebrity birthday party. As luck would have it, I was even dressed for the occasion, in a ratty, pilling, black-and-white Norwegian sweater, tattered jeans, and blue-and-yellow jogging shoes that I had fished out of the garbage can twice when my grandma tried to get rid of them.

The party was in Hamburg's most elegant neighborhood, at a posh bar. At the entrance Otto ran into Frank Zander, and introduced me to him as the future of television.

Glamorous VIPs as far as the eye could see. Boney M. and Drafi Deutscher beat a path to Otto. Otto was eager to introduce me to the lead singer, Liz Mitchell. She evidently didn't share his enthusiasm, and scowled at me as though I were a banged-up old VW parked in a tow-away zone. Then Otto announced to everyone within earshot, in that inimitable way of his, "This is our up-and-coming comedian! You all just have to meet him!" Most of them were probably thinking, Such a card! What is Otto doing with this nobody in a shrunken Norwegian sweater?

Next I met Michael Holm, who chuckled when he saw me but hastened to excuse himself. I also met Nino de Angelo, Dagmar Berghoff, and countless others who would come to play an important role in my life over the coming years.

Otto gave me a formal presentation to high society. This was my opera ball, and I was not prepared for it in the least. The singer Isabel Varell was sitting in a corner with Carlo von Tiedemann. Isabel's career was just starting to take off. One year later, she became my best friend, and she has remained so to this day, although we weren't introduced at the party. Frank Zander looked me up and down and seemed to be considering the possibility that I might be witty. He and I could not have imagined back then that over the coming two years we would be spending most of our waking hours together in front of the camera.

Otto had to take press shots with the North German Broadcasting bigwigs, and he dragged me along to the photo op. He plunked me right next to NGB manager Werner Buttstädt, who gaped at me in confusion. "How did you get in here?"

I cheerily replied, "I'm a friend of Otto's."

"And what are you doing at my birthday party?" was his very justified retort.

"Oops! Happy birthday," I came out with, and the photographer snapped the shot. The next day, this photograph was splashed all over the Hamburg newspapers. Everyone's name was listed except mine. There I was, standing next to the host with a goofy grin on my face.

The odd thing is that nearly everyone I met at this party came to be an important part of my life. In retrospect I feel as though I was watching the preview for the motion picture of my life.

In Otto's house, I slept better than ever. At breakfast, he and Manou gave me sound advice for the future. You might say that on this evening, Otto laid the foundations for my career.

These are the kinds of thoughts that are now running through my head. Still, the story I'm trying to tell is not the story of my life but the story of the Camino de Santiago—though I've begun to think that in many respects, they're one and the same!

While I limp through the streets of Pamplona, I wonder if the Holy Scriptures on our planet are like complicated instruction manuals for a high-quality Japanese DVD player that have been poorly translated into German. Everything is explained nearly correctly, but a combination of mistranslations, complicated explanations, missing words, distortions in meaning, contradictions, and absurd formulations make it impossible to make the DVD player work—

and it won't work until I start experimenting for myself. Sometimes it's just a matter of resetting a single switch.

Hang in there—I'll find the switch.

Toward evening, I sit down in a classic tapas bar and enjoy a well-earned, exquisite appetizer plate. On the wall of the building across the street, I read a graffiti sign that asks in huge letters: "Why are you happy only in front of a camera?" Once again I get the feeling that the wall means me. It's certainly true that in front of the camera I am never as grumpy as I am here!

I hope that I'll be able to continue on tomorrow; my feet really hurt. By the end of this pilgrimage I will have invented as many different words for aching legs as the Eskimos have words for snow.

Insight of the day: Lighten up, sweetie!

June 13, 2001

Pamplona

There is no way I can continue on this morning. Everything still hurts. I have to stay in Pamplona one more day.

So I take a stroll through town, past the bullring, and buy a ticket to Viana on a bus scheduled to leave at 7:30 tomorrow morning. Given the battered condition of my legs, I have to opt out of at least the next three segments of the Camino, totaling thirty-seven miles. It has several mountain passes, and I think that if I try to tackle them, I may have to throw in the towel altogether. I also have to keep an eye on my schedule. I can't spend the next two years hobbling through Spain.

After Viana the road continues on somewhat flatter terrain for four days. I'll manage that.

Later today I'll go to the movies to unwind a bit.

Went to the movies!

Saw a comedy with Warren Beatty and Diane Keaton dubbed into Spanish. The first five minutes of a foreign language film are torture for me, but when I finally relax into it and stop straining to catch every word, I get what's going on. Even when I watch German movies, I often find that I'm not following all the words, or I can't figure out whole parts of the plot. I don't know whether to blame it on my stupidity or on the quality of the film.

We don't understand life right off the bat either. Maybe I ought to approach life the way I deal with a movie in Spanish—I just sit back and relax, and before I know it I catch on to the essentials. What good is it to pounce on one silly word, as I did today with the word *chapado* (have to look up the meaning of that one later), only to miss the rest of the actual scene?

The movie was a wonderful comedy about a marriage. I was howling with laughter! I love to laugh when I can't figure out what to do. A laughing fit that sends you flying across the room is sheer delight. Humor prevents a situation from escalating; it's a way of venting. A hearty laugh signals that you are not dangerous. If you try to coax a laugh or a smile out of someone, you're really asking: Are you a friend or a foe? Laughter has to come from the heart.

People who laugh at racist jokes laugh from the throat. Their laughter is literally stuck in their throats. They don't *open* up—they *clam* up. And so-called dirty jokes don't come from below the belt; they tend to be complex mental constructs. People who tell those kinds of jokes are typically repressed, and experience sex in their heads rather than in reality. They use jokes to overcome their inhibitions. I think this is why intellectuals may go for dirty jokes that have all the ingredients of real humor but are trite in content. When I attend mediocre Shakespeare productions, I often notice sophisticated academics roaring with laughter over the most vulgar jokes. They are so closed off that it takes an extraordinarily strong stimulus to coax a laugh out of them.

Good jokes have one thing in common: wisdom, coupled with a dose of love and fear. Humor has to come from the belly, and it should open and broaden your perspective. A belly laugh makes for sensual humor.

It's amazing what kinds of thoughts run through your head when you're walking through Spain all alone.

I keep comparing Spain to Italy. Italy always comes out ahead, especially because of its food. But when I'm in Italy, I think Germany is great. If I'm in Germany, I consider Spain wonderful. Why can't I be content with the situation I'm in? I guess I'm just a grouch. Well, now I'm here . . . and that's a good thing!

I also like to hear the language. I keep thinking about something a Spanish king once said:

> *In Italian you sing,*
> *In English you write,*
> *In German you negotiate,*
> *In French you love,*
> *And in Spanish you pray!*

Well, this trip seems to be turning into one long prayer for me. Tomorrow I'll continue by bus to Viana and then resume my journey on foot, on the Camino de Santiago.

Insight of the day: Laughter is the best medicine—end of story.

June 14, 2001
Viana and Logroño

At 7:30 this morning I took the bus to Viana. I'm now at the border of Navarre.

After two hours on the road, the bus arrived in Viana. The bright sunlight makes the flat landscape, punctuated by an occasional hill, look hazy and reddish or earth-colored rather than green. I am quite grumpy. I perk myself up with a *bocadillo* (a roll with ham and cheese), coffee, and lots of water, then I march off. The sunshine does nothing to lift my spirits. My bones are aching—I know I'm repeating myself, but the aches keep on coming—and I'm feeling guilty for having just skipped three segments, which is not actually a problem, because you are considered to have completed the pilgrimage along the Camino de Santiago if you can show that you've gone the final sixty-two miles to Santiago on foot or the final one hundred twenty-four miles by bicycle or on horseback. Your evidence is your pilgrim's passport.

But once you've decided to hike this Camino, it demands to be hiked on foot, and if you travel any other way, you feel uneasy. There are people who get hooked and repeat the pilgrimage year after year.

In the next village, two mischievous locals send me off in the wrong direction, and I spend several senseless miles trudging

cross-country over fields in the quest for yellow arrows that are
nowhere to be found, even though my travel guide assures me that
the trail is marked at frequent intervals with the *flecha amarilla*
(yellow arrow) and/or the familiar scallop symbol (*vieira*).

Two of the coveted signposts right next to each other

At some point I spy two *campesinos* across the field, farmers
who start gesticulating wildly and shouting something. I give them
a friendly wave, then realize that they are trying to tell me something. So I walk over to them and they promptly send me back in
the direction I just came from, onto the right path.

Later I realize that every time I deviate in the slightest from
the path, the butterflies disappear. No sooner am I back on the
pilgrims' trail than I see swarms of colorful butterflies. Maybe it
has something to do with the vegetation? Did the Spanish tourist
office engineer this? Twice I nearly miss the yellow arrows, but at
just the right moment, a butterfly settles on a faded yellow arrow
at the side of the trail and catches my eye. Don't worry—I am not

calling that a mystical miracle, but I *am* duly impressed. I forge ahead through the flat Rioja vineyards.

My handy travel guide says, "Shortly before you reach Logroño, you will find Doña Feliza, a Spanish woman as old as the hills, standing at the side of the road in front of her little hacienda. She will stamp your pilgrim's passport in exchange for a modest donation. Anyone who does not get a stamp here has not done a proper pilgrimage."

Sure enough, as I approach Logroño, I make out her crooked house on a hill. She is out in front, dressed in black, sitting on an old folding chair at her kitchen table, which she uses as a stamping station. She spots me from a distance and rises solemnly from her seat, stamp in hand.

The view over the orange-tinged city is breathtaking. Logroño's claim to fame is its status as the capital of La Rioja, the premier wine-growing region in Spain. Logroño might have remained a one-horse town forever if an eleventh-century ruler, King Sancho, had not had the clever idea of making the Camino de Santiago cross through the town. I begin to notice that the farther westward you go, the more the landscape opens up.

Evidently the old lady and her daughter, who has just come out of the house, are always up for a chat. Doña Feliza calls out an exuberant *"Buenos días, señor!"* When I tell her that I'm from Germany, she is eager to inform me that her grandson lives in Minden. Now, isn't that interesting?

I enter my name in her pilgrims' guest book, and take my leave with a *"Buen camino."* I also throw in the medieval pilgrims' battle cry: *"Ultreya!"* It means something like "ever onward!"

While I slowly make my way down the trail, two German men arrive at Doña Feliza's home to get their stamps. I'm still close enough to hear her pulling her German trump card out of her sleeve, namely her grandson in Minden, who of course makes quite an impression on the two Swabians as well. But they appear to be more impressed by my entry in the guest book. I hear one of them declare in a broad Swabian accent, "Unbelievable! Somebody signed the name Hape Kerkeling here! Funny guy!"

With my beard and my silly hat I think I barely resemble myself at this point. I love that! People think I'm someone or other, but not the person I am. Or am I no longer that person? I'd better watch out—the sun is blazing down on my head like crazy!

In my hat, sunglasses, and denim shirt,
I barely resemble myself.

Before I know it, I'm standing at my destination for today, Santa María de la Redonda, the majestic cathedral of Logroño. Its brilliant yellow façade makes it look like the finest marzipan, and I get the feeling it might melt away in the sweltering heat at any moment.

Once again, I am barely taking in the sacred structure before me. Instead I'm focusing on my decidedly secular physical state.

I'm on the verge of hypoglycemia! I find a nearby ice cream parlor—*heladería*—and fall into conversation with an equally hypoglycemic French man about my age. He started way back in Arles and has hiked every day for the past thirty days. He must have either a will of iron or an unshakable belief. Admirable.

After three and a half hours of trekking in the scorching sun through the flat Rioja vineyards, I call it a day. The important thing is to keep making progress. I am truly grateful for every reasonably pain-free step I take.

At the main square, which is bright yellow like the cathedral, I finally take a breather and enjoy a *café con leche* while writing my first postcards. Sitting at the next table and also busily writing postcards is an amusing little pilgrim with close-cropped red hair and granny glasses. Her bright red freckled skin tells me she has to be British. For the first time on my trip, I've found someone who might be truly interesting. I would very much like to strike up a conversation with this woman in the purple FC Barcelona T-shirt, who looks to be about my age.

I give her a series of big silly grins to signal my interest in striking up a friendly conversation. The first two times she responds with a friendly smile, but by the third time she has clearly come to regard my grinning as an idiotic come-on, and she turns her back to me. Boy, did she take that the wrong way. I certainly did not intend to come across as lascivious!

Back at the ramshackle balcony of my little hotel in the historic city center, I consider making a longer trek tomorrow. For now I'll wash my clothes, take a little stroll, and snap some photos.

Insight of the day: I have to stop looking so lascivious!

June 15, 2001

Navarrete and Nájera

The weather is unpredictable, but so far it's a great day for hiking. Finally I'm feeling plain old cheerful, if still a bit unsteady on my legs.

This morning I don't get going until 11:30. After a long phone call to a friend and a good hearty breakfast, I stride off to Navarrete. Today's segment starts along a highway service road on the dreary outskirts of Logroño. I'm not surprised to see no butterflies.

The traffic is fierce, and since there is no sidewalk, I do what every German is taught to do: I walk on the left side of the road, against the traffic. Suddenly a driver slams on the brakes and a car screeches to a halt beside me. A Spaniard in his sixties leaps out and snaps at me in German, "Wrong! What you're doing is wrong! Are you from Germany?"

"Yes," I admit.

"I thought so!" He laughs in triumph. Then, out of the blue, his finger traces the number *1952* on the hood of his dusty green Spanish car (an old SEAT) and he announces, "That's when I was in Germany, in Heidelberg. Horrible. All of Germany was razed to the ground. You weren't even born yet."

"Thank you for the compliment," I reply, and wonder what he's after. Traffic behind him has come to a standstill. He keeps talking. "Only Heidelberg remained intact, as if by miracle." In the course of a long monologue he tells me how wonderful the German women found him back then, how wonderful life is, how important it is for me to bear that in mind . . . and how I'm walking on the wrong side of the road. By the end of this street, he assures me, I'll be very grateful to him if I follow his advice and walk on the other side.

He gives me a hug and wishes me "*Buen camino*." I dutifully switch to the right side of the street, a bit befuddled but with a smile on my face and a feeling of having encountered an old friend. When I reach the end of the street, I truly am grateful to him. If I'd been pigheaded enough to stay on the left side, I would have found myself in the inane situation of needing to cross several lanes of the service road.

After about two hours of walking, I'm ready for my obligatory break. I'm at the Pantano de la Grajera, Logroño's reservoir. The town is behind me, and the landscape is getting wilder and somewhat hillier. While I sit on a bench and smoke a cigarette, I see an odd couple of elderly pilgrims walking along in slow motion, holding hands. The short, gaunt, dark-skinned woman, who looks about seventy, wheezes breathlessly in Portuguese, while he, an Anthony Quinn wannabe with a gigantic straw hat on his head and a big crucifix around his neck, tries to soothe her in Spanish. Both are wearing white Santiago T-shirts and leaning on sticks. They have no baggage. They are straight out of a surreal film.

Later I catch up to them again on the way up to Navarrete. I have rarely seen anything so poignant. The woman is having great difficulty managing the slight uphill climb. But she keeps moving along at a snail's pace, gasping for breath and clasping her friend's hand.

As I come closer, I see that the back of her blue peaked cap says, in Portuguese, *"O Senhor é meu pastor."* The Lord is my shepherd.

This faith in God is fabulous, and I forbid myself to mention or even to notice my aching feet—starting right now!

Today I finally stick to my schedule, and three hours later I arrive at the pilgrims' hostel in Navarrete. There I am greeted with a big hello by two beaming young Danish women who volunteer here. The hostel is a medieval building in the center of town and very inviting. It smells of fresh coffee and cherry cake. The Danish women and I settle in for coffee and conversation. I'm no longer feeling exhausted, and after this refreshing break I find I'm able to move on. I get my *credencial del peregrino* stamped, fill my water bottle, and make the daring decision to tack on an additional day's walking right now. By now the Spanish sun is once again blazing down. According to the travel guide, Nájera is a mere five hours away. I can manage that.

Just past Navarrete, the Camino takes you over gentle hills dotted with vineyards to the top of the Alto de San Antón pass. From here you can catch a first glimpse of the famous Valley of Cairns. If you squint, this assortment of rock piles begins to look like a fossilized penguin colony.

Pilgrims construct little cairns from the rocks lying all around the plain. Some hikers even bring colored stones with them. Though I'm alone here, looking around this infinite expanse, I get a sense of the vast numbers of people who have already made pilgrimages along this path. As far as the eye can see there are stones piled up by human hands. Each cairn is different. One suggests a wish, the next a call for help, and yet another, a thank-you. Every pilgrim takes the time to leave his signature in this dusty heat, after hours of walking.

Suddenly I feel a bond with all the people who have traveled this path, with their wishes, yearnings, dreams, and fears, and I am keenly conscious that I'm not, in fact, traveling alone. These little towers, thousands of them, extend all the way up to the hilltop. And each little structure seems to be saying: "I made it, and you'll make it too!"

At the end of the plain, I build my own little cairn. My disposable camera stays in my backpack, because I have decided not to take a picture. No one would understand an image like this. If I were to show people a photograph of this valley, they would likely say: "So, what's that compared to Niagara Falls?" This place imparts strength only to pilgrims, and this valley is special only to them.

Once I get to the hilltop, there is a majestic view of Nájera, the former residence of the Navarrese kings. And while I gaze down into the valley, I think: What I wouldn't give to be able to talk about this experience with a good friend, in my own language!

I stare into the magnificent sun-flooded valley, silent and amazed. The grayish-green town seems so close from up here, but it is still more than an hour away. I start off again. The shadeless gravel path down to Nájera is difficult to walk on, and my heavy steps send up clouds of dust.

Shortly before I reach Nájera, I find a gigantic thirteen- by thirteen-foot billboard in my path. It's smack in the middle of nowhere, like something in a Fellini film. Word must have gotten around that I look at all the advertisements. You never know what kind of interesting information they'll contain. But what made anyone think of setting up a huge advertisement on this gravel path?

I am quite astonished to read what's on it. A poem—in German!

Only in German! The anonymous poet describes his feelings during the pilgrimage. It goes something like this:

> *Why do I deal with the dry dust in my mouth,*
> *The mud on my aching feet,*
> *The lashing rain and the glaring sun on my skin?*
> *Because of the beautiful towns?*
> *Because of the churches?*
> *Because of the food?*
> *Because of the wine?*
> *No. Because I was summoned!*

While reading the poem, exhausted and covered in dust from top to bottom, I have no choice but to believe every word. These words are true in some mysterious way.

Being a pilgrim agrees with me. I am on top of the world!

Some abstruse amusement park clairvoyant once told me that I have "ancient Gypsy blood" that will never let me attain inner peace. I really like the idyllic little places I pass through where people live their lives in peace, working, having children, and celebrating holidays, but I couldn't live like them. I have to keep on going. I just have to hike, and the rest will fall into place.

The longer I hike, the less I think. Sometimes I just burst out laughing. When my feet start to hurt more than usual, a little tear might roll down my cheek, and I smoke the occasional cigarette . . . and somehow I manage to heal.

My travel guide calculates that the second leg of the journey, which I hiked today, ought to take five hours. I did it in three and a half hours. I seem to be finding my rhythm. All in all, I have walked roughly eighteen miles, but I again took too little water with me. I've got to drink more.

While I now sit here in the hotel and stare at the TV, I find out that today there was a major attack in Logroño by the ETA (Basque Homeland and Freedom) separatist group.

After doing my laundry, I take another stroll through the medieval town of Nájera and look at the relics in the village church. A thorn from Christ's crown of thorns.

Insight of the day: I really must hike and drink more!

June 17, 2001

Santo Domingo de la Calzada

I'm now up on the hill in Cirueña, enjoying a wonderful view of the bluish green valley. This morning I set off at nine o'clock. Magnificent weather for hiking—scattered clouds and a gentle wind—lured me onto the trail right after a good solid breakfast. My feet are also being quite cooperative.

Today I notice, for the first time, that the entire path is lined with red corn poppies, my favorite flowers.

And whom do I run into on my hike? The little red-haired British woman from Logroño. Her FC Barcelona T-shirt glows at me from a mile away. I guess she's also afraid that she'll keel over along the way and blend into the landscape. Her cropped red hair and her Harry Potter glasses further ensure that she will not go undetected in this endless expanse. The big safari hat on her shoulders gives her the aura of a future Nobel Prize winner. I'd love to know what she's doing here! She doesn't seem Catholic, and her look suggests an eccentric but witty entomologist. She seems far more interesting than the other pilgrims.

When I pass her on the trail, I say a quick hello, but I'm not overly friendly this time around; I do what I can to look as unlascivious as possible. I want to avoid confirming the false impression she already has of me—assuming she remembers me at all. She replies in a pleasant tone of voice, but once she recognizes me, her face falls. I whisk past her and see that her gaze is fixed stoically on the road ahead. She's looking rather jittery. I can well imagine the scenario playing out in her head. A man and a woman alone in the wilderness. That can mean only one thing. I seriously contemplate striking up a conversation with "Hello, I'm not after sex!"

I get the chance to do so in a saloon-like bar in the next one-horse town. How she managed to get here before me is a mystery to me, since I passed her on the road. My surprise is written all over my face. Flushed and exhausted, she's standing at the counter and enjoying her latte. The look she shoots me makes me feel like a convicted sex offender, but I sit down with her anyway, since there are no other customers. I force her into conversation by introducing myself: "Hi, my name is Hans Peter." She looks aghast: "What? You've got two names? Are you a member of a royal family?" Judging by her accent and her sense of humor, I now know for sure what had been no more than a wild guess before: She is British, and how! She reluctantly extends her hand. "Hi, I am Anne. Just Anne!" I make a feeble joke that her name sounds more royal than mine, but she probably chalks that up to another stupid pickup line. She gulps down her latte, doffs her big safari hat, and strides out of the saloon like the sheriff of Dawson City. I, the scoundrel, stay behind.

I'm going to spend tonight in a pilgrims' hostel. It's time I mingled and chatted with people, if not in German, then at least in English. I'm getting to be as much of a nuisance as a lonely old man in the corner grocery store.

After more than twelve miles of hiking, I'm not as wiped out as usual. I think I'm getting the hang of this routine. I have to make

Anne from
Liverpool, in her
FC Barcelona
T-shirt

sure not to walk too fast in the mornings, and I need to take breaks
and drink quite a bit. Now both my legs and my feet are cooperating quite nicely. I've already had a look at the trail I'll be on tomorrow. It shouldn't be too strenuous and ought to take about seven
and a half hours, which is one and a half hours longer than today.

I reach today's destination, Santo Domingo de la Calzada,
eager for a chat. I decide to spend the night at the pilgrims' hostel,
which is in a gloomy, rather forbidding sixteenth-century Cister-
cian monastery behind the town gate. It is a fortress, completely
self-contained.

A stern-looking nun assigns me bed number seven in an eight-bed room. When the nun brings me to the room, I find that the only other pilgrim there—occupying bed number six, diagonally across from me—is Anne. You can bet she's glad to see me! Her astonished look is so funny that I can hardly resist the urge to burst out laughing. I'm astounded that a convent permits males and females to sleep in the same room. I had not expected the Catholic Church to allow such radical progressiveness along a pilgrims' route. I do my best not to foist any more conversation on my bunkmate.

While I wordlessly make up my bed, which is directly beside the bathroom door, the nun guides an elderly woman and a good-looking young man to our room, and they head for beds four and five. Anne's face lights up and she greets the two newcomers like old friends. "Lori, Brad—how did you get here?" The American named Lori flings her arms around Anne. Then I'm introduced, there are handshakes all around, and Anne makes a point of mentioning that she can't picture me as a member of a royal family. The three of them know one another from the pilgrims' hostel in Saint-Jean.

We start chatting, and I learn that Brad and his mom are from Seattle. Anne is from Liverpool, which explains her funny accent.

All three of them were inspired to become pilgrims by reading Shirley MacLaine's *The Camino: A Journey of the Spirit.* By odd coincidence, that is the very book I brought along to read, in addition to my often-quoted travel guide. My roommates think Shirley MacLaine failed to convey a realistic sense of the trials and tribulations pilgrims face along the way. I'm happy to pick up where she left off. This route is indescribably strenuous!

The conversation is quite amiable. Anne even lets me in on

how she got to the saloon before I did. "I just wanted to see an old Western movie set, which is off the Camino! And that path is quite a shortcut!" So there are shortcuts! It's too bad my ultra-Catholic travel guide has been silent on the subject.

Lori wants to hear what Anne has been learning along the way. Anne freely admits that she has been attempting to separate herself from material objects; she realizes that she is too attached to them. Well, what do you know—we have something in common after all. The three of us nod in agreement at her wise insight. And while she's talking, I get the feeling she's also letting go of the idea that I want something from her.

I tell them that my backpack has come to seem like a luxury yacht. Let's be honest here! I need only a third of the things I'm carrying with me. And why did I let myself get talked into bringing this camping mat? I'm not sleeping outdoors or on the floor, and have no plans to do so. Tomorrow I'm going to give it away. It weighs more than a pound—twenty-five ounces, to be precise. That's quite a lot to haul for a full month. I paid a small fortune for this little number. The things you really need here are water, a couple of oranges, bananas, some bread, toilet paper, and the all-important walking stick. Clothing (aside from underwear, of course) can be washed every second day. The fact is that I brought far too many things.

When Lori and Brad head off to dinner, I stay behind in the room with Anne. She's now fiddling around with a yellow plastic tarp and clearly needs help: "Gosh, I don't know how to deal with this bloody tent!" I try to help her squeeze the partially assembled one-man tent into her backpack. "You sleep in a tent?" I ask, concerned about the chilly weather. "It's too cold outside, isn't it?" Anne grins. "Oh yes, it is! So once in a while I sleep in a *refugio*.

Although I rather like sleeping alone! You know what I mean?" Anne is slipping into her pajamas under a towel while saying this, so there's no point in inviting her to dinner. I call out: "See you later!" in a tone that cannot possibly convey the wrong impression.

I have to be back by ten at the latest, because that is when things shut down here and I need to be tucked in bed.

The cathedral square in Santo Domingo de la Calzada is straight out of a storybook. The Romanesque-Gothic cathedral is named after St. Dominic de la Calzada, who built a hospice for the poor in the Middle Ages and selflessly devoted himself to caring for them. Visitors to the church are greeted with an odd spectacle of a golden cage containing a live rooster and hen. A medieval legend explains this practice.

One day, back in the Middle Ages, a German couple on a pilgrimage with their son, Hugonell, came to the city. They spent the night in the local *refugio* and planned to continue on in the morning. During the night, however, some gold coins were stolen from the innkeeper, who accused the son of this crime. The legal situation being what it was back then, the innocent son was found guilty and condemned to death. The boy's distraught parents appealed to the bishop of Santo Domingo to pardon their son. The bishop, who was in the middle of enjoying a chicken dinner, denied their appeal with these words: "Your son is as guilty as this chicken is dead!" No sooner had the bishop spoken than the dead chicken flew from his plate. The boy's innocence was proved, and since that time a rooster and hen have always been kept in a golden cage in the cathedral.

One variant of a nice story. But I think a little skepticism may be warranted. Sheesh! Who would come up with a story like that—and who would believe it?

Even so, I pay a visit to the little feathered fellow. According to another legend, if the rooster begins to crow when you enter the cathedral, you will enjoy a successful pilgrimage to Santiago. Maybe a little superstition can't hurt. I enter the house of God expectantly, and . . . nothing! Silence!

When I leave the impressive cathedral again after a quick tour, I bump into the Spanish Anthony Quinn wannabe, the one wearing a sombrero and a crucifix so gigantic that he seems to have torn it off the wall of a Bavarian school. His gaunt dark-skinned companion is not there, which piques my curiosity, so I call out to him: *"Hola, como estas? Soy Hans Peter."*

He doesn't make an issue of my double name, and introduces himself as well, displaying his perfect etiquette by removing his hat. *"Soy Antonio, encantado!"* Bingo. Anthony Quinn. His name goes perfectly with his appearance. I come straight to the point: *"Nosotros nos hemos encontrado ayer, te recuerdas? Donde està tu compañera?"* (I remind him that we have met earlier, which is unnecessary, since he's already placed me, and I ask where his friend is.) Antonio begins to weep bitterly, throwing his arms around me and giving free rein to his emotions. I feel a bit awkward standing here with him, so I ask him to come with me to the little restaurant on the square.

I order him a glass of red wine, and he tells me his story in a voice choked with tears. He, Antonio, fifty-six years old, from Andalusia, has walked the Camino de Santiago every year for the past twenty-six years. And this year, just before reaching Viana— the part I skipped—he had a close encounter of the unbelievable kind. On a high mountain pass, he found a short dark-skinned woman lying on the ground, gasping for breath, dying. He resuscitated her and somehow managed to carry her unharmed to the nearest pilgrims' hostel. She is a Benedictine nun from São Paolo whose Mother Superior ordered her to walk the Camino de Santiago in Spain. This frail sixty-eight-year-old woman, who weighs just sixty-six pounds, was carrying a thirty-three-pound backpack on her thin shoulders.

For a reason that I have to admit I didn't catch—I've been pushing the limits of my Spanish—she was told to take this journey as a penance. Not only did she suffer from chronic asthma but somewhere along the line she injured her foot so severely that she wound up with blood poisoning. She was barely able to communicate in Spanish, and since she spoke the Brazilian variant of Portuguese, virtually no one understood her here.

Antonio walked alongside her for six days at a pace of less than a mile an hour—five times as long as it takes the average pilgrim—until he was finally able to persuade her to see a doctor. The doctor ordered her to return to Brazil immediately.

Shortly before her departure from her homeland, Antonio tells me in tears, the nun's order purchased a life insurance policy for her in an amount equivalent to one million euros. Antonio mournfully informs me that the Mother Superior does not want this nun to return alive. I can only hope that she gets home to Brazil in good shape. The story sounds implausible, but when I look at Antonio's weepy face, I cannot discount it altogether. I did see the woman with my own eyes, and she did seem more dead than alive.

The way he cared for her was truly touching. The two of them seemed so well coordinated, radiating harmony and even affection.

After the meal he asks me for some money, and I give him two thousand pesetas. He promises to repay me at some point along the way. I doubt I'll ever see him again.

The peal of the cathedral bells calls the people to mass, and I decide to give that foul fowl a second chance. The very second I enter the church, the rooster crows four times in succession at the top of its voice. There you go! I can't recall ever having witnessed such a peculiar mass. The rooster's racket rarely lets up, and the priest simply interrupts his sermon—a good ten times—when his voice cannot be heard above the animal's shrieks. The pilgrims are doubled over with laughter. That's entertainment!

After mass, I leave the church with a spring in my step, only to be hit with a shock at the door. Who should be standing there but Antonio? He is plastered and has his hand outstretched; he is begging for money. Of course, he recognizes me at once, and blushes deeply. To spare him any further embarrassment, I act as though I haven't seen him. It's plain to see that this man has been eking out his existence for twenty-six years by begging on the Camino de Santiago. He simply walks back and forth along the trail. And in all probability he's not the only pilgrim out for profit. You're allowed to spend only a single night in each *refugio,* but your stay is free, and the food, mediocre as it is, is gratis for the needy. Many *refugios* accept voluntary contributions to help cover the costs, but there are no set prices. When I return to my eight-bed room at nine o'clock, the remaining four beds are occupied as well. The atmosphere is starting to remind me of the 6 A.M. Lufthansa shuttle from Munich to Düsseldorf. People greet each other with a clipped hello and then promptly ignore everyone in the room.

A few pilgrims are still awake and reading, while others, such as Anne, are already snoring away. The seven adjacent dormitories are also fully occupied, and since there are no dividing doors, the noises of my invisible neighbors are also reverberating in the high-ceilinged old rooms. The same can be said for the toilet, which makes an earsplitting racket when flushed. I rummage around for my sleeping bag to spread it on the cot, in accordance with the rules. When I pull it out of my backpack, a mildewy smell comes wafting toward me. The sleeping bag is soaking wet! Damn! Back in Roncesvalles I forgot to spread this thing out to dry. I quickly shove it back in. But it stinks something awful! Anne is tossing and turning in her sleep, then she squeezes her eyes shut several times and wakes up. Since I'm in the middle of trying to yank my unnecessary mat out of the side pocket of my bundle to use as a blanket, for lack of a better option, I get an idea, and I whisper: "Anne, do you want my . . . uhh . . . ?" Damn—how do you say *Isomatte* in English? If I could only get it out of my backpack, I could simply show it to her. Instead, I say: "My iso-mat? You know what I mean?"

Anne is wide awake in a flash, scowling at me as though I'd just propositioned her, and she asks: "What? Your *what*?" I stammer out in Pidgin English: "My iso-la-tion-mat . . . or how do you call this?" I pull really hard, and the mat comes loose and flies out at me. Anne stares at me in disbelief. "Your Therm-a-Rest? You want to give me your Therm-a-Rest? Are you kidding?" She seems to think it's a ploy, so I say: "I don't need it anymore, and to be honest I never did!" Like a child eager to open her Christmas presents, she jumps out of her bed and plops down on mine.

"Oh, God, of course I want it! Now I can sleep in my tent every night and I don't have to be . . . here!" she adds, in disgust. That sounds convincing, so I give her my "Therm-a-Rest." Cradling the mat like a cuddly teddy bear, she snuggles up to it and beams with happiness. I decide to sleep with my clothes on, and am happy to shed twenty-five ounces from my backpack! Shortly before Anne slips back into her sleeping bag, she turns to me one last time and whispers: "Sorry, Hans Peter, for being so rude to you today . . . but you know . . . pilgrims aren't necessarily nice just because they're pilgrims. But *you* are nice!"

Mesón el Peregrino (in Santo Domingo de la Calzada)

I can't help thinking that my British bunkmate bears an uncanny resemblance to my British host mother in Eastbourne, where I learned English twenty-one years ago. Her name was also Anne, she was the same height, wore glasses, and had a similar accent and red hair. So I somehow feel that I know this Anne.

Anne has certainly given me the cold shoulder, but my British host mother was the same way at first. We eventually got to be good friends, and we stayed in touch for many years.

Just when I'm about to fall asleep at 10 o'clock, I'm awakened by brisk steps and a loud drone.

I can't believe it. The Mother Superior is walking through the dormitories and counting the pilgrims. She does not wish us a good night or say anything else—she's simply counting her sheep. I hope I can fall asleep again. It's damned loud and stuffy in this room. This eight-bed room is connected to seven additional dormitories, in which a total of fifty more people are sleeping. Any noise, any movement can be heard, and the closed windows cannot be darkened. Oh well—good night!

Insight of the day: Now and then it pays to have brought something along with you after all.

June 18, 2001

Santo Domingo de la Calzada

It's now four in the morning. I haven't gotten a wink of sleep. My whole body is itching; something's bitten me.

The counting nun now knows how many sheep she is tending, and she's probably fast asleep, but sheep number seven (yours truly) has not been able to doze off since the counting ritual. This room doesn't really get dark, and everything is grimy. It's hard to sleep in a room with seven strangers and to be privy to their sounds and smells as well as those of the fifty people in the adjacent rooms. To top it all off, my bed is right next to the door leading to the only bathroom. Ghastly. Every five minutes, someone or other goes to the bathroom, and the flushing never stops. Someone's snoring over there in the corner, the air in the room is stuffy, and people are talking in their sleep. My euphemistic travel guide calls this setup "intense human interaction in pilgrims' hostels."

I seem attuned to the etheric bodies of my bunkmates, their fears, wishes, and yearnings. These thoughts are not conducive to sleep, and I have no idea how to shield myself from this sea of humanity.

Pilgrims' hostels are meant for people who have no money. None at all. No vacation could be cheaper than this, because pilgrims' hostels cost nothing. My grandma always said: "If it costs nothing, it is nothing."

And it's gotten chilly! I must have been out of my mind to subject myself to a hostel like this. How old am I, anyway—fifteen? Even when I was in school, I hated sleeping in youth hostels. So why would it be fun twenty years later? All I can say is, I've got cabin fever! These bathrooms! And the rooms are cubicles. That's all I've got to say. I don't need to wade through other people's athlete's foot to find illumination! Though, incidentally, athlete's foot glows in the dark under infrared lamps.

This is no longer an option! I can treat myself to a hotel, so from now on I'm going to. I cannot and will not play the pauper. Hans Peter! Be yourself! This is not who you are.

Since sleep is out of the question anyway, I get up and pack my things. Anne is one of the few to be fast asleep, so I set off without a word. I figure it can't be long before the sun rises. I make my way through the convoluted labyrinth of the monastery passageways leading outside. A big door leads to a brick passage that lets you out of the monastery and into town. I stupidly let the door slam shut behind me. I am now stuck in an oppressive entrance tunnel that leads to the street through a big wooden gate on the one side, and to the monastery garden through a wrought-iron gate on the other. Both gates are bolted fast. Now I get what it means to be in a Spanish convent. The way back to the monastery is also blocked, since the entrance can be opened only from the inside. I am trapped between the walls of this monastery! Just a single step separates me from the street.

I'm hoping that this is an order of early risers. I've been lying awake for seven hours and am really beat. Damn!

I will never again sleep in a monastery or on the ground—unless I have to. I'd rather stay awake or sleep outdoors on a bench. I simply cannot believe that Shirley MacLaine spent even a single night in these *refugios*. And if she did, she's nuts. I want out of here! Directly across the street there's a wonderful inn, about fifteen feet from where I'm standing.

When, for heaven's sake, do they open the monastery gate around here? It's horrific, like being in jail! Let's see how long I'll be stuck in this twilight realm. I'm neither in nor out; I'm just trapped, this time literally. I spend two hours sitting around in the cold.

At the stroke of six, a nun comes to my rescue and opens the gate to freedom. I may not be passing Go and collecting $200 when I get out of this prison, but I'm heading straight to the inn across the street, where I collapse into a freshly made, clean, lily-white bed and slumber until eleven o'clock.

Since the sun is once again blazing down mercilessly from the cloudless sky when I awake, I decide to rest in Santo Domingo for a day. Forging ahead in this heat would be idiotic anyway, so I idle away the sweltering day in the shady streets of this Spanish dream town and feel sad that I was not able to say a proper good-bye to Anne.

When I catch sight of my reflection in a pharmacy window, I burst out laughing. Who in the world is that scrawny bearded creature with the greasy felt cap on his head? No wonder Anne was afraid of me! I've got to get a new hat, pronto!

I hunt for a suitable store and find one near the edge of town. A gregarious elderly gentleman, who appears to have spent his life poised behind the counter of his chaotic general store, waiting for me to arrive, chats with me about his shop, then gets down to the

In Santo Domingo de la Calzada

business of measuring my head. The unusually large size of my head does not leave us many options, and after weighing the few we have, we decide on a wide-brimmed green cotton hat.

Since I'm wearing the new hat, the gentleman asks me, "Might I perhaps hold on to your old hat, if you're not going to wear it anymore?" This strikes me as peculiar, but if it's so important to him, where's the harm? Still, I ask him what he wants to do with it.

The answer appears to embarrass him. His eyes are trained on the ceiling as he explains, "Well, you see, I collect cast-off pilgrims' hats!" I look up, and my jaw drops. There are a good one hundred old caps and hats hanging over me. He pulls out a felt pen and holds it out: "You have to sign it for me, and date it; otherwise it's worthless. Do you mind?" So I sign and date my yellowed baseball cap, and can't resist pointing out: "You may find this a bit conceited of me, but . . . this is not the first autograph I've given. In Germany I'm . . . something of a . . . well . . . star is perhaps the wrong word, but . . ."

He interrupts me: "You're famous? That's fantastic. That makes my collection even more valuable!" He submits my old hat to more detailed scrutiny, and is as happy as a little kid to see my legible signature! "I'm going to show this hat to every German, believe me. This cap is getting a place of honor!" And since he sells not only hats but also drugstore supplies, he gives me two tubes of Yves Rocher face cream. Just before I leave the shop, he remarks, "It's funny: Every German has a big head like you. You Germans think a lot. Too much!"

He's right. This cursed thinking machine tries to maintain constant control over our hearts and bellies. I try to tune out the impulses from my head. Click—I'm switching it off now. I'll go into the cathedral and wait until the rooster crows again. Stop! Don't think; today's the day for my heart!

During the mass in the cathedral I mimic all the other pilgrims, kissing a relic of St. Jerome. I have no idea what purpose that serves. Remember—no more thinking today.

Afterward, when I'm heading back through town to my hotel, invigorated by the mass, who should suddenly stop his car, loudly honking, right next to me? It is the man from the hat store, and he invites me to his house in the country to enjoy a bottle of Rioja. My heart rejoices—yes, I would really like to go. But this invitation is likely to result in a long night, and I want to get an early start tomorrow morning, so I reluctantly turn him down. The man is a little disappointed, but he drives on. I could kick myself

for not having accepted his invitation. Why di[...]
enjoyed it. I let my stupid head decide!

The nicest spot in town is the little ca[...]
down on the steps to the town hall acro[...]
watch the pigeons flutter in the dusk. My atte[...]
a one-legged snow-white pigeon whose handicap makes [...]
out from the others. It can't keep up. Its movements are gawky,
yet it seems quite dignified, to whatever extent this is possible for
a bird. Suitably impressed, I find a bakery on a side street, buy
some bread, and then approach it cautiously. All the other pigeons
are frightened away, but the white pigeon inches closer to me and
eventually eats out of my hand.

Afterward it coos, satiated. It understood that it had no choice
but to come up to me, a huge, dangerous-looking creature, if it
hoped to survive. Braving me was quite an achievement, and I
imagine its fellow pigeons are regarding it with admiration and
envy.

My travel guide tells me that this path is a path of illumination, but
I think it doesn't come with any guarantee of illumination, just as
taking a vacation doesn't guarantee relaxation. Fine: I won't set
my hopes too high, but illumination wouldn't be bad. Whatever
it is!

I picture illumination as a gate you have to pass through. You
needn't be afraid of stepping through the gate, but it shouldn't be
your heart's desire, either. Maybe the more detached you are as
you pass through the gate of illumination, the faster and simpler
the process.

You can't yearn for what lies behind the gate, nor can you be
repulsed by what lies before it. It ought to be a matter of indiffer-

Maybe detachment is the key to the joy of life? No expecta-
s, no apprehensions.

Expectations result in disappointment. Disappointment leads
to apprehension, and apprehension winds up where we started,
at expectation. Hope produces fear, fear produces hope. Detachment? Yup, this old guy is waxing philosophical today.

Wheat fields, as far as the eye can see

I've already taken a look at tomorrow's leg of the journey on a
trail map. It shouldn't be too exhausting and ought to take about
seven and a half hours.

Insight of the day: Open your heart and canoodle with the day!

June 21, 2001
Castildelgado

When I set off this morning at nine o'clock, it was already scorching hot, and in the distance the sun was lighting up the snowcapped Cantabrian Mountains. An almost holy vision!

During the several hours I spend hiking, the ground gets drier and drier, and way out in the distance I see vast golden wheat fields interspersed with green and orange hills. This landscape is exquisite.

In Grañon, I strike up a conversation with a pleasant, rather stocky Dutch woman in front of a bar that is about the size of the average German bathroom. As soon as we get inside, she orders two cold beers. She guzzles the first one on the spot and takes the second outside with her. Steering her pink parasol, which is flapping in the stifling wind, she comes over to me and plops down with a laugh on the rickety plastic bench.

"I know you!" she says to me in Dutch.

Since I am able to speak some Dutch, I reply in that language, "How? From TV?"

The flaxen-haired woman in her late fifties clad in strikingly bright colors finds this response hilarious, and she continues to

81

giggle as she gets two more beers from the microscopically small bar. After plunking herself down again, she says: "I'm Larissa, from Gouda! I know you from Saint-Jean-Pied-de-Port! Don't you remember?"

Is that so? Her name doesn't ring a bell. She points to her walking stick, grinning—and finally it dawns on me that we bought similar walking sticks in the same shop!

When we were paying for our walking sticks, we found it funny that even with the huge selection, we both opted for this style. Now she points proudly to her stick and remarks, "This one's good, isn't it? Don't you think so?" Sure enough, I've grown just as fond of our style of walking stick as she has. Ever onward!

Larissa treats me to a beer, and we start to talk. Her face clouds over as she tells me that this is her second journey on the Camino de Santiago. In 1999, she hiked this trail with her daughter Michelle. Michelle was then thirty-two, and had breast cancer. Mother and daughter were quite devout, and they were determined to walk the Camino. Since Michelle was unable to carry a backpack, they bought a donkey named Pierrot in southern France on the spur of the moment, then spent two weeks hiking to Santiago with the donkey as best they could, until Michelle was no longer able to endure the pain of her tumor and had to break off the journey. Larissa and her daughter headed home to the Netherlands, where Michelle died fourteen days later.

This year, Larissa began her trek at exactly the spot in southern France where Michelle stopped in 1999. Larissa is determined to make it to the end to honor her daughter's memory. She dedicates each day of hiking to one individual—and she has decided to devote tomorrow to me.

After our intense discussion, we both find it a bit difficult to go our separate ways, but Larissa is set on walking the Camino all alone, so she wants me to get a forty-five-minute head start before she continues down the road.

When I leave, she places her hand on my shoulder and says: "Each of us eventually gets to the point of bursting into tears somewhere along this route. The Camino does this to everyone. You just stand there and cry. You'll see!"

A few miles later the hiker is faced with these options: to go left, following the main road, or to turn right onto a back road, which continues straight for a couple of blocks, then forks. Once again, there are no yellow arrows to be seen, and I can't make heads or tails of my map, no matter which way I hold it.

Maybe I shouldn't have quit the Boy Scouts back in 1978 until I'd completed my training in cross-country orienteering, instead of leaving after just one week, simply because I couldn't see myself running around in that paramilitary uniform.

Now I'm in a fine pickle—smack in the middle of all this vegetation!

I don't want to walk along the main road, so I opt for the nature trail, then for the left fork. Three young Spaniards who are wandering around looking just as disoriented as I am trail along behind me. The dirt road ends in a gigantic grain field after a couple of miles.

The pilgrims who got lost here before us were nice enough to cut a swath in the field. I might as well give it a try. Evidently you wind up somewhere, because the tracks lead in only one direction, meaning that no one returned this way—not that this is necessarily a good sign! But it's hot, and no way am I hiking back an additional pointless eight miles. I follow the path for about a mile until it's impossible to go any farther, and I find myself in front of another gigantic field with seedlings—onions, I think.

The Spaniards, who are still traipsing behind me, are real wimps. They lose their faith in my ability as a travel guide and soon head back. There are no more footprints—not to mention a path—left by any previous pilgrims. I guess this is where pilgrims ascend to heaven without a trace! Except for yours truly. Since no one's getting beamed up today, I venture out onto the virgin field and eventually wind up in some nameless village. On the paved little main street I see the first yellow arrow again, and I am once again on the trail.

Walking along the main road, I learn from a tipsy *campesino* in the village pub, would have been wrong too. So I must have gotten lost even before the fork in the road. This whole way, I have not seen a single butterfly. It's crazy but whenever I veer off the Camino, I don't see a single butterfly. Maybe I should have paid more attention to that! It sounds absurd, but even most songbirds seem to stick to the trail. And never in my life have I seen so many storks. I find them nesting on every church cross along the trail, thereby establishing a peaceful coexistence between the symbols of death and birth. The cross—the symbol of death—is the only place high enough here to give the stork—the symbol of birth—a place to build a nest way up in the sky. Might this exemplify the close affinity and mutual dependence of the two fundamental experiences in human life?

Today is the first day of summer, and the heat is outrageous; it must be close to 100 degrees, and it stays that hot well into the early evening, when I reach today's destination, which is Castildelgado. I am in Castile; hurray!

Castildelgado is more than 2,500 feet high, in the middle of nowhere. I'm relieved to find a decent motel for truckers with good solid Spanish cooking. There is no pilgrims' hostel here. The town consists of five—how shall I put this?—houselike structures, a megalomaniacal village church that has the makings of a cathedral, the motel, an unsavory club with a pink neon sign, and two combine harvesters.

Every way I turn, I find nothing but bright yellow fields and the aforementioned snowcapped mountains in the distance, growing closer. And I'm finally in Castile, the place where the Spanish I learned in school is spoken.

When I look out of my motel window, I see an old woman unlocking the church. I just have to go down there and have a look at the only attraction in town. When I arrive at the church, the old lady is still there.

She is puzzled to see me, which makes me think that pilgrims virtually never find their way here. It's really a pity, because the few old people who live here are obliging and hospitable. She is delighted to learn that I want to have a look at the jewel of Castildelgado, and she comes inside with me. Our sightseeing tour is over when we get to the altar, so the woman asks me to take a seat in one of the wonderfully cool pews. Gradually, five other old ladies and an old man join us in the church.

The elderly woman begins to recite the rosary. The monotonous singsong is soothing, and the repeated lamentation gives me a sense of strength, security, and serenity. Once I catch on to the text, I join in the mantra and cannot help but think of Larissa.

After the prayer there's a brief get-together on the sandy square across from the motel, and the congregation tacitly accepts me into the group.

I find it quite comic that no one pegs me as a foreigner. They think I'm Spanish, which makes me seem less foreign even to myself. I guess these folks don't have very good hearing.

The longer I continue along this path, the more I feel at ease. This is not home to me, but it's no longer so very alien. Maybe I'm drawing nearer not only to Santiago but also to myself.

I would certainly be able to go on walking today, but I'm not up for any more experiments, and I want to take it easy on my legs. I haven't had a single blister on my feet, but my biorhythms are not promising for the next few days. In the motel I got a readout from one of those machines. No improvement for the next six days.

Insight of the day: I am at home within myself.

June 22, 2001

Belorado, Tosantos, and Villafranca

I've made ten miles! I'm now in Tosantos, sitting at the microscopic town square and taking my siesta while bathing my swollen red feet in the village fountain.

This morning I got going at seven o'clock. It's much better to hike early in the morning. The sun is not as intense, and you make much quicker progress than in the afternoon. Today I'll walk as far as Villafranca, another four and a half miles from here.

It has been an eventful day: Shortly before the descent to Belorado, a very athletic man from Madrid named Victor passes me by. He's a real head-turner! It's hard to figure out how old he is; he might be a little younger than I. The man is a professional pilgrim, not an amateur like me; his nimble walking and lightweight Nordic walking sticks give him away. We hike together for quite a while, then eat a mid-morning snack in a mill in the woods of Belorado. The guy has a great sense of humor; every second sentence ends with a surprising punch line, and we hit it off right away. He tells me that walking the Camino de Santiago is the fulfillment of his childhood dream.

While we're eating, we decide to continue walking together. Distracted by our animated conversation, we are able to cover two and a half miles in no time at all. It's nice to see that my Spanish is improving by the day. I understand just about everything Victor says; it just takes me a little while to express complex thoughts.

The village fountain—ideal for swollen red pilgrims' feet

But after a while, our conversation takes an unexpected turn. *Casado?* He wants to know whether I'm married. I leave the question unanswered. His inquiries get more and more personal, and a bit intrusive. He's too Madrid-macho to say what's on his mind. Still, I get the distinct feeling that Victor is not all that chaste; he's looking for adventure of the four-letter-word variety. But at this point in my pilgrimage, I don't have the slightest desire to descend into soft porn. Since Victor is stepping up both his flirtation and his walking pace, I realize that I can't keep up with him for long on either score.

He has calves like an ox, and is simply far more athletic than I. I get to thinking that if I zoom along for one more mile at this outrageous speed, I will twist my ankle on the bumpy trail and break a bone, so I stop and say, "Victor, *perdón*. I can't keep up with you. This is not my pace!" I get the feeling he's about to suggest we walk at a more leisurely pace, but I'm not offering him any encouragement, so he shakes my hand, bids me a cordial farewell, and promises to wait for me in Villafranca so we can have dinner together. Then he vanishes as quickly as he had appeared earlier. And I know for a fact that he will not be waiting for me in Villafranca, because you don't give a proud Spaniard the brush-off.

So here I am, still sitting on a bench and cooling my feet in the fountain that was donated to the little town by none other than Generalissimo Franco. The water in the fountain is oblivious to that fact; it is fresh and clean, not the kind of brown bilge one might expect from a dishonorable donor. I could do with an hour of sleep right about now. But I want to get to Villafranca.

So I trudge on very slowly through the heat.

During another brief stop at a country inn in Espinosa, I am joined by Stefano, a very stylish older gentleman in an exquisite designer hiking outfit. Without further ado, he begins to bend my ear as we walk along. Listening to his flawless Castilian, I think I hear a slight northern Italian accent coming through, so I ask: "*De donde eres?*" Where are you from? He challenges me to guess. So I say, "Well, you're not Swedish. You're from northern Italy, from Piedmont or Lombardy!" Stefano is clearly affronted that I solved the mystery so quickly, and admits that he is from Milan, which gives me the opportunity to switch to Italian, which I speak much better than Spanish.

Stefano is a sixty-three-year-old retired telecommunications engineer. He tells me that last year he made a pilgrimage along the Via Francigena from Piacenza to Rome. That route is nearly four hundred miles long, and I consider walking it next. He seems quite nice, but under the surface he's a bit arrogant. It seems to irk him that my Italian is better than my Spanish, and he tries to keep me in my place by speaking only in Spanish. I ask him several times to use his mother tongue, which he finally does, reluctantly—and I discover that he's far less interesting than I'd thought. In his mother tongue, he sprinkles his statements with clichés (though I will admit that they are brilliantly formulated; he is, after all, a communications engineer).

He keeps badgering me with questions, asking why I'm not married at my age, arguing that it's just not proper for a Catholic. Of course, it's not proper for a Catholic to be boastful and arrogant either. Then, out of the blue, he suggests that I consider marrying his daughter, who, like me, is single. What is going on with my fellow pilgrims today? It's like a marketplace here.

Even though it's nice to hear and speak Italian again for a little while, at some point I let Stefano, who is determined to beat his future son-in-law in today's segment of the rally, go on without me as well.

It doesn't take long to reach Villafranca, which is an enticing place from a distance, situated in a lush green valley with gleaming white houses and colorful roofs. But the closer you come, the more the gleam fades, and you find yourself smack in the middle of a gray, dead dump with all the charm of a Belgian industrial town. Villafranca is really nothing but a mirage with a melodious moniker.

It's too bad that I haven't struck up any friendships yet; friends would make it easier to face this dreariness. But my solitude doesn't get me down. In a way I even enjoy making fleeting acquaintances every day and gaining brief but deep insights into the lives of strangers.

I wonder whether I'll ever make it to Santiago on foot. The trail is still quite strenuous, and this experience is no walk in the park. And if I make it, will it change my life? Maybe I'm simply expecting too much! Probably I am. I just have to learn the art of indifference.

I get a room in a dilapidated but pleasant inn for truckers. An antique dealer would be thrilled with the turn-of-the-century furniture that is scattered randomly throughout the house, although it is in poor condition and keeps getting in your way. But everything is very clean. Am I turning into a caricature of a German? In front of the inn there's a gigantic empty gravel parking lot, in the middle of which is the only telephone booth in town.

I have no choice but to head for the *refugio* to get my pilgrim's stamp. This one, like the others, is a sheer horror. Of course, there's no sign of Victor anywhere. I figure he kept on walking and chose not to subject himself to this grimy, tiled dormitory with all the charm of a rendering factory. Thirty cots are squeezed into four hundred square feet, in a building that only a wrecking ball could improve, directly on the main road. The windowpanes are already smashed and patched up with cardboard. For centuries, this has been a place where pilgrims gathered their strength for the arduous, perilous hike through the Demanda Mountains, in whose forests robbers and bandits lurked.

Perhaps one reason I avoid the *refugios* is that I really do care where I sleep. I muse about my modern-day hang-ups. Should I be more flexible about this? For me, sleep is the only recovery time from the daily stress. I'm sticking to my resolution; I will not subject myself to pilgrims' hostels—especially not in this oppressive heat!

The place is full to bursting. My future father-in-law, Stefano, is strutting about as though it were the presidential suite in the Hotel Principe di Savoy in Milan. He comes running up to me, his face beaming.

"It's terrible here, isn't it?" he asks me in Spanish, and for simplicity's sake I reply in the same language. "*Orible*! Why are you sleeping here? I'm sleeping over at the inn near the entrance to the village for fifteen marks, and it's *grandioso*!" He wants to see my room right away, and to dispel any notion he may have of moving in with me, I say, "They still have a couple of vacant rooms!" The pompous Milanese skinflint was probably hoping for a night free of charge, and figuring he could find out whether I snore, so that he could pass the word along to my future fiancée. I find that I can't hold back, and I start bragging to Stefano that there are three toilets, two showers, and a lounge with a color TV just for me!

Why do all the other pilgrims—many of whom are not poor—subject themselves to these horrible lodgings, in which you're often treated rudely to boot? I don't get it. Twelve-mile hikes in scorching heat on dusty asphalt and rough terrain are quite enough of a challenge for me. Here and there, of course, there are also very nice hostels run by terrific people, such as the *refugio* in Navarrete, where you're more than willing to overlook a few faults.

An elderly American couple, clearly well-to-do, has decided to slum it tonight. A homeless shelter would be luxurious by comparison. Privacy is invaded to an extreme in this *refugio*. One toilet and one shower for thirty people! People have known for centuries that this kind of crowding is not healthy. Even so, wealthy people like to play the pauper here, and during the day, chubby American women in their fifties torture themselves with twenty-five-mile treks under the blazing sun. How guilt-ridden must they be feeling to undertake all this? Or do they simply want to look forward to getting home at the end? For now, all I'm looking forward to is my nice room.

Stefano walks me back to my hotel, and is thrilled by what he sees. He hasn't set eyes on anything like this for weeks: simple clean rooms with sanitary facilities in accordance with European Union hygienic regulations. Still, without saying why, he opts to remain in the *refugio*. I'm speechless. But we'll have dinner together here. I simply don't feel like being alone again this evening, and I've met far worse than Stefano along the way. The bar downstairs offers a hearty meal, which makes Stefano and me long for Italian cuisine. After dinner, Stefano wants to call his unmarried daughter at home, but he—a telecommunications expert—has no cell phone, so I walk with him to the telephone booth in the parking lot in front of the hotel. I picture him telling his daughter that I slurp my food and that she should forget about me.

However, the telephone booth has vanished behind twenty parked trucks, which have now taken over the lot. Their running motors make an earsplitting racket. Stefano and I eventually find the telephone booth in the mass of vehicles. But an audible phone call is out of the question. Stefano, former expert in telecommunication, runs from one truck driver to the next and asks them to keep it down.

The truck drivers have no intention of turning off their motors, since nearly all of them are transporting freight that will rot in the beastly heat without refrigeration. Unable to call my intended and fuming with anger, Stefano tramps back to his cot.

My nice little hotel has turned into an acoustic nightmare. I'll have to stuff wet toilet paper into my ears tonight. It is only now that I realize I'm the only pilgrim staying here.

Tomorrow Stefano (who is sixty-three) intends to walk the full twenty-two miles to Burgos, because the nearest destination, San Juan de Ortega, has no decent lodgings. I am tempted to do the same. But this section is also challenging, and if the heat doesn't let up, I won't make it.

I return to my room and wash my clothes in the bathtub. The air is so hot that they're bone dry in forty-five minutes.

Insight of the day: What makes us human? Our minor faults and major flaws. If we didn't have them, we'd all be little angels.

June 24, 2001

Burgos and Tardajos

Yesterday morning was cold and foggy in Villafranca, and I was too wiped out to take a single step. I was so tired the whole day that I couldn't think clearly or write a word. My biorhythms are at an all-time low.

Those rumbling trucks made it hard to sleep. I had wild dreams about Stefano, trucks, and Stefano's daughter. I dreamed that the universe was expanding and contracting all at once. I didn't really understand it myself. It was like a VW Bug turning into a miniature truck—contracting but growing larger all the same. What an absurd dream.

When I went downstairs to the truckers' bar, a miserable little place in the light of day, the truckers were munching away at an elaborate fatty breakfast, having a good loud discussion, and smoking. Some were already drinking red wine—great way to set out on a long drive—and watching the color TV with the volume turned way up. I figure I'm the only one who knows how tiny their trucks really are, then feel a bit absurd. I order a cup of coffee and a biscuit and, since there are no seats available, take it outside. Besides, the cooling units in the parking lot are quieter than the drivers in the bar.

Then, suddenly, as if by magic, a short-haired blond angel with bright blue eyes and a perky smile is standing in front of me.

Now that I've had nearly two weeks of practice in figuring out the nationality of pilgrims, I'm able to peg her as Swedish. Sure enough, she asks me in perfect English, tinged with a sweet Swedish accent: "Oh, do they serve breakfast there?" and dashes into the greasy spoon. That gives me a reason to go in and order another latte. She's standing at the counter next to me, and trying in all this racket to order her breakfast. Her English may be perfect, but she can't make herself understood.

The fat, unshaven barkeeper stares at her openmouthed. He doesn't catch a word of what she's saying, and the idea that she might simply be asking for food seems unthinkable. Her voice grows louder and more forceful: "Do you think it may be possible to have breakfast outside? Maybe you could set up a little table for us [here she points to me] with a nice white tablecloth?" The man doesn't seem to understand—he's still coming to grips with this blond, ethereal being. So she keeps at it, and even tries to lift up a table, whereupon the barkeeper waves his hands about to make his point that the tables have to remain indoors. My quick translation does nothing whatsoever to solve her dilemma. She gives up and, without another word, takes her little breakfast and follows me outside. We sit on the curb and burst into laughter.

While we laugh, the Swedish woman looks me over. She notices my scallop sticker, which identifies me as a pilgrim, and asks in English, "So, what wonderful things have you experienced so far?"

I look at her and say, "I think . . . nothing."

She looks at me doubtfully and says, "I don't believe that. Something happens to everyone, even if it's just a modest insight."

Sure enough, something occurs to me. "Did you know that the universe is expanding and contracting at the same time?"

She explodes with laughter. "You are funny!"

I say, "Oh, I know!"

She stands up and says, "If that is the case, I'd better get going to find out if my friend has shrunk since I last saw her." She blows me a kiss, and off she goes.

After breakfast, I make my way to the bus station and, without a trace of guilt, ride the bus twenty-two miles to Burgos. Several centuries ago, there were sheep pastures on the horizon; today you ride through a major industrial area.

In Burgos I stay at the best hotel in town, directly in front of the medieval town gate. I have a magnificent view of a place that could have been plucked from a Robin Hood film. I spend half a day in the Gothic cathedral of Santa María and its museum and have the chance to admire only a fraction of what's inside. When I leave the church, I see a thin, bespectacled, itinerant preacher who looks as though he's just stepped out of a Woody Allen movie. He belongs to a sect called Corpus Christi. He's running a scam that works like the sidewalk game three-card monte. Whenever he asks the passersby for a volunteer confession, the same three people always step forward, one at a time. A plump, pimply young man confesses all his sins a total of three times to the bellowing preacher.

It's horrible when people try to profit from the faith or the misery of others. But none of the passersby is taken in by this shifty loudmouth, who is now hollering out the story of Zacchaeus the tax collector.

I then buy my first German newspaper, my beloved *Süddeutsche Zeitung,* and sit down with it on a shady bench on the banks of the Arlanzón and with great relish read reports from my chilly homeland. And my good mood, enhanced from all this hiking, brightens even more. During a Social Democratic Party press conference, Franz Münterfering called upon all gay politicians to come out publicly—on the grounds that "gays are people like everyone else, and can fill any office, even that of pope."

I almost fall off my bench laughing! But when I read the reactions from the Bavarian Christian Social Union, I am hopping mad. This reactionary party declares Münterfering's statement an insult to the pope. Not that the CSU has anything against homosexuals; it's just that sexuality is a private, individual matter. What?? Sexuality is a private matter? Since when?

In our society, nearly everyone assumes that the guy next to him is hetero. Why, for heaven's sake, do people get married in public? And why do most women continue to take their spouses' names? That is a public profession of one's own sexuality and a clear avowal: "Just so everybody knows, we're sleeping together!" There you have it!

Amnesty International ought to put the CSU on some kind of list—maybe not a blacklist, but how about a nice dark gray one?

And the way the Catholic Church avoids questions pertaining to homosexuality and many other important issues is inhuman and rife with disgraceful double standards.

I know that my natural proclivity puts me in complete harmony with the world and myself, so why should I be forced by anyone into disharmony? Because a Catholic God aims to make me, and countless other millions, desperately unhappy and unnatural? Do they seriously believe that God is just as small-minded and ideological as they?

Old men in flowing silk robes with expensive red and purple velvet appliqués want me to become what they themselves are not: a cowboy! That is flat-out absurd.

When will a pope finally realize that the Gospel is not an adhesion contract! Still, there is one amusing parallel between the gay subculture and the Catholic Church; nowhere else in the

West has there been such a strict segregation of the sexes. Both of these two small societies feature separate women's and men's circles.

I think that any pronouncement supported or established by dictators is inhuman and culminates in disaster. And any authority that claims to represent humanity and peace in this world must roundly condemn every one of these pronouncements.

Man, am I furious! I chuck the *Süddeutsche Zeitung* into the garbage can, even though I'm not angry at my newspaper. Still, this is the first and last German newspaper I'll read on the Camino. Blessed are the meek!

Yesterday was my name day, by the way. St. John is much admired in Burgos. I think he's the patron saint of the city. The whole town is one glowing circus bathed in torchlight. Later there are fireworks, which I unfortunately don't catch because I can't raise the stupid window shades in my hotel room. I practically burn my fingers trying to pull them up, but I can hardly get them to move. I guess fireworks and illumination have something in common. To see the fireworks of illumination, perhaps all it takes is to get the shades up!

This morning the sun decided again, on the spur of the moment, to blaze down on the parched ground. I got off to a late start in Burgos, leaving at about 11:30. The trail is tough and the landscape barren and monotonous, aside from a few stunted birch groves. It looks like Holland, if you can imagine Holland on the brink of smoldering.

Today I've set aside and dispensed with all negative thoughts. I don't want them to weigh me down here anymore. I can bear the weight of my backpack, but that's it.

When I'm coping with sweltering heat, dust, legwork, and thirst, I have no other choice anyway.

After just seven tough miles, I have arrived in Tardajos, and I will stay here. There is a very nice *refugio,* which an older woman has polished into a real jewel. She puts fresh linens on the beds every day, and no more than four people share a room. I actually have a room all to myself.

Evening setting

Tomorrow I should be back up to twelve miles. If I go beyond twelve, the summer heat will bring me to my knees. Anything over twelve knocks me out and I can't continue the next day.

Insight of the day, freely adapted from Lore Lorentz: My fury is young!

June 25, 2001

Hornillos del Camino and Hontanas

This morning I loll about in the Ruiz, a saloonlike bar in Tardajos. I am close to the breaking point. I had a good night's sleep in the middle-aged señora's house, but the heat and the dust weigh me down even before I begin my daily stint. I am flat-out exhausted and grumpy! I am on the verge of cutting short my pilgrimage. Yes—that's my decision: I'll finish off the pilgrim in me!

While I'm absorbed in thoughts of this kind, the waiter suddenly appears before me, and I read this saying on his T-shirt: *Keep On Running!* I figure this is probably a Spanish tourist office ploy, but—numbskull of a pilgrim that I am—I fall for it. Taking this motto as a command, I order my coffee, gulp it down, wrap up my indispensable biscuits, and get out of there. This is a clear message, and before I have a chance to think it over rationally, I'm making haste. By pure coincidence, then, I won't be cutting the trip short today. *Keep on running!*

That's the way it goes; you have to expect a physical and emotional low here and there. Still, a pilgrimage has to be completed alone, or at least begun alone. Along the trail, I keep running into couples arguing loudly, or people who tell me that they have separated from their partners on the Camino. Some people grouchily match their partners' incompatible rhythms for miles until they brim over with resentment. Good friends decide on impulse to go their separate ways. In the end, nearly all pilgrims who are in it for the long haul walk alone. I virtually never see groups. Rhythm and pace are what separate most people on the trail. It is hard to find someone who dances to a similar beat. If you hike in a slow waltz, the way I do, you can't join up with a speedy flamenco pilgrim. Once you're quite sure of your own pace, you might be able to link up with someone. The pilgrims' walking styles reflect their feelings and thoughts and their very essence.

Sure, I could simply go home, throw a party for my friends, and recount my nice little travel anecdotes, and everything would be fine and dandy. But I've resolved to walk this trail, and once I begin something, I usually finish it. I want to know what the Camino de Santiago will—or won't—do to me. At least then I'll know. So: *Keep on running!*

Actually I begin my pilgrimage anew each day. I don't feel as though I'm on one continuous journey, but rather on a thousand short trips. Every day I have to fire myself up all over again. I'm convinced that the daily task of the pilgrim is this: Just be yourself, no more and no less!

This is one tough task. The directive itself is straightforward, but putting it into practice is not, which is better than the other way around. It's a test of your patience, like Labyrinth, that classic wooden game where you try to maneuver a small silver ball into a hole in a series of back-and-forth movements. Very simple task— and yet . . .

This journey seems to be teaching me the value of brotherly love. Although there are certainly differences between the pilgrims, I find that I'm compelled increasingly to focus on our similarities rather than our differences. Brotherly love, arguably the most secular of all virtues, can be learned only in the here and now with the acknowledgment that we all do the best we can.

I feel as though I'm building a spiritual house of cards here. Every card I add makes the house seem more impressive, but it gets harder and harder to position the next addition so as to prevent the structure from collapsing on itself. The challenges intensify. The least of them, namely constructing the basis of the house of cards, had the highest priority, and I somehow had the feeling of being supported in my efforts. Now I feel more and more as though I have to fend for myself, but my house of cards is still standing! And who knows—if the creator is in especially high spirits tomorrow and blows down the house of cards, none of what I have ever believed will be valid any longer.

My own naïve spiritual map of the world resembles world maps from the Middle Ages that were missing entire continents.

After three hours of uninterrupted hiking through tiny, medieval villages and grain fields, I take a break in Hornillos del Camino, then embark on a two-hour trek through dry, spectral hills that lead me to a high plateau. I would imagine that Mongolia looks much the same way. It's 95 degrees, and there's no shade as far as the eye can see. In the middle of this steppe, in a little forest oasis with a brook running through it, there's a mosquelike building with a gigantic cross of the Knights of St. John of Jerusalem on the roof. It is the San Bol *refugio*.

When I get there, I find that my Swedish angel from Villafranca and her equally Scandinavian-looking friend are dipping their feet into the brook. I accept their invitation to join them and stick my feet in too. It's kind of funny that I am getting to know only women pilgrims, but they are in the clear majority, and anyway, most of the men are weirdos—as I probably am by now.

The angel's name is Evi (pronounced EE-vee), and her friend is Tina. We don't talk very much. We just sit under the trees full of songbirds and daydream—until a brassy Brazilian woman barges in on our group and rants at us in Portuguese. Normally I would flee on the spot from a South American woman, who more often than not is out to snare a husband, but I can't, since I'm still a bit weak. Surely the presence of the two Swedish women will convince her that I have all the women I can handle.

Since the two Scandinavians are pretty annoyed by this Brazilian bundle of nerves, I come out with the only sentence I can muster in Portuguese: "I don't speak Portuguese!" I couldn't have picked a stupider thing to say, because now she really starts in! I just give her a silly grin without an inkling of what she is desperately trying to convey.

Evi and Tina figure I'm coming on to her and beat a hasty retreat from our oasis. I would like nothing better than to follow suit, but I haven't regained my strength, so I'm at the mercy of this exuberant Brazilian woman. She seems to be telling me the most exciting story I've ever heard—but I don't understand a single word of it. For all I know she's cluing me in on all the essentials of this pilgrimage, and I will fail to find the illumination I'm seeking just because I picked the wrong courses in high school, opting for pointless advanced-level Spanish. *Muchas gracias!* Finally, she sees from my blank face that I'm not following her story, and she takes to the road again. I decide it's time for a real breather and, for the first time since beginning my journey, I simply lie down in the pampas and sleep. Now, that's what I call mellow!

On the way to Hontanas I pass by many construction sites and torn-up streets. That's exactly how I feel: I'm tearing down some things and building up others! The trail seems to reflect my frame of mind, or vice versa . . . or both.

In the early evening, after about twelve miles, I arrive in Hontanas, which cannot be reached by car. I didn't realize this kind of thing was still permitted in the European Union. The locals have to park their cars far outside the village because of a medieval path that is off-limits to cars and is strewn with horse dung. Consequently, this hamlet is absolutely silent. The air may smell like horses, but it's clean.

My travel guide does not recommend the only hotel here. Rightly so, as it turns out! I go into this place—made of coarse, brightly colored sandstone—and feel as though a time machine has catapulted me smack into the Middle Ages.

I'm standing in a world that could have been dreamed up by Hieronymus Bosch. A sweaty innkeeper, short and fat with a greasy apron tied around his bulk, prances through a gloomy room of tipsy locals and weary pilgrims to a fireplace filled with garbage, while balancing on his head a *bocale,* a glass wine bottle resembling a watering can. Then he pours a liter of red wine over his hair, inhales it through his nose, and blows it into his mouth while warbling a tune. Formidable, but revolting!

After this virtuosic performance, the innkeeper, whose name is Vitorio, shows me to a room on the upper floor. Six rotted mattresses are scattered on the floor and covered by four gray military blankets eaten away by moths and dust, next to a porthole window. This room is straight out of the Bible; the only thing missing is a manger. By now I've mastered the art of showering without touching the bathtub, but in this dump, that skill would be of no use at all. True, our Savior was born in a similar room, but I am not going to sleep here. If I'm to be downstairs, it'll be all the way down! The temperature outside seems to be holding steady tonight, so I announce to Vitorio that I will simply sleep in front of the house on the wide stone stairs. He will not hear of it, and he shows me a second room, pointing out that it will cost twice as much as the first. Twice as much as a pittance is not very much, so I have a look at the room, which now seems on a par with the aforementioned Savoy presidential suite in Milan.

The bed is surprisingly clean and well made, although I get the feeling that no one has slept in it for some time. Next to the bed is a bottle of suntan lotion that expired four years ago. It's as though the wife of the innkeeper, who appears to have died in the interim, made up this room one final time shortly before her death.

Next to the bed there's an admission ticket for the Burgos cathedral museum, dated 1998. I nod to Vitorio, indicating that I accept his offer, and he returns happily to his restaurant, while I try to make myself as comfortable as I can. Once again the shower will demand a great deal of physical effort.

When I enter the dimly lit dining area, I see Tina and Evi, paralyzed by the horror of their appetizer platter, a greasy flowered plate holding undefinable bits of meat. I sit down with them, and Evi says, "What are they trying to do to us? This is supposed to be *carne con pimientos.*"

Tina and I consider the little brown mound on Evi's plate, and it is so unfathomably disgusting that we burst out laughing. Evi laughs along with us, but her laughter is mixed with tears, and she has to keep blowing her nose. Finally she sobs, "Let's go somewhere else!"

Now we really let loose! Tina and I cannot hold back at all, and we throw our arms around each other with hoots of laughter. Tina asks me, suffocating with giggles, "Will you tell her or shall

I?" But then neither she nor I can utter a single sensible word, and Evi, flushed with anger but chuckling all the same, asks, "Tell me . . . what?" Through my paroxysms of laughter, I manage to shout out the words: "There *is* no other place!" Evi lets out a howl, and we all split our sides with laughter.

Vitorio attributes our laughter to a happy pilgrim mood, and he asks Tina and me whether we'd like to order something as well. We respond with screams of laughter and pound our fists on the table. When we finally quiet down, Tina makes the only sensible suggestion: "We'll simply order everything he has to offer. Something will have to be edible. For each dish, we'll ask for three extra plates, which we'll wash with our drinking water, and we'll get a bottle of whiskey so we don't catch any diseases!" And that is precisely what we do.

Each dish is more horrible than the last, and the plates have never come in contact with dishwater. Tina and I force ourselves to try something. There's no way around it. The three of us have walked about eighteen miles today, and our hunger is very real. And what do you know—it doesn't taste as horrid as it looks, although it does have an unusual aroma. The scrambled eggs can almost be identified as such right off the bat, so we make a grab for them.

And our whiskey not only staves off illness but raises our spirits. Just as the three of us are valiantly choking down every bite virtually unchewed, the Brazilian woman walks up to our table. Evi nudges me and says, "Look who's coming to see you!"

Before I know it, the Brazilian has sunk her hooks into me and is talking a mile a minute. First she pushes Tina aside unceremoniously in order to sit next to me. She stops chattering for one brief moment when her blank stare lands on the ten platters we've been nibbling at. It's do or die for her now; her stomach is growling and she wants a culinary recommendation from the menu. So she starts speaking to me in a slow Portuguese-for-dummies, in accordance with my linguistic abilities. After two or three double whiskeys, I'm evidently able to understand her childish version of Portuguese just fine, and since what I'm hearing sounds closer to Italian than to Spanish, I reply in Italian, "Have the scrambled eggs!" She understands me and places the order, then, at the sight of the half-empty bottle of whiskey on the table, she asks us in all seriousness whether we're alcoholics. I'm able to assure her in somewhat slurred speech that we're not, whereupon she treats herself to a double from my glass. It slowly dawns on Claudia (for that is the name of the olive-skinned beauty from Rio) that we are in a restaurant no gourmet guide has ever praised, so she goes into the kitchen to see for herself what the cook is preparing. She returns to the table looking as ashen as her complexion allows, and stammers: *Sucio, sucio!* Once again I hear a distinct resemblance to Italian. When Romans consider something really repulsive, they say, *zozzo!* which means "filth."

When Vitorio places his sorry effort on the table, Claudia takes the plate and flings it back at him, cursing and swearing. Vitorio is able to grab the plate just in time, but he is unable to reply. I'm almost a little sorry for him. Evi, Tina, and I ask Claudia to take it easy, but her pride is wounded. Evidently she's never been served this kind of muck.

To make amends for the meal, Vitorio offers us bananas soaked in whiskey. He also seems to consider us high-proof tipplers by this point. Even Claudia from Rio tries some of the new *creación de la mesón*. The evening is lovely, the atmosphere is improving, Vitorio does the trick with the bottle again, and Claudia is not as annoying as she first seemed. Later a young Slovene (whose name is something like Mirjo) joins us at the table. We take care to fill him in on Vitorio's cooking secrets and turn him into a tippler as well.

At dusk I walk with the four of them to the *refugio*. On the bench in front of the lovingly restored building, Claudia's friend Sonja is sitting stony-faced. She's been waiting for Claudia for hours, and she vanishes rather quickly into the *refugio,* muttering Portuguese curses. Man! These Brazilians are hotheaded. Claudia doesn't feel like going straight to bed anymore, so we make ourselves at home on the bench under what is now a clear night sky.

She doggedly continues speaking Portuguese to me; after all, she doesn't speak any other language. The funny thing is that I understand quite a bit of her nutty Portuguese. She doesn't even have to speak slowly anymore.

This pretty woman must be about my age. For South Americans, the Camino is one big marriage market. Strict Catholic parents send their children off with orders to return with a potential marriage partner. I hope Claudia has not seriously chosen me for this role.

She asks me if I've had any magical experiences on the pilgrimage. Like others around here, she thinks it's absolutely normal to experience something extraordinary. But none of my experiences to date fit into this category.

Claudia launches into the exciting story from the afternoon all over again, this time in slow motion. She found a little half-dead sparrow, then carried it three miles through the blazing sun into a shady grove and washed it—hmm—and after a few hours it was able to fly again. What I could actually understand was more along the lines of: sparrow almost dead—found—pick up—walk three miles with sparrow—lots of sun—then forest—cold—wash bird—wait—then bird fly.

That's a nice bedtime story, so I say good night to this Brazilian patron saint of the animals—a regular Francis of Assisi—and head off into the balmy night.

There's a slight breeze as I walk back to Vitorio's bodega, wondering where all the people I have already met so far on the Camino are by now: Antonio, Larissa, Stefano, Victor, and Anne.

I'm sure to see Claudia tomorrow—but maybe not. You never know. People turn up, then they seem to vanish from the face of the earth.

Insight of the day: Keep on running! I can take more than I think!

June 26, 2001

Castrojeriz and Frómista

Vitorio spent last night carousing with two friends downstairs in his bar. I took the precaution of double-locking my door and slept quite well. This morning I set off at 6:30.

Chubby little Vitorio wanted to brew me a latte before I took off, but I was happy to tell him no once I saw my Spanish breakfast biscuits lying unwrapped on the greasy counter between a bunch of stinking empty beer bottles. As I turned to go, he grabbed an unwashed plate, put something indefinable on it, and fed the cats on the street. I assume he'll just rinse off that plate with cold water—if he cleans it at all.

Slowly but surely, the mess and the filth are getting on my nerves. Germany is really clean, and that's a good thing. Call me petty bourgeois, but I say, long live German cleanliness.

I make a quick getaway so as not to throw up, and hike in double-quick time to the next town, which will take me two hours to reach if I take the main road. I can hardly wait to get a good breakfast. Seven miles! I'm really no good at all without breakfast, but I have no choice.

Once I'm on the trail, I hear only birds chirping. It's simply fabulous, and I'm at one with the world. Cuckoos, turtledoves, sparrows, all kinds of songbirds, punctuated by the rattling of storks. This planet would be unbearable without birdsong.

En route to Castrojeriz, I see Claudia far ahead of me, near the *castillo,* the enormous fortress of Castrojeriz. She's moving along slowly with Sonja. Claudia keeps turning around to see who's behind her. I'm sure she wants to know whether I'm anywhere in the vicinity. The two of them keep coming to a standstill, and when I suddenly catch up to them, the Girl from Ipanema acts startled. The first thing she tells me is that she's seen two cobras this morning. I try to explain to her that as far as I know there are no cobras in Spain—although I *have* seen twelve eagles! But if she insists that she's really seen cobras, maybe it's symbolic. Devout Catholic that she is, she may be spending too much time thinking about sex.

Once Claudia and I start chatting again, her friend Sonja moves away from us gracefully but resolutely, and it is obvious that Claudia wants to know once and for all what my intentions are. What does this vivacious Brazilian woman want with a wimp like me? Well, she's not about to make any headway here! I'm flattered, of course, but her quest is futile.

We continue to carry on a strained conversation, which soon peters out. She is obviously waiting for me to say something suggestive, but that is not about to happen. The magnificent fortress of Castrojeriz, the chirping of birds, and the parched landscape are my diversions this morning. All in all, my conversation is not especially imaginative, and doesn't seem to match Claudia's agenda.

Suddenly, out of nowhere, she stops short and erupts in fury. Looking deeply offended, and adopting the tone of voice I heard last night when she attempted to cut Vitorio down to size, she makes it perfectly clear to me that she will be continuing on alone. She tells me to wait fifteen minutes so that I won't catch up to her, because she never wants to see me again! She turns on her heel and disappears.

I dutifully wait out the fifteen minutes, because I'm not all that eager to see her again either. I find the whole thing quite surprising. Still, I can't be angry with Claudia. I am willing to wager that I'll never see her again.

The medieval breakfast café in Castrojeriz is sensational. The owner is incredibly friendly, and a funny parrot named Kathie flies around to the beat of a Viennese waltz in a sun-drenched room adorned with flowing multicolored curtains. I sit down at a table across from a rough stone wall hung with a big photograph of a friendly Mediterranean guy, which I am forced to stare at while eating my sumptuous breakfast. I dig in and gather my strength for the day. Suddenly my greasy innkeeper Vitorio from Hontanas is standing in the doorway. He orders a cup of coffee and says to me, "Yes . . . it's quite nice here too, isn't it?"

The sight of him takes me right back to his grotesque medieval inferno, and I can't continue eating. So I decide to head straight out to the meseta, which is nearly three thousand feet high and leads over the Alto de Mostelares.

The trail brings me to a dry, dazzling yellow, but desolate countryside. The landscape is spectacular, but how people ever got the idea of settling here is a mystery to me. I should have brought my camcorder along and made a documentary film. It is simply incredible, and exquisitely beautiful, and the people I meet in a village are extremely friendly and attentive to the pilgrims.

Who knows where I'll wind up today? All I need are a clean bed and bath—but please don't make me go without them!

During the 3,000-foot mountain ascent to the shadeless meseta, I meet a middle-aged, colorfully clad American woman who weighs about four hundred fifty pounds, hobbling over the very rough, pebble-strewn trail. She has no backpack, and she's wearing flip-flops and clutching a walking stick. This woman's baroque voluptuousness is the antithesis of the austere, emaciated landscape. I would have placed her in a snack bar in Dallas, but here her stout and colorful presence is the perfect complement to the land's monotonous barrenness. By now I chat with everyone I run into. She seems similarly inclined, so we both stop and act as though we had arranged to meet in this semidesert—which is 105 degrees—to enjoy some small talk.

She tells me that her husband drops her off every day at a street that cars can drive along reasonably well, so that she can hike for a mile or two alone up to an arranged meeting point, where her husband waits for her with the car. This American woman from Seattle seems even more overwhelmed by this tedious task than yours truly, so after our chat, I walk extremely slowly, wanting to make sure that the lady makes it over the pass safe and sound. I pretend to take a rest here and there so I can check that she's still alive. There is no other pilgrim in sight anywhere, so it's up to me to keep an eye on this portly lady. Finally, off in the distance at a country-lane crossroads in the valley, I see a white Jeep with the motor running. In the car is a man looking eagerly in my direction and obviously waiting for someone.

Now I pick up my pace and forge ahead. The slow crawl sapped my energy, so I stay in the hiking mood by singing songs. First I pep myself up with an aria from *Don Giovanni:* "Là ci darem la mano" ("There you'll give me your hand"). Mozart, I tell myself, will somehow make my body lighter and more agile.

Whenever I find my strength ebbing, I break out into loud song. Musicals, hymns, folk songs from around the world, from "Hava Nagila" to "Blowin' in the Wind," maybe an aria or two, marches, and pop songs. Usually I spend hours walking alone without encountering a soul, so why not?

German folk songs are well suited to hiking and propel me ahead. Today, before I ran into the American woman, it was Strauss's "Radetzky March" that got me to the meseta. My feet are hurting quite a lot. I know I'm repeating myself, because my feet always hurt, but today it's worse than usual, and I find that note-worthy! It would be impossible to overstate how much your feet hurt when you walk the Camino de Santiago.

By 4:30 in the afternoon I've covered an astonishing twenty miles. So I treat myself to a break at a bar in a sandy little village, and enjoy a tasty *bocadillo* and a *Spezi*. The other pilgrims always look at me as though I'm crazy when I mix lemon soda and cola, so I explain to them that this is a German specialty called *Spezi*, also known as cold coffee. Evidently it has never occurred to any of the Norwegians, Swedes, Spaniards, Italians, or Brazilians to try this combination.

At the village fountain in front of the bar, I strike up a conver-sation with two robust Norwegian women from Telemark, and tell them in English about my encounter with that temperamental Claudia from Brazil. I just have to get the story off my chest! Just for the fun of it, the two of speak to me in Norwegian—not Portu-guese, luckily—and I reply in German. We try to find out whether we can communicate that way. And what do you know—it works. The two women understand nearly everything, and I take a crash course in baby Norwegian this time. I have to say that the cool language of the fjord glaciers feels refreshing in this heat.

There is a *refugio* here in the boondocks, and I'm really pooped, but I want a nice bed today, and the hostel is both spartan and jam-packed.

I still don't see how it is possible for hikers to spend the day trekking alone, then when the sun goes down and they've reached their destination for the day, spend the night with hundreds of people who have walked the same trail at the same time.

I have to walk just three more miles to get to Frómista, and—lucky me!—there's a hotel. I'll manage that somehow. The journey to Frómista is tough, however. I find myself plodding along a canal that never seems to end, feeling dog tired. The water meanders along just as sluggishly as I do. I can't feel my feet. My body is emitting so few endorphins that I have to depend on sheer will to bring me to my destination. After nearly twenty-three miles of walking, I reach my destination for the day. I am amazed at myself.

About two weeks ago I probably would have fallen over dead after twenty-three miles. Now I'm just tired, and my feet . . . well, no more about that!

The trek has tested me sorely today, but the landscape was the most beautiful to date. I cannot believe that I did twenty-two miles in just eight hours, rather than the eleven miles I'd anticipated. Twenty-two divided by eight is 2.75, so I did about 2.75 miles an hour. Not bad for a guy who was always horrible at sports.

Still, I get the impression that it is my mental rather than my physical condition that has improved. I now know how to gauge the exertion and to conserve my strength. Even so, I cannot walk at too leisurely a pace when it reaches 105 degrees in the shade.

The faster I get out of the sun, the better. But when I walk too quickly, sooner or later I can't go on, and I get stuck in the sun. My consumption of liquids is enormous. Today I drank about six liters. Oddly, hunger is not really a problem. In fact, I do even better when I'm hungry. It's amazing what I can get out of my couch potato of a body. I don't think I've lost a single additional ounce over the past few days, but that's not the point.

This trail has been teaching me a great deal about my strength. I'm learning how to use my energy properly, to apportion it sensibly, to take breaks when I need them, and to treat myself well no matter how hard I'm working. This evening I'm rewarding myself with Hotel San Martín, a beautiful little building across from the gleaming Romanesque church of the same name. The square has little flags fluttering every which way, and it looks quite dignified, as though awaiting a high-ranking guest of the state who will be arriving at any moment.

When I go for dinner, whom should I find but Tina and Evi, my squeaky-clean Swedes! They are the only guests dining here. It's like a dream come true. The dining room has a fine red terracotta floor, and the candlelit table is elegantly set. Marvelous! We spend another enjoyable evening together. These two gracious and witty ladies from Stockholm really lift my spirits. They are also sick and tired of the tortures of pilgrims' hostels, and are treating themselves to nice hotels. Bravo! The triumph of Swedish reason!

After a series of quarrels, Evi and Tina have also decided to walk separately. Sometimes they even spend the night in different places. After all that solitude, the two suntanned blondes and I are eager for a chat, so we talk, gripe, and laugh our guts out.

Tina has a wonderful pilgrim story to tell. Earlier on the trail, she couldn't find laundry detergent in a tiny town. Since she doesn't speak Spanish, she made a series of wild gestures to show the saleslady what she wanted. The saleslady gave her a package of something or other, which Tina happily purchased and brought to the pilgrims' hostel. When Tina later opened the little package over the sink, she found out that it contained liquid vanilla pudding. So she washed everything in vanilla pudding! "My clothing may not have been clean," Tina explains, "but it smelled very good!"

Tina and Evi are also put off by the fact that many pilgrims staying at the hostels hike at night. Many people set their alarm clocks for 2 A.M. and make a terrible racket in the dormitory. It's hard to believe that people choose to hike at night. Everyone is always on the hunt for the next free bed, because if the undersized pilgrims' hostels are full, it's hard to find a place to stay. Little groups form to split up the quest for beds. Some walk during the day, and the others at night, and in this way they keep beds available for one another. And then there are the really wacky lone wolves who arrive at their destination at 8 A.M. and line up to wait for a bed to open up.

How do they do it? They probably have searchlights with them, because the trail has no artificial sources of light, and a full moon occurs only once a month. Not to mention the stray dogs and other animals lurking in the brush!

I have absolutely no desire to do anything of the sort. I prefer to make my way at my own leisurely pace, and not to chase after a bed. Night-shift pilgrims—astonishing! That is probably the reason I am not running into other pilgrims these days.

We try to guess each other's professions, and we all do quite well. Just as I suspected, Evi is an English teacher. Tina is an executive secretary in an agency in Stockholm. Once I've told them the saga of my Brazilian fiancée, in all its racy details, right down to the punch line, the two of them guess that I'm a comedian.

In the further course of our conversation we realize that in key spots along the Camino we are always greeted by animals.

In Saint-Jean, the first station of my route, an old dog was sitting and staring at me when I set out from the train station. Today, when I arrived in Castrojeriz, a dead owl was lying next to the town wall, and in Frómista a black and a white stallion were there to greet me on a pasture. Shortly before I got to Belorado, I nearly stumbled over a dead cat. Thousands of butterflies fluttered around me in Zubiri, and in Logroño, five storks were perched on a church spire. These observations might mean nothing, but when you're walking alone, you pick up on things like this.

Evi recounts how she was "saved" during her first pilgrimage on the Camino de Santiago. Alone in the mountains on a Sunday morning at 9 A.M., she broke her foot. The next thing she knew, two uniformed Spanish nurses hiked by. One began to administer first aid while the other used her cell phone to call the fire department. It is hard for me to buy the part with the uniforms, so I press her on that several times, but Evi sticks to her story, even though she has no idea (since she doesn't speak a word of Spanish) why medical personnel would be hiking through nature in full regalia.

Tina also went solo on her first pilgrimage, and, like most of us, she miscalculated how much hydration she'd need. On the verge of collapse after walking for three hours in the blazing sun without water, she found a big juicy orange on the trail, which a pilgrim must have dropped. Everyone has a funny tale to tell about the Camino. Neither Evi nor Tina made it all the way to Santiago the first time around, but this time they have resolved to get to Santiago in just twelve days—an almost superhuman task.

After the fantastic meal, I return to my room feeling quite content, and while washing my dirty clothes, I laugh out loud when I think of the vanilla pudding. It was a fabulous evening. Tina and Evi are wonderful.

If all goes well, I plan to reach my destination in nineteen days. Then I'd like to spend a couple of days in Portugal, relaxing by the sea.

Before I fall asleep, I think about the portly American from Seattle. She was so happy, and hiking to the meseta meant so much to her.

Insight of the day: Friends! Sometimes we have to make a point of surpassing our own limits.

June 27, 2001
Carrión de los Condes

The two Swedish women and I really tied one on last night. I wasn't out the door until ten today. Great weather for hiking. Cloudy and rather cool, somewhere around 60 degrees.

When I set out this morning, an elderly gentleman stopped me at the way out of Frómista and said, "You're having good luck along the Camino, aren't you?"

I asked, "Why do you say that?"

"Well, if the apostle is sending you such good weather, he is accompanying you on your way."

I said, "I hope he's accompanying me."

He answered with a smile, "There's the difference between us—I *know* he is!"

The county and the towns of Población de Campos and Villovieco through which I am hiking look almost exactly like the little farming community on the outskirts of Recklinghausen where I spent the first six years of my life among flat Westphalian beet fields and sturdy little farms. The dreary weather contributes to this impression. Unbelievable. It looks just as I remember; even the people seem similar, gruff but sincere. I feel as though I'm heading home! It's awesome. I keep thinking of our old neighbor Bödeker, a retired mine worker who made six-foot-tall naïve concrete statues. Unfortunately, he did not achieve world renown until after his death. Today everyone in the art world has heard of Bödeker. He is known as the Botero of the Ruhr Area. I always got along well with him, and when I was a child he let me play among his fairy-tale statues. Why am I thinking about him now, after such a long time?

Yesterday's twenty-two miles really got to me, as did last night's wine. Today I'm aiming for only twelve miles; I've already made four or five.

In that bar in Boadilla del Camino, where I was hanging around yesterday feeling thoroughly exhausted and sipping on my *Spezi*, I felt at peace with myself and the world. Everything was just as it should be. I wasn't at my destination, but I had just arrived at my stopping point and was poised to leave again shortly. I had no doubts about the point of my pilgrimage.

A friend once said to me, "You shouldn't entertain doubts. You should simply rely on God! He somehow solves all problems in His inimitable way."

Today I had luck on my mind; in particular, a stroke of luck I had in Prague back in 1989.

On the second day of Christmas, three Italian friends from Bologna and I got the brilliant (and novel—or so we thought) idea of going to Prague to celebrate New Year's Eve and the Velvet Revolution. On December 30, we drove to the Czech border from Munich and arrived there at about 10 P.M. in the midst of an awful blizzard. The border gate was raised, and the customs office was dimly lit. The next thing we knew, ten more cars had lined up behind ours, nearly all filled with Italians who had seemingly also decided to visit Prague on the spur of the moment. Since no officer emerged from the customs office, I got out and walked over to it. The officer inside brusquely informed me that the border was already closed, and that as a German I wouldn't be eligible to enter at this crossing point anyway; it was only for Italians. I would need to use a crossing point thirty-seven miles to the north—which was also closed.

I went back to the car and told my friends and the others in the line of cars: "This isn't going to work; we all have to go back." But Italians can be marvelously headstrong. None of them made the slightest attempt to turn around. The Italians started hollering, "Damn it, you're a democracy now. Let us in."

But evidently the old conditions for entry still applied, and the guard wouldn't budge. It was cold and dark, and we all wanted to cross into Czechoslovakia, and so, buoyed by the spirit of peaceful revolution, we decided simply to pass over the border. My friend Anna was nervous, and ventured to ask, "What happens if they shoot at us?" This fear struck me as absurd, and I replied with a laugh, "They can't gun down two dozen Italian tourists here the day before New Year's Eve! Vaclav Havel would surely not approve of that!"

The gate was still open, so we all drove over the border in quick succession. The road was pitch black, and it took us half a mile more to reach the actual border crossing point, which was illuminated with menacing floodlights. In a flash, we were surrounded by the military as though smack in the middle of a 1970s James Bond movie! The soldiers kicked up a frightening fuss, and since we were in car number one, we were the first ones targeted.

We explained to the officer on duty, or whoever he was, "The other guard sent us over."

"That is impossible," he snarled in his Czech-tinged German, and waited for a more plausible explanation. So I said, "We're not out to get killed here; we're just driving over the border to get to a Warsaw Pact country!" He bought that argument; I didn't look like much of a hero. Anna was relieved that there wouldn't be a shoot-out in the snow, which had now piled up to eight inches. We all had to turn off our motors and step out of our cars. Our personal data were recorded, and then the aggravation started in earnest.

After one and a half hours of deliberation, they deigned to hand us visa papers written in Czech and Russian, which we were told to fill out accurately. Unfortunately, none of us knew these languages, and since the Colonel-General-Major-or-whatever-he-was understood a little German, I ran over to him and asked him politely for a document in a language with which we were familiar. He was starting to get fed up with us but dug up some Spanish visa documents.

We were standing there with the snow coming down like crazy, filling out these papers on the roofs of our cars in the freezing cold weather. We weren't allowed back in our cars, presumably because we were a flight risk, although just where we'd flee to was a mystery to me. The Italians and I had no trouble understanding the Spanish. My name was my name, in Spanish or any other language. My address remained the same, and I indicated my height, date of birth, etc., in numbers. I abbreviated "Germany" as F.ederal R.epublic of G.ermany. That ought to work anywhere in the world! But then came the kicker: *Color del coche*. Color of car?! What was I to write in now? Czech, Spanish, or English? So I trudged back to the hefty lieutenant and asked for his friendly advice. He shouted at me: "Czech!"

I humbly inquired of him, "How do you say 'white' in Czech?"

"Figure it out for yourself!" he hollered back, while I disappeared into his cloud of breath. Sure, at midnight, in the snowy Bohemian Forest!

One of the Italians walked up to each car and translated its color into Czech. He was, in fact, a Czech emigrant. (*Bila* means "white.") At some point we were granted permission to enter, and we spent the night in the nearby city of Pilsen.

We arrived in snowy, icy Prague at three in the afternoon the following day. All the hotels in the Golden City were full, and there were loads of other impulsive Italians also on the quest for a place to stay. There were no beds at the inns. There were no rooms even on the outskirts of the city. There were simply no rooms, although we spent hours looking for one.

Toward evening, we four decided with a sigh of resignation that we'd just go have something to eat, celebrate somewhere, and to hell with the consequences. I slipped a hotel porter a 150-mark bribe so that we could join a big New Year's gala in a luxury hotel on Wenceslas Square. In the ballroom, each of us had to fork out an additional 150 marks, which meant that we wouldn't have been able to afford a reasonable room anyway. But the hotel was warm, and we could stay out of the cold until the party ended at 1 A.M.

It was great fun, and we partied hard, drinking plenty of alcohol until the dot of one, when we ventured out onto Wenceslas Square, where people were embracing and sobbing for joy. It was an unbelievable New Year's Eve. The Czechs were celebrating their hard-won freedom, and we were right there with them—drinking, weeping, and laughing!

At about three o'clock, we again realized that we had no place to sleep, that we were too drunk to keep driving, that the weather made it impossible to keep on going anyway, and that we would be unlikely to survive a night in the car. We were really in a bind, and Anna started blubbering when I suggested we simply spend the night in the train station concourse. The situation appeared hopeless, and we fought. How could we spend the night outdoors in the icy cold and snow?

Suddenly, out of the hullabaloo of the Velvet Revolution and the New Year's celebration, a smiling, long-haired blonde roughly my age appeared and said, "*Dobri novi rok*."

I looked at her and answered, "Huh?"

She replied with great excitement, "Televisha!"

I said, "Televisha? Yes, of course!" I got what she was saying. This lady from Prague knew me from TV. To my surprise, she then switched to fluent German. "What are you doing here?" I sprang to attention. "I'm celebrating New Year's Eve with three friends, and here's the thing: We have no hotel. Could we sleep at your place?"

The woman laughed. "Of course you can. Why not?" She called over her friends—two women and a man. The man was a sculptor and, as chance would have it, the grandson of an Italian immigrant, so he spoke Italian quite well. Veronika, our rescuer, was also a sculptor, and it turned out she really did know me from TV, as did her girlfriend, a Czech immigrant to Nuremberg. When I told them that my grandma was born in Marienbad, the Czechs adopted me.

Veronika let us stay in her studio, which offered a splendid view over the historic city center of Prague, for four days. We kept in touch for years afterward.

Dobri novi rok means Happy New Year, by the way.

~

I had an equally bizarre stroke of good luck when I was in Egypt, at a hotel in the middle of the desert, and suffered a near fatal poisoning. A renowned cardiologist from Cairo on vacation was staying three rooms down the hall, and he saved my life.

When things like this happen, you wonder: Could all this be pure coincidence?

Today's route is extremely taxing: twelve miles in one straight line. No wonder my mind keeps wandering. I'm now walking along the main road through the Tierra de Campos, passing by endless grain fields to my left and right.

At one point I'm so tired, and have such burning pains in my legs, that I begin to see strangely bright beams of light all around me, and I get the sense that two of these are like gigantic white wings bearing the weight of my backpack. I no longer feel its weight. Now I'm not slowing down; I'm speeding up, and it feels as though someone else is doing the walking!

The sensation of being on my last legs is fast becoming a form of meditation. This colossal light, this insanely bright light stays with me for the entire day. Every once in a while I check to see whether my sunglasses are really on my nose. Everything is so bright: the trail, the fields, my body. Without this light I would drop from exhaustion. Or is this light nothing but an outgrowth of my exhaustion? No idea. Probably my endorphin production is diminishing, and I'm getting warning signals in white neon. Walking thirty-five miles in two days may be too much for someone like me after all.

My dreams grow more intense with each passing night. My dream apparatus has become a well-oiled mechanism. Last night I woke up with a start because someone in my dream advised me to make a clean break with three of my friends. I couldn't get back to sleep after that. As a precaution, I deleted those friends' telephone numbers from my cell phone listings; I can fish them out of the trash bin if I come to regret this decision.

I'm aware that what I'm doing now exceeds my physical strength, but I keep on with it, and I no longer think I'm going to drop dead, because something seems to be conveying me along. Maybe it's my will? Despite my bodily weakness, I feel mentally fortified. Maybe this long period of solitude agrees with me? I'm starting to like being alone! This luxurious opportunity to focus on myself, just this once, is starting to bear fruit. I'd never known that some of these fruits existed, but they're interesting.

I hike through Carrión de los Condes, a hilly, light gray little town, cross an old Roman stone bridge over a torrential river, then reach the former Benedictine monastery, Real Monasterio San Zoilo, which has been converted into a hotel. I take a room there. From the outside, the monastery is nondescript, almost ugly, and does not seem monumental in the slightest. But once inside I discover impressive cloisters, a staggeringly beautiful white courtyard, an expansive rectangular cathedral, and a gigantic park.

Loudspeakers playing Gregorian chant transport you into a kind of perpetual meditation. This hotel has umpteen rooms, but apart from three Spaniards and me, there is no one staying here. The four of us have the entire monastery to ourselves. The town and the pilgrims' hostel are honestly not worth mentioning, but the Real Monasterio, where the martyr Zoilo is buried, is justly considered a world heritage site (although actually it is *other*worldly).

Alfonso VI, Alfonso VII, and Alfonso VIII, all Spanish kings, retired here after abdicating the throne. I can see why. This place is a great comfort for my battered body and weary soul.

I'm more impressed by monasteries than by castles, because the latter are usually just ostentatious. A monastery combines magnificence and modesty in perfect harmony. In Carrión de los Condes, the blend of these two apparent opposites is especially successful.

Real Monasterio San Zoilo, a retreat for kings and pilgrims

While walking through the large, deserted cloisters, I keep thinking about how often along the Camino de Santiago the outside world has mirrored my inner life, so when I see all the grotesque figures and symbols chiseled into the columns, I wonder what significance the cloisters of this monastery have for me, and what they are telling me about myself.

I sit down on a bench in the shade and contemplate the column from which a skull gawks back at me. That suits the occasion. I'm dead tired and consequently unruffled, so I don't bother fending off the associations that now spring to mind.

A skull . . . Does that mean I ought to muse about dying and death here? I look up at the big church clock; it has stopped. Time stops here, I think, so I can enjoy the leisure of meditation.

Should my journey be taking me through my own netherworld and bringing me to a symbolic death? Maybe I'm meant to stop time and prevent night from falling, but that would mean there'd be no new morning.

Those in search of illumination may have to experience the exact opposite first, namely darkness.

I have to have a closer look at my dark side. What is my night like? What do I see there? The Gregorian chants and my radiant exhaustion form a perfect backdrop for this nighttime meditation, which features all kinds of grimaces and contortions—shadows of myself. So I sit tight and, with as much detachment as I can muster, I let the spectacle drift past.

Later, befuddled, I go to the other side of the cloisters and again sit down on a bench, this time in the sun. I look at the column in front of me now. A newborn baby is carved into the stone. Naturally my first thought is of dying in order to be reborn, heading for the morning by way of the night. Life is marked by birth and death. You cannot have one without the other.

Waking up—going to sleep, starting work—finishing work, training for a job—entering retirement. Everything begins and ends, although it is always Now, and everything really does happen in one single gigantic moment.

From the cloisters I make my way into the cathedral. I'm alone there, watching a pigeon fly onto the altar. Directly about it is a huge crucifix, and for the first time I become aware that Christ on the cross is clearly looking in one direction. Most depictions of Jesus Christ have him looking to the left. To the west: sundown, night, death.

But from his own perspective, he's looking to the right, to the east: to sunrise and to life. What appears to us as a gloomy end is actually a bright beginning for him. We humans can never truly grasp this idea.

The cloisters in Carrión de los Condes

All of us will have to face our nights one way or another. Better to do it freely and serenely than wait until we're forced by fate. Maybe those pilgrims traveling on the night shift are doing the right thing by surrendering to darkness.

The less we're delighted by and attached to the constant symbolic births in our lives, the more easily we may be able to accept the symbolic deaths as well. In any case, I really must confront my shadow head-on!

I have eighteen segments left to go, and I've already completed eleven—one hundred thirty-seven miles—on foot. I did one of them by hitchhiking, and four by bus, which amounts to about sixty-two motorized miles.

Tomorrow will be the end of the first half of my journey. I'm exhausted this evening. I feel like an empty bottle that needs refilling.

Insight of the day: I will face my shadow!

June 28, 2001

Calzadilla de la Cueza

This morning I didn't get out of bed until 7:30, and I'm still dead tired. It took quite an effort to drag myself to the marathon awaiting me today, which begins on an unpaved Roman road. At a gas station, shortly before starting out on the dusty, ten-mile dirt road to Calzadilla de la Cueza, I grab another cup of coffee. And since I have only two liters of luke-warm water with me, I order seltzer, too. However, the plastic bottle turns out to contain nothing but a rock-hard clump of ice. At first I feel like complaining, but then I simply mutter under my breath and stuff the mini-glacier into my backpack. What good would it do: it's either this or nothing at all!

The part that now follows is pure hell. The sun begins blazing down mercilessly and early in the morning. There are no trees or bushes. I see nothing but identical fields and this straight, dusty road, and there is no end in sight. Ten endless miles in the same direction without any variety or even a hint of shade. Today I'm guaranteed not to encounter my shadow! Normally you can stop off somewhere at least every six miles to sit in the cool shade for a minute and take a rest, but not here. The sunlight on the trail nearly blinds me, and though I'm wearing sunglasses, I have to close my tearing eyes for several seconds at a time to spare them from the glare. My breathing is getting louder and my throat more parched. I eventually become oblivious to everything but my pathetic panting.

It would be insane to take a rest in the blazing sun, so I have to do the thing I dread: I step up my pace drastically to get out of this glaring grain-field inferno as quickly as I can.

Luckily I have my bottled clump of ice on hand. Every once in a while I pour some of my lukewarm liquid into the frozen bottle, and then I have a cold drink handy for the next two and a half hours. Even so, this segment is brutal, and when the ice water is all gone, I start to panic, because the little village of Calzadilla de la Cueza, which is clearly marked on my map, refuses to appear on the horizon, even though the land is as flat as a pancake and you can see ridiculously far into the distance. My experience as a pilgrim thus far has taught me that I will not last much longer at this pace. I wonder if I am I lost again, but the butterflies are still fluttering around along the side of the road, and I'm resolutely keeping my head above imaginary water by singing gospel and marches.

After what feels like fifteen miles rather than ten, Calzadilla de la Cueza suddenly appears before me, less than fifty yards away, in a hollow on an incline. For ten miles you go on thinking that this stupid village will never appear, then suddenly it's there. All at once—out of nowhere!

That was one awful trek! I'd sooner drag myself over the Pyrenees in the fog than try this part again.

I have now walked ten miles in exactly three hours without taking a break. That's a record, and I suddenly feel like an Olympic champion. This whole one-horse town ought to gather around and give me a tear-stained standing ovation. And after that maybe I'll spring for a round of beers.

No bushes, no trees, no shade

But there is no sign of life. My zoologically minded pilgrims'
guide tells me that at the very minimum there ought to be wolves
howling at night! At the moment, the only sound is of a dry, hot
wind whooshing the dust through the town's two streets.

Whether I like it or not, I have to stay in this dumpy place,
which consists of five dilapidated houses and a tidy little hotel. The
next hotel is fifteen miles down the road.

When I enter the simply decorated hotel restaurant, where a
gigantic ceiling fan is doing quite a good job keeping the place
cool, a pretty dark-haired woman is sitting over a cup of coffee
and writing in her diary. I say a friendly hello, get a room key at

the reception desk, which also serves as the bar, and join the young
woman uninvited.

Calzadilla de la Cueza comes into view suddenly,
like a mirage.

We don't need a lot of small talk to get our conversation going;
we just jump right in. The longer you hike, the less interest you
have in superficial chitchat about the weather or similar trivia, and
I have developed a sense of who will be a suitable companion for
me and who might find me a suitable companion.

Jose, who is from Amsterdam, is one of these. She tells me that
she temporarily parted ways with her girlfriend yesterday in Carrión. Both decided to hike the route alone. Tomorrow Jose will
continue on to the next *refugio,* which is a few miles down the
road. Her friend will remain in Carrión and have a look at the

monastery cloisters, which will give Jose a twelve-mile head start. They plan to meet up again in eleven days.

This Dutch woman has one thought in mind as she treks along: Be yourself! And the key question for her is: "Who am I?" Our conversation develops into the kind of lovely intense exchange friends have. Jose is like me; she doesn't feel too comfortable with the pilgrims' hostels and the people there. It's good to know I'm not the only one.

Jose tells me how she forges ahead on her pilgrimage without giving up: "You know what? When I need something, I simply order it from the universe!"

"That does the trick?!" I ask her dubiously. This sounds a bit nutty to me, although Jose doesn't seem to fall into the category of "psychologically peculiar." She grins from ear to ear, and her eyes and teeth sparkle: *"Probeer het!"* Try it! she challenges me in Dutch.

After two more cups of coffee, Jose gives me a peck on the cheek and goes on her way.

My wonderful darkened room makes me forget how worn out I am, so I start washing my things with a song on my lips. I hate it when my clothes start to smell. If I could, I would wash them en route.

Yesterday in Carrión de los Condes I bought myself a no-iron, wrinkle-free "city shirt," because I look quite a sight in my old denim. Whenever I enter a village, I have the feeling that everyone's gawking at it, horrified. The city shirt is a bit more impressive. I now use the denim shirt for hiking and the city shirt, obviously, for the city. But here in Calzadilla, I leave my denim shirt on. Not only is it barely a city, but I'm still mad at the place because it hid from me until the last minute.

It's so hot! While the wash I hung up drips loudly into the bathtub, I try to catch up on my sleep—which is hard to do in this oppressive heat, even with closed shades and wide-open windows. Some neighbors have moved into the room next door. A German couple. Judging by their voices, I'd say they're in their late fifties, and I hear them prop their walking sticks against the wall with a clatter. This town may not have a church, but the hotel has the acoustics of the Cologne Cathedral. The place has such thin walls that I can hear every word, no matter how softly spoken, as well as every step—whether I want to or not. I'm reminded of my grandma's words of wisdom: *The eavesdropper's the one to blame / when, ear to wall, he hears his shame.* True enough! But I'm an unintentional eavesdropper. All I want to do is sleep. And it gets boring when you can't doze off. Luckily the newcomers want to take a rest too. I hope they have well-functioning soft palates.

After five minutes—they are already lying in bed—I hear the following dialogue, which I will write down here without a twinge of guilt, since the speakers shall remain anonymous.

She (gruffly): "Stop doing that."

He: "I'm not doing anything."

She: "Yes you are."

He: "I'm not doing anything at all."

She (shouting): "Stop it, damn it. Quiet!"

It stays quiet for over two minutes. I can't sleep by this point anyway, and I'm dying to find out what happens next. Sorry, Grandma! And sure enough, it continues.

She: "Stop it."

He: "Oh, come on." He mumbles something incomprehensible.

She: "Put a lid on that beak of yours and turn the other way."

Then she gets hysterical and yells something incomprehensible. The Camino seems to be doing wonders for these two. I fall asleep.

Thirty minutes later, I wake up to the sound of the same voices, but this time they're under my window. Evidently they couldn't fall asleep, and are now going for a stroll through town. Once again, I hear only their voices. This is like a radio play. The woman's voice rises as she addresses someone parking her car. The following high-decibel dialogue ensues, from which I infer that for now, there is a truce.

My neighbor ("she"): "Are you German?"

Another, somewhat younger woman replies: "Yes, how did you know?" In the background I hear the voices of German children at play.

She: "Because you have a German license plate."

Good thinking, I say to myself with a laugh.

The other woman: "Yes, we're German."

She: "We're German too."

That never would have crossed the other woman's mind.

Other woman: "Nice place, isn't it? Are you staying at this hotel?"

She: "Yes."

Other woman: "And how is it?"

She: "Clean."

As a fellow German with the same petty bourgeois mind-set, I have to agree, and I nod to myself.

Other woman: "Do you know your way around this area?" Then she goes on to say, more testily, probably to her husband: "Günther, would you please open up for me?"

I guess she's referring to the trunk or the car door; but I have no idea. Maybe she's sitting in the car and wants to get out, or the other way around. It's a radio play, after all, and I am ashamed of my insatiable curiosity. In any case, Günther does not reply.

She: "Nah, we don't know this place."

Other woman: "We want to get to Burgos. Do you know a hotel there?"

She: "Yes, we've just come from there. There's an Art Deco hotel right in the center of town."

Other woman: "Is it easy to get there by car?" Then, impatiently, to Günther: "Can you open up for me now?"

Addressing herself to "she" again: "Do they have a parking lot too?"

She: "Yes, I think so; we don't have a car here."

The other woman does not react.

She (waiting for expressions of admiration): "We've come on foot."

Other woman: "Oh! You're *walking* the Camino."

She: "To Santiago."

Other woman: "We've come from there by car. Keep up the good work! Have a nice trip; we're going on as well."

Then she says to her husband: "Can you open up here now, Günther?"

She: "All the best."

"She" seemed disappointed that the "other woman" wasn't more impressed by her pilgrimage. Meanwhile, the other people zoom off with their children.

My neighbor speaks to her husband, and from the sound of it I gather that it's something disparaging about the people with the car. Five minutes later, my married couple comes back to the room next door.

He (quite resolutely): "So, now I'm going to sleep."

Obviously it didn't work before, just as it didn't for me. She again says something I'm unable to make out, and then screeches out the name of a Galician town ("La Coruña, La Coruña, La Coruña!"). Her voice carries throughout the hotel.

Then it's quiet. I hear her yawn one last time before they evidently go to sleep.

Five minutes later, however, two Spaniards get into a shouting match in front of my door. And my two next-door neighbors wake up again. My God, what kind of place is this?

She shouts to the people outside, "Shut up!" Then she turns to her husband with this puzzling remark: "There was nothing she could do about it either!" and adds, even more bafflingly, "Shut up, you old billy goat!" I didn't hear him say anything.

Now what? I know this is none of my business, and yes, Grandma, I do know the saying, "Don't stick your nose into other people's business!" But the two of them are intruding on my life. There ought to be a law against people like those two staying together! Downstairs, they played the suave, well-informed Germans (at least she did; he didn't say anything), and now, a mere five minutes later, she is out for blood.

I shudder to think about how many people may be living like that. I sincerely hope these two go their separate ways; any other outcome would be disastrous. I wonder what they look like—and picture retired assistant principals clad in gray and blue. Maybe I'll see them today. She must be skinny and uptight, and I'm assuming he's tall, a bit stout, and very tired. Let's hope they don't bump each other off here. If I think about all the things the Camino has made them do already, I wouldn't put it past them.

~

I manage to get in another half hour of sleep before I'm awakened yet again by a terrible racket. The doors to all the rooms in this hotel are directly above the restaurant, on a wraparound balcony that bears a slight resemblance to a cloister. I hear a Spaniard race into the bar, distraught. He orders a whiskey and tells the innkeeper that he witnessed a terrible accident on the way here. On the main road to Burgos, a German family riding in a car collided head-on with a Spanish truck. All the passengers died on impact!

Were these the people I heard not half an hour earlier, under my hotel window?

Sleep is now out of the question, so I get dressed and walk down the staircase, which looks just like the one in that old TV soap opera *Dynasty*. I head for the bar.

I consider asking about the car accident but decide against it. I've been privy to enough things that have nothing to do with me for one day. I order a cup of cocoa and my standard *bocadillo,* and enjoy the cool room while leafing through the *El País* newspaper.

Up on the balcony, a door opens. At first I just hear voices, but then I see them! My next-door neighbors! They stroll over to the staircase and slowly descend.

The two of them look pretty much the way I pictured them. They're dressed in grayish blue with a hint of ocher. She's taller and even more unpleasant than I'd thought. A giant Germanic grayish-blond sourpuss. He is dark-haired, nicer-looking, and shorter, but even more weary than in my fantasy. I can hardly stand the sight of them, because I'm ashamed to know so much about these total strangers. So I decide to take a stroll around town. Otherwise I would have no choice here but to continue listening in on their conversations.

I'm half expecting to meet a shadow of myself in her! My acoustic shadow! I am too nosy!

It takes very little time to walk through the two streets in this town, though I have to keep dodging brambles. It's like a Sergio Leone spaghetti Western. I take one final glance back to the dirt road and snap a photo of the indescribable view. On the shaded stoop of one of the houses, I make friends with a stray dog, a pregnant, snow-white pointer who is bedraggled but beautiful. This flea-bitten dog is scratching her skin raw. I pluck two empty plastic bottles out of a garbage can. (You find these at every street corner.) I can't tell whether many pilgrims find the illumination they were seeking here, but they sure do leave quite a lot of garbage along the way. I go over to the village fountain with the intention of filling the bottles with water so I can wash the dog. Naturally, she has no desire to be washed. But she trots over to the fountain herself, figuring cleverly that since I was there and opened the faucet, there must be some overflow, and she can now drink.

At a little store in one of the modest huts, I buy a pound of cold cuts and feed the emaciated animal. Then she goes back to the entryway to her house with a full belly. I hope I don't have any fleas on me!

Even at night the stifling heat makes my body feel feverish. It's no longer tolerable outdoors, and I have yet to see a single villager.

On the way back to the hotel I almost have a heart attack. Suddenly, in the middle of this ghost town, an indescribably ugly animal, like a monster in a horror movie, is standing in front of me. It sends shivers down my spine! Roughly the size of a Great Dane, it looks like a mishandled genetic engineering experiment, a cross between a wolf, a hyena, and a Himalayan black bear. Of course, it might be nothing more than an insanely fat dog, although I have never seen anything like it in my life. I am really scared. Unfortunately, there is no way around this monster, so I approach with my right hand outstretched, fibbing in a purring baby voice: "You are soooo sweeeet!" I figure this horrid animal would not be able to handle the awful truth. He even lets me pet him, though his coat is quite revolting. What kind of an idiot am I to touch this thing? Yuck! But the hyena-wolf-bear is very trusting, and I get the vague feeling that he doesn't have the foggiest notion of his brutal effect on others. There is no doubt that this dog has not been petted since he reached sexual maturity, as I can tell from the fond look he gives me.

I've had it for today. I go to my room, watch a little TV, and then fall asleep despite my "chronic fever."

I hope the German couple keeps it quiet tonight.

***

Insight of the day: Yes, you even have to draw near monsters.

June 29, 2001
Sahagún

This morning I get up at six o'clock and head straight down to the bar for breakfast. I discover to my horror that it doesn't open until eight.

Without breakfast I'm insufferable. I'd rather have a bad breakfast than none at all. Without breakfast I am nothing and can do nothing! I still have two brownish bananas, and there's plenty of lukewarm water in my bottle, but I'm just in the mood for something more substantial, accompanied by a nice cup of coffee. So I swipe a piece of marble cake from the counter and devour it.

In front of the hotel, I cuddle up with a white cat and at 6:30 I'm on my way.

My petty culinary larceny wasn't a real breakfast, though, and I'm grumpy. The hiking book claims that I'll have to walk six miles until the next stopping point, in Ledigos. My mood sinks with every step I take; I'm barely moving ahead, and I'm fuming all the way. I am furious at everything!

The landscape all around me bores me. Nothing but wheat fields. How much bread must the Spaniards be baking with all this grain? The farther I walk, the more it looks like Hesse in Germany. I might as well have trekked through southern Germany. It certainly would have been cooler and less complicated!

I want to smash one of the route's ubiquitous scallop signposts. But I don't want to splinter my walking stick, so I stop myself just in time. Instead I start cursing aloud. I really don't want to go on. Sheesh; I am fed up once and for all with this stupid pilgrimage, and I want my breakfast now!

My hiking outfit is ridiculous. This idiotic denim shirt and this huge hat. I can't bear myself in these clothes anymore. Washing my clothes by hand never gets me the results I want. And wearily wringing them out at the sink will never be the same as a good spin cycle. I want to wear something truly clean.

I stop walking and give myself a good talking-to: "OK. Either I keep whining and give up, convinced that everything I'm doing here is stupid, or I forge ahead and believe in the possibility of a small miracle."

Once I hear myself saying that out loud, I realize that I can't give up now. I'll always regret it. I'm nearly halfway there. So I tell myself to shut up and keep walking. A last spark of reason tells me to persist. Now I'm waiting for a miracle!

I walk along a beaten path until I get to Ledigos, the farming community listed in my pilgrims' book, and look for the only bar in town. Guided by my enormous hunger, I soon find the bar. When I look through the grimy window, I see not only that the bar hasn't been cleaned up from the previous day but that it is closed today. I feel like bashing in the window. I tell myself to shut up and keep on going.

The next town, Terradillos de los Templarios, is another two miles down the road. Frustrated, I start to understand why some people, like my German neighbors, might want to pick a fight.

Farther down the road through Hesse, aka Andalusia, four grim, ragged men come my way in quick succession. They are walking along barefoot in tattered clothes with plastic bags in their hands, staring vacantly ahead. One is carrying a bucket. What are they doing here? Looking for mushrooms? Gathering berries? Robbing pilgrims? They won't find any of those things in that direction!

When I get to the next tiny town I'm covered in dust, worn out, and in a foul mood. Terradillos has nothing but earth-colored adobe houses, which is not surprising given that the name of the town translates to something like "earthen." The buildings seem to be made of cow dung, giving off a pungent sweet-and-sour smell. It's silent as the grave. I will never find anything to eat here! I stand in the middle of this town and decide to take Jose's advice. When she needs something, she simply orders it from the universe. Ha, ha, ha! Next thing I know, I'm saying out loud: "Universe, I want a nice breakfast in the next five minutes, or else!"

At that very moment, a deafening racket erupts behind me. People are shouting, singing, and banging on drums. Someone is playing the flute off-key. I look at my watch: it's nine o'clock. I turn around and follow the noise. Six tipsy teenagers with colorful hats and musical instruments are standing in front of one of the adobe houses. I feel as though I'm seeing things; and they are bound to have the same reaction when they see me. I look so dumb in this hiking hat. One of them holds out his colorful hat and asks me for money. They are collecting for this evening's village festival to honor St. Peter, the village's patron saint. Today is St. Peter's day? Then it's my name day all over again. I quickly wish myself a happy name day.

Since I'm not in an especially generous mood today, I give them a hundred pesetas and ask, "Is there a bar here?" Their reply is roaring laughter. "Here? A bar!?" One of the drunken teenagers offers me his half-eaten ham sandwich. I'm on the verge of taking it, but I don't. This is not what I ordered! When I asked the universe for a delicious breakfast, I was clear and unequivocal.

I traipse down two more blocks in this hamlet and wind up in front of a very run-down *albergue*. These *albergues* rarely offer anything but a place to sleep. I walk across the overgrown garden, enter the building through the back door, and wind up in a cramped kitchen with a low ceiling. A short, dour Spanish woman, an apron wrapped around her buxom middle, is frightened out of her wits when I enter her inner sanctum and ask, "*Perdón, señora,* is there any chance of getting breakfast here? I would be willing to pay you handsomely." The woman peers at me crossly. It would appear that no one has ever made her such a stupid offer. "Of course there's breakfast!" she snarls at me, and makes a vague gesture in the direction of another room, where I hear muted conversation. The dining room! That's a first.

Several exhausted pilgrims are seated in a brightly lit room, at tables with lovely place settings, and I smell freshly brewed coffee, scrambled eggs, and buttered toast. My mouth starts watering like crazy, and I promptly order a *desayuno grande,* an extra-large breakfast. I drop my backpack on the floor and sit down at one of the room's five tables Then I look to the right and do a double take. Who should be there at the next table but my loud next-door neighbors from yesterday, whom I have now dubbed Beaky and Billy Goat. I flinch and decide to keep my hat on, in the hope that they won't recognize me and start up a conversation.

My food is served, and even under the circumstances I enjoy every bite.

I find it a bit creepy that these two have also found their way here and are stuffing their faces just like me. But I can say without exaggeration that this breakfast is the best thing I've eaten on the whole journey so far. All those boring biscuits!

Beaky and Billy Goat are sharing a table with an Austrian woman, the only person I have kept running into from the beginning of my journey. She's a sunburnt beanpole of a woman, and she wears a perpetual grin. Her Tyrolean hat is bedecked with colorful stickers from places she has breezed through and others where she was probably forced to stay when she was too exhausted to go on. Evidently she is progressing as sluggishly as I am! The Camino seems to spirit away most of the other pilgrims I've met, but she keeps popping up. Why am I just noticing that for the first time? We have been walking in tandem for weeks.

Her method of seeking companionship is unvarying. She approaches people and asks, "Is there a little store around here?" I have been asked this question twice already, and both times I gave her a friendly brush-off. I find her too intense and too superficial all at once, so I don't want to encourage any intimacy.

The three of them are having a very animated conversation, or rather, the two women are. Billy Goat isn't saying much. He is sitting at the table stripped to the waist, covered in sweat, and stuffing a jelly sandwich into his mouth. To the left of me there's a motley group of young American women and a German woman. The German woman recognizes me right away. She stands up, comes to my table, and—oddly—uses English to ask me: "Are you from Germany?" I answer, "Yes; hello." The woman, who is wearing blue shorts that are much too short—or is that underwear?— fixes her gaze on me, then returns to her group without another word. What was that? Either she's too awestruck to speak, or she is put off by my idiotic "Yes; hello."

These pilgrims and their manners! My curiosity gets the better of me again, and I go back to listening in on Beaky, who is far more entertaining. She's acting as though all is fine and dandy and playing this role to the hilt, but I can't help noticing that her eyes look despondent. I almost feel sorry for her. She always talks so loudly that everyone is forced to listen.

Now she's saying to the Austrian woman, "But Vienna is absolutely wonderful. I don't understand you. The cultural capital of the German-speaking world: everything good comes from Vienna . . . Ludwig Hirsch, for instance."

That's true, I'm thinking. His song about suicide is called "Come, Big Black Bird." Beaky, Beaky, that's really deep!

The Austrian woman admits, "I like him too."

Well, what do you know!

Beaky appeals to her husband, "Right, Gerd? Vienna's great."

So that's Billy Goat's name: Gerd!

Gerd replies indifferently, "Vienna's wonderful."

Austrian woman: "Have you ever been there?"

Beaky: "No, we haven't."

That takes the cake! I feel like screaming with laughter! You can't make this stuff up—it's so marvelously idiotic.

Apparently the Austrian woman lives in Vienna and considers it abominable, but Beaky does not want to confront abominations, least of all her own. Beaky, I am now certain, is my shadow! Things will never get dull with her around.

The Austrian woman orders another cup of coffee from the ill-tempered Spanish woman in halting Spanish, and once again grins at me from ear to ear. Gerd is trying to figure out where he knows me from. I hope he's suffering from TV amnesia.

Beaky is now standing at the gigantic map in the dining room and calculating loudly how many miles she has already walked and how many she has left to go. For a minute it feels like geography class, and I'm fully expecting Professor Beaky to call me up to the board to mark the mineral resources on the map.

This woman is authoritarian, and I have a problem with that.

Then she sits back down and announces, "We always watch *The Literary Quartet* on TV."

The Austrian woman says she doesn't know that show. This abrupt change of topic makes me think that Beaky has recognized me and now plans to bring the subject around to me. I feign oblivion and continue eating my breakfast.

Beaky: "Sure you do; you have to. They show it in Austria, too. Right, Gerd? She *has* to know it."

Why has she started using the formal *Sie* to the Viennese woman, when they've been on informal terms up to now?

Gerd: "She knows it."

Austrian woman: "I don't."

Silence.

Beaky: "You speak good Spanish."

She says this to the Austrian woman, who correctly assesses her limited abilities in her terse reply, "I get by."

Beaky: "No, it's outstanding. But I like Italian better; it sounds nicer."

Meaning: My dear Austrian, you wasted your time learning this ugly language!

As if on cue, a beaming southern European man and woman in their late fifties enter the room and walk up to my table. The woman asks me very politely in Italian whether the two of them can join me.

I invite them to sit down, wanting nothing more than to stop listening to Beaky.

I strike up a lively conversation with these Italians, who are from Friaul. Like me, the wife is struggling on the Camino and feeling grouchy today. She's sorely tempted to throw in the towel. It's a relief to chat with these two open-minded, refined people. She lifts my spirits, like the good Italian mama she is. Her husband says a few kind words, and my grouchiness dissolves. To commemorate my name day, I order another coffee.

Shortly thereafter, a nice but rather dejected young Englishman joins us. Beaky sits at the next table, looking daggers at me and soaking in every word.

My shadow is just as much of a snoop as I am!

She says to Gerd, "Listen, that man is Spanish."

She means me.

The Austrian woman hastens to correct her, "No, he's speaking Italian to that couple."

Well, Beaky, how can you think Italian sounds more beautiful than Spanish if you can't even tell the two languages apart? Beaky and I may well lock horns today.

The conversation at our table is a happy hodgepodge of Italian and English. The British guy tells us a funny story about a toad he rescued, and the Italians raise my spirits by praising my Italian again and again.

Even so, I find myself identifying with Beaky. She wants constant affirmation of her heroism in hiking the Camino de Santiago. And so I decide that it is absolutely inconsequential whether I can do this or that, or whether I hike or not—from here on in, I'm just out for fun!

Beaky's expression reveals that the good cheer at our table is grating on her nerves. The German and American women begin to apply their sunblock. Beaky seizes this opportunity to weigh in again. The more intently I look at her, the more she resembles

Liv Ullmann's evil twin. Beaky comments with a slightly ironic undertone, "Look at how they're all rubbing cream on themselves. They must really love themselves. See how they're putting cream on their feet, and their necks . . . They sure do primp and pamper themselves, don't they? Huh, Gerd?"

The Austrian woman now asks her standard all-important question, "Is there a little store around here?" I can't believe it; she's said it again. And she's in luck. There is indeed a store in one of these adobe huts, as Beaky is happy to report.

Gerd has his eyes glued to the young women daubing sunblock onto their bodies. The Austrian woman, Beaky, and Billy Goat drink another cup of coffee, and decide to hike together.

Ah, well. Eventually we all go our own separate ways.

My hike to Sahagún goes quite well. The crisis of the morning has passed. I realize that my anger at things has nothing to do with the things themselves. It takes only a minor attitude adjustment to spare myself some tantrums. But I do have to wonder whether this trail really is a path of illumination. For the most part, I'm still groping in the dark.

After some cheerful hiking, I reach a hilly landscape that looks like a scene right out of southern Germany. Off in the distance, at the fork in the road, a group of pilgrims suddenly starts shouting "yoo-hoo" and "hello" in my direction. They must be drunk or suffering from sunstroke . . . or maybe both. I am a bit annoyed, but I wave back and approach the group with a smile on my face, until I make out who is standing there. At a cattle trough under a willow rustling in the wind are Beaky, Gerd, the Austrian woman, and the German woman in the blue underwear, accompanied by the German woman's sunblock-smeared American gang!

When I arrive at the lineup of my fans, I say a quick and

Is there a little store here?

friendly hello, just as I did earlier in the dining room. The German girl with the hotpants invites me to a picnic, as though we'd been the closest of friends for decades. It appears that Miss Tanga couldn't wait to tell everyone who I am and what I do, which explains the big emotional outburst! Well, I'm sure I would have done the same if I were in her shoes.

Since they have yet to see a vision of the Blessed Virgin Mary on the pilgrims' route, they have to settle for seeing me. Even the American women are ecstatic; they're acting as though they're getting George Clooney in a tux instead of me in my torn denim shirt. Evidently they now consider their German acquaintance far more interesting; to judge by her pushy behavior, she has now definitively risen to the rank of alpha dog in the pilgrim pecking order. She's the one who discovered me, so the spoils belong to her, the victor! But I have no interest whatever in playing the highlight of the day here. Gerd and Beaky are welcome to do so; they are much better at it.

I look down at the sandy dirt road and see that Beaky's shadow and mine are forming a misshapen lump. How dreadful! The couple is staring at me as though expecting a miracle. I guess I could whip out my diary and read their hilarious dialogues aloud, but that would be cruel.

Come on, folks. This is not the way to find illumination.

Of course, I could stand here in my dusty hiking boots on a dirt road at a cattle trough and bask in my fame . . . but that would be flat-out ridiculous.

It shouldn't matter who is standing before you! I'm not saying you should be gruff and dismissive, but to act as though an encounter of this kind is the highlight of your life is just plain unreasonable. No way am I going to burst out in a fit of glee.

I thank them for the invitation, doff my greasy hat, and continue on. The silence of the group behind me speaks volumes, even though I did nothing to offend them. I was unfailingly friendly, and raised neither hopes nor expectations. Too bad I didn't get to hear Beaky's comments about my grand exit.

These pilgrims were a little test for me and I was a test for them.

If Beaky and Gerd had been there alone, though, I would have stayed.

I feel sorry for Beaky and Gerd, and I can't get them out of my mind. I was able to look so deeply into their personal life and now I have to bear witness to their public personas. I have a weird kind of access to them; I'm like an all-hearing ear. I would enjoy chatting with them over three bottles of a good Spanish red wine.

The worst part is that the two of them hold up a dreary mirror to me, and I don't want to look into it. I'm not exactly like them—at least I hope not—but does that make me any better than they are? I can't disdain people just because they're in desperate straits! I feel for them, the way I would for a close relative. I've given her the cutesy little nickname to make her seem less insufferable.

"Beaky" sounds rather sweet, like a gawky little duck with an oversized beak.

When afternoon rolls around and I see from a hill the imposing town of Sahagún off in the distance, I weep for joy. Halftime!

I did fifteen miles today, and I have half the journey behind me.

I'm not going to be like Beaky and run down a list of all the miles I've walked—but if I hadn't met her, I'd probably be tempted to do just that.

As I'm walking toward the magnificent town with trancelike sluggishness, a long-maned creature leaps out of the bushes off to my left. I'm afraid that I'm about to be assaulted. But the creature turns out to be a lovely young woman, who freely confesses that she was in the field because she had to go to the little girls' room. This field is not Lara's natural habitat; she's from Vancouver, Canada. I think Vancouver is one of the most beautiful cities in the world. I bought my hiking boots at a little shoe store in Vancouver.

We start walking together, sweat pouring down our bodies, while chatting about Canada, our trials and tribulations along the trail, and people we've met along the way. I ruefully admit to her that earlier today I felt sorely tempted to give one of the pilgrims a good thrashing. She laughs, saying that she's run into this woman too. She asks me how far we've come; like me, she started out in

Saint-Jean. I say, "Today is halftime; as of today, we're halfway there. Didn't you know?"

She stands still, breaks down in tears, and flings her arms around my neck. She has neither map nor hiking guide with her; she simply walks without any concrete idea of when she will arrive where, and how many miles she has covered in a given day. In this respect she's miles ahead of me!

Then she says, "Did you know that only fifteen percent of the pilgrims stick it out to the end? Each year, thousands of pilgrims' passports are issued, but only fifteen percent are actually stamped in Santiago. It is a path of illumination for the select few. What do you say to that?"

I look at her and say, "Maybe."

Lara tells me that she has stopped taking photographs of herself. Every photo shows her in the same clothing, and she always looks the same. That is the very reason I also have stopped taking pictures of myself.

It's funny, at home you look different on the outside with each new day, yet on the inside you stay virtually the same. Here you're always the same on the outside, but on the inside you change by the hour.

As we get closer to Sahagún, I ask Lara, who strikes me as being quite intelligent behind her glasses, the question that keeps preying on my mind: "What do you think God is?" She looks at me skeptically and asks, "Do you really want me to tell you?" I nod. "Do you have time?" she asks, with a giggle, and I nod again.

Lara takes a deep breath: "Okay; I don't like to talk about it, because sometimes I get the feeling that my ideas are well-defined, only to find that when I put them into words, they've turned dull and vague. I think God installed a safety valve in my mouth to make everything sound distorted and untrue when I shout my inner truth from the rooftops. I don't know!"

"On the Camino," she explains, "I have developed a very naïve notion of God—or of the sole truth, however you want to put it. I believe that for millions upon millions of years, there was only a heavy black void, and in a process of eternal endurance, 'It' came to life in a lucid moment as though after a long sleep, the way a stinking dung heap eventually ignites in a fierce blaze. A spark of light was born! This spark comes into the void with a scream of horror and of bliss, like a newborn, and expands infinitely. It devises, invents, experiences, and puts everything to the test, like a small child. This light pursues a single, innate, clear aim—complete happiness. To do so, it carries out all kinds of experiments in every dimension. We are parts of this expanding light but so far removed from the origins that we can no longer recall the source, and only vaguely the call: 'Be completely happy!' This spark soon conjures up suffering, because only suffering leads to true consciousness. Light does not want to be happy just unconsciously, like a small child at play, but knowingly happy, the way only a person who has been sorely tried can be. A summer's day is doubly beautiful once you've survived a difficult operation. After an extreme experience, a sunny day is not only beautiful but absolutely wonderful and holy. So if this light expands infinitely and has fulfilled everything, it goes out again and goes back to sleep. As everyone knows, perfect happiness doesn't last long. It dies, because this ultimate experience of the infinite conscious expansion is unique. In its final moment, it enjoys the bliss of explicit happiness, and forgets all the suffering that preceded it. 'It' has come to terms with itself and attained perfect bliss. And then it falls asleep, only to reawaken at some point all on its own."

"You mean suffering is the key to happiness?" I ask in confusion.

"Exactly! Everything serves just one goal: to give joy to God and thus to oneself. You may well laugh. I know that sounds like a childish notion. But the Bible says: 'Become like children!'"

I don't say anything at first. But somehow this idea gets me back on an even keel. And since God embodies all opposites, it would stand to reason that He must also at some time be dead or asleep—or am I mistaken here? But we count the hours we're asleep as part of our lifetime; we don't subtract them.

I tell Lara that her idea of suffering as the key to happiness is a really hard nut to crack here at the halfway point of our journey. I ask her whether she thinks we might better endure suffering or perhaps even prevent it with awareness training. She grins again:

The pilgrims' route to the grave of St. James

"Yes! The darkness can be complete without light. When you are in a room without windows and electricity, you don't see anything. But there can't be light without darkness. Look, today's a brilliantly sunny day, but our dark shadows always come right along with us, and we have to be aware of them. Only the source of light itself is spared any hint of a shadow."

Oh, dear; let's hope Beaky doesn't round the bend right now!

Lara and I walk to Sahagún side by side in silence, like an old married couple. Lara plans to spend the night in the hopelessly overcrowded pilgrims' hostel. I don't try to talk her out of it, because she's obviously come to terms with the conditions in these places and accepts them uncomplainingly. I'm not prepared to do so. I need a single room with a shower, so we part ways after getting our pilgrim's passports stamped in the *refugio* and exchanging telephone numbers and addresses.

In the middle of town, there's a reasonably priced, charming hotel. A colorful, medieval sort of mosaic in the foyer displaying the Camino Francés makes it painfully clear to me how many miles still lie ahead. This hotel will be my home today. As time goes on, more and more pilgrims opt for hotels.

After all the time I've spent in dusty villages, I'm very impressed by Sahagún. This town has fabulous buildings dating back to Roman times and the Baroque period. Several monuments from the Arabic era make some streets look like a little mecca. By the late eighteenth century, though, Sahagún's heyday had ended. Everything built afterward is lackluster by comparison. It figures that halfway along the Camino de Santiago you come to a town that spends centuries on an upswing, only to be followed by centuries heading downhill.

~

The bulletin board at the hotel desk says that David, the local physiotherapist, offers massages to pilgrims at special prices. I grab the phone and call him, and get an appointment on the spot.

What luck! For the first time in two hundred miles I can get a massage.

After an ice-cold shower and a ham sandwich, I race over to the massage studio, where David the masseur is waiting for me on the street. I recognize him from his photo.

I greet him by saying, "*Hola,* David! I know your face from a picture in the bar in Castrojeriz, where Kathie the parrot wings her way around the room!" He laughs, and explains to me that the owner there is his best friend. I recall that the bar had a big picture of David hanging on the wall right over my table, and I stared at it the whole time I was eating. He looked pleasant, so I remembered his face. It's funny how things sometimes come together.

In no time, I'm lying half-naked on the massage table, having my swollen feet kneaded. While the radio crackles away, David tells me how he met Kathie's owner on one of his own two pilgrimages. I have no idea what else he says, because the reflexology massage on my aching feet sends me into a zone of utter bliss.

Just as I nod off, I'm jolted into the here and now by the sound of my own snoring and an old Kate Bush song playing on the radio: *Don't give up / I know you can make it.*

I like this song, so I start singing along to myself, but when I get to the second chorus I realize what I've been saying. I can't believe it! Yet another wonderful challenge. *Don't give up / I know you can make it*— along the Camino de Santiago!

Maybe the Camino is wonderful simply because I will it to be wonderful.

Shortly before David finishes massaging all the kinks out of my feet, he asks me when I started my pilgrimage—yesterday, or the day before?

I sit up, astonished and wide awake: "What? Yesterday or the day before? I'm halfway through." He examines my feet skeptically and somewhat more thoroughly. "That is not possible," he states matter-of-factly. "But I'm telling you I am!" I insist, although it doesn't make a bit of difference to me whether he believes what I'm saying. The foot expert sticks to his guns: "No—you don't have a single blister or scar on your feet. That's not possible!" I answer honestly, "I know that's not possible, and it surprises me as well. Normally every new pair of shoes gives me blisters on the very first day, but on this journey I haven't had a single one. I guess my Canadian hiking shoes are simply the best in the world." David grins, and keeps on massaging in silence.

Don't give up / I know you can make it!

After our session I feel as good as new, and drink my usual *café con leche* on the plaza under the shady colonnades. I also order an insipid *bocadillo* with cheese.

Today's breakfast was the culinary high point of this journey. Apart from that, the cuisine is almost universally bad, not bad in the nutritional sense. It's good, nourishing food, just not creative or well prepared. After all, I suppose this is a pilgrimage, not a gourmet tour. You do learn to appreciate a simple ham sandwich.

While I gobble up the last bit of my roll and wipe my mouth with a napkin—who should round the corner? The Austrian woman. She is doubtless on the prowl for an open store. But this is siesta time in Spain, and shopping is a no-go! But the big surprise is still to come; the Austrian woman has Beaky and Gerd in tow! And then the inevitable happens. The Austrian woman starts in with her chatter, and asks to sit down with me. I have no real grounds for objection, so I set up some chairs. But Beaky doesn't want to sit down. Gerd wouldn't mind—not that he says anything. Beaky is probably still sore at me because of the picnic snub this morning. The Austrian woman notes this and no longer dares to sit down; Beaky can really give you the evil eye. Still, the Austrian woman is nothing if not consistent, and she asks me, "When does the *panadería* [bakery] open?"

I tell her that all the shops in Spain wait to reopen until siesta time is over, no earlier than 5 P.M. One thing you're sure to know by heart after three weeks on the Camino is the store hours. No earlier than 5 P.M.!

The Austrian woman acts as though this were news to her and she had never come across such a thing.

The way she keeps changing the subject is both chaotic and creative. Now she wants to know how many languages I speak. She starts counting: "French, Spanish, Italian, and English are what I've heard you use so far. What else do you speak?"

I'm tempted to mimic her Viennese dialect and count that as another foreign language, but instead I go with a matter-of-fact reply and give her the information she wants without showing off too much—adding Dutch to the list. Before this trip, I would have considered that an affectation, but it's true, so why not say it?

The Austrian woman is paying far more attention to me than I am to her, but she didn't catch my conversation with Larissa from Gouda. I realize how excited I am to get to know the three of them at long last. They're the sorts of characters I develop for screenplays and sketches. I'm starting to feel as though they're an outgrowth of my own imagination.

The Austrian woman with her Tyrolean hat and her obsession

with shopping is so comical. I love it when people repeat the same silly sentences in inappropriate situations the way she does, especially here in the middle of nowhere. Crazy mixed-up Beaky and Gerd are actually wonderful; it turns out that they are from Remscheid, in North Rhine–Westphalia. I've been enjoying the way they've been gabbing away without sitting down, but now Beaky raises her dark, heavy voice.

"I have something to tell you now too." She doesn't just say what's on her mind, she announces her intention to do so! Like the queen of England or the pope.

Gerd cradles his head on his walking stick, which has to mean that this story will be a long one. We wait to hear what she has to say. I am so curious that I ought to blush with shame! Beaky begins: "Three years ago my husband and I were hiking the Camino, though not all the way to the end. We met two strapping young men in training for the priesthood." She manages to make this sound risqué. "And after walking from Saint-Jean-Pied-de-Port to Roncesvalles, we went to mass in the evening, and there the two of them had to limp up and support each other as they received their blessing at the altar. I was directly behind them, and walked to the front standing tall, with my head held high!" She laughs, and I'm speechless. What a triumph, I think, to wrest victory from the defeat of others. It depends on how you look at it, I suppose, and there's no obvious victor, but how often have I entertained thoughts of this kind? Beaky gives me a devastatingly clear picture of what may be my worst shortcomings! I have to be grateful to her.

While Beaky continues her self-righteous chatter (I've quickly lost interest in her), I get ravenous again, even though I've already wolfed down a fatty hamburger and two big *bocadillos* since I got here. Now I know why she doesn't want to sit down. In this position she looms over the rest of us; if she were to sit, she wouldn't be able to look down on us anymore.

On the other side of the street, a stunning woman strolls by, and even I can't take my eyes off her. She sees me, smiles, and waves. This time I hold back on waving and keep my distance. I don't know her, so I don't react. She comes running up to me, and says in English: "Hi, Hans Peter, it's me, Lara!"

How embarrassing! I didn't recognize her without her hat and glasses. I jump up to offer her one of the chairs we've set up, and she sits down. Fresh from the shower, with flowing blond hair, she looks like Miss Canada.

Beaky gives her a quick hello and turns the focus back to herself: "I liked the cleanliness of the Basque country, but I don't understand why they're still throwing bombs when they get to live in such pretty houses!"

Now it's getting creepy. Not only do I have a window into Beaky's inner world but she has one into mine, which is only fair, I suppose. Is she a mind reader? I was thinking, and even writing down, the exact same thing when I was in the Basque country. Coming from Beaky, it sounds dreadfully dim-witted.

But I don't change my mind. I think Beaky's right, and I tell her so, which clearly pleases her. Thankfully, Lara agrees, which eases my self-doubt. I'm growing quite fond of Lara.

It's still appalling that I think like this Rhenish Valkyrie from Remscheid! Beaky and I have more in common than I'm comfortable with.

I'd like to be rid of these three weirdos and get something to eat with Lara. Lara seems to want that too, because she no longer deigns to look at the German-Austrian trio. Beaky picks up on that right away and makes a point of coming to a dead halt on the curb with her entourage. My subsequent remarks to Beaky, Gerd, and the Viennese woman sound pretty feeble. I hear myself telling some tedious story about my knee. Beaky wants to know which one! What good is this information to her? And while I say "the left one," I think about how I'd like to know Beaky's real name. Something Teutonic—Ursel, Hildegard, or Inge—would suit her. But I don't dare ask for fear that she might sit down after all. It's silly that the three of them know my name, yet they don't introduce themselves. So she'll continue to be Beaky.

The Austrian woman finally gets a complaint off her chest: she finds it appalling that everyone on the Camino thinks she's German. Maybe that's why she's wearing that Tyrolean hat, but it doesn't do the trick, because the Spaniards figure it's an Oktoberfest costume. Beaky and Gerd are clearly taken aback by her German-bashing, and nasty repercussions could easily follow. The trio soon takes off, and I picture Gerd grabbing the patriotic Austrian around the next corner so Beaky can beat her up. I guess I won't be seeing them again.

Lara and I stay in the café for quite a while, getting something to eat and basking in the sun. We don't say very much, since we've already hit the high points. But Lara does mention that that middle-aged woman from Germany is awful, and she feels sorry for the husband. Ditto!

When I get back to my hotel room, I relax with a bit of TV. German television is often dismissed as pathetic and trivial, but it doesn't hold a candle to Spanish TV in either respect.

Every channel features hour after hour of pseudo-experts grouped on imposing, candy-colored stage sets, blathering about paparazzi videos of the Norwegian heir to the throne, his fiancée, and their son. That is the theme of the day on all channels, and these inane images are shown again and again. Some idiot films the heir to the throne and his retinue and sells this mediocre material to TV stations around the world. Nobody bothers to ask what point there is to this footage. The paparazzo is praised to the skies for having taken these sensational pictures of aristocratic offspring.

To make matters worse, Spanish celebrities evidently love to accept dubious invitations from blouse manufacturers or cookie makers to announce their upcoming liposuction or divorce while posing in front of an advertising logo. For a fee, of course. A cookie maker positions the celebrities in front of the company logo, and the celebrities get big bucks to leak intimate details of their personal lives. These shows must get top ratings, or there wouldn't be so many of them.

I'm watching some famous singer's wife with blond dreadlocks stand in front of a poster advertising sherry, while an interviewer asks, "Did you have morning sickness during your pregnancy?" Instead of stomping off at this intrusive question, she smiles and says, "No, not during this pregnancy." But when she was pregnant with her first child—you'd better believe that she threw up. I can't believe what's being shown on the screen. All I can do is laugh!

A liposuctioned woman in her midforties stands in front of the poster of a pen manufacturer and says she's gone to bed twice with the new Mister Spain. Then Mister Spain, at some other get-together, stands in front of the poster of a cosmetics firm and says no, she didn't go to bed with him, but he does know her, and knows she likes to spread the rumor that the two of them had a fling.

Is anyone going to buy that pen just because she was or wasn't in bed with this guy?

I switch the channel to a Spanish quiz show, where a boisterous buxom blonde manages to keep a straight face while posing this multiple-choice question to the contestants: "In 1982, what did the German mass murderer Hans Whatshisname turn his victims into? A: Meat loaf, B: Tripe, or C: Meatballs?" Then the contestants take a guess, and there's a cool prize. I won't give away the answer—to do so would mean gratifying primitive instincts and encouraging out-and-out voyeurism. Horribly enough, though, I find it hard to turn off.

These people who stand in front of cookie or sherry posters and dish out details about their sexual and vomiting habits, as self-important as the American president bombing Baghdad, are robbing themselves of the most important human quality: dignity!

On a different station I find another unseemly spectacle. Naomi Campbell is in Madrid, visiting a hospital for children with leukemia. The caption reveals that "Naomi is here to comfort the children!" Ten camera crews, bodyguards, and hundreds of newspaper reporters with flashbulbs popping are along for the ride. You see a little boy, stricken with leukemia and looking utterly distraught, sitting in his bed next to Naomi Campbell with the flock of picture vultures shouting to the supermodel, "Sit down and put your arm around him." She does what she's told. Or tries to. The boy does the only sane thing—he pulls back and refuses to let her touch him.

Why does something like this run on TV? Who benefits from this stuff? Why do millions of people tune in, and how can they not find it sickening? And that's exactly what we read in Ms. Campbell's eyes.

Some woman who underwent surgery on some other body part is now sitting down on a sofa in a set decorated like a news studio, next to a morbidly obese man who evidently has yet to be liposuctioned, and the two of them dissect every little detail of Naomi Campbell's life, including her suicide attempt and her recent breakup. Now, that's what I call instant karma. No sooner is Naomi Campbell recognized as the supposed good girl than she is punished for her good deed. And these hypocrites punish her exuberantly, against the garish candy-colored setting. The two of them deserve a public slap in the face.

I think about that child with leukemia. A brave little boy is fighting the fight of his life, and some ditsy yuppie whose only interest is to thrust her silicone-enhanced boobs into the camera has the nerve to intrude on his crisis and yap like an idiot in a ridiculously expensive Gucci outfit for one reason only: to be in the picture!

I am furious, and now I know why.

The next notable segment consists of secret footage of topless women on a luxury yacht that belongs to some self-important hotshot. Evidently this topic is more in line with this chick's interests, because she offers up concrete information. I was half expecting a report from Sahagún about a murder committed by an aging couple from Remscheid; their victim, a hapless Austrian woman. That way I would finally have learned Beaky's first name. But no such luck.

I hope we won't be getting programs like that in Germany. What do they accomplish? This stuff will make people stop worshipping so-called stars and start regarding them with disdain, and eventually with utter indifference. Maybe this program is like homeopathic medicine: the symptoms grow worse when you first take it, then subside. So be it!

~

This rage. Everyone has one problem or another. Right now mine seems to be suppressed rage. No wonder my gallbladder acted up. But what is rage, when you come right down to it? Am I rage? Is rage the object I'm enraged about? Is rage even an element of my character?

Let us assume the object I'm enraged at is a chair, and I smash it. The chair is not the object of my rage and cannot have triggered it. When I get a chance to drop down into a chair after hours of hiking, which, I might add, is the story of my life these days, it's a great feeling, and I think the chair is fantastic. But the chair is a chair. The truth of the matter is that if I have a problem with it, I actually have a problem with myself.

When I'm outraged at a dumb TV show, it means I have a problem with myself! I can't be truly enraged at people I don't even know, and who have no direct connection to me. Perhaps I'm annoyed at myself because I don't contribute enough to good causes.

It's important not to jump to conclusions. Nowadays everyone forms an instant opinion, and the media push us to do so. Opinion polls, surveys. What do they tell us? Nothing, absolutely nothing. An opinion about something cannot take precedence over the thing itself.

I lie in bed with the window wide open and wonder what God actually represents for me.

Many of my friends have been estranged from the Church for quite some time. They find it far-fetched, antiquated, frayed, rigid, and downright inhuman. Consequently they are also estranged from God. If His ground crew is in such bad shape, how must He himself be . . . if He exists at all! Unfortunately, most people say, "Don't talk to me about God!" I view the matter differently.

I think there is a God—be He a person, an entity, a principle, an idea, a light, a plan, or whatever else. I view God the way I do outstanding films like *Gandhi:* award-winning and superb!

And the Church hierarchy is merely the local movie theater showing the masterpiece: God's projection screen. The screen may be crooked and crinkly, frayed and full of holes; the speakers may crackle and sometimes stop working altogether, or there are annoying announcements during the picture, along the lines of "Will the driver with Remscheid license plate number SG 345 please move his car?" You sit on uncomfortable, squeaky wooden chairs, and nobody's even cleaned the place. The person sitting in front of you is blocking your view, and the constant chatter makes you miss parts of the plot entirely.

It probably wouldn't be much fun to see a blockbuster like *Gandhi* under these circumstances. Many audience members would walk out and say, "A bad movie." But a closer look reveals that it's really a supreme masterpiece. A rotten showing does nothing to alter the significance of the film. The screen and the speakers reproduce only what they're able to.

God is the movie and the church is the theater that's showing it. I hope that some day we can see the film in 3-D and stereo quality, uncut and unadulterated. Perhaps we'll even be in it!

I figure I'm pretty gutsy to have taken on this pilgrimage without any guarantee that I will experience any personal gain at the end.

Insight of the day: Masterpieces can be seen in the most astonishing places at the most astonishing times.

June 30, 2001
León

I am really beat. At 2:30 this morning, a wild mob of Spanish teenagers planted itself in front of my hotel window and made an unbelievable racket. Everyone goes berserk on St. Peter's, my name day. On this humid night, the whole town is reveling and dancing up a storm. But aching feet make it hard to celebrate, so here too I opt for bed and a nice long slumber.

My wide-open window on the second floor is directly above the main street, and once again I am privy to a radio play, this time in Spanish. And now it's a good thing that curiosity gets the better of me and that I hang on to every word.

One of these cute kids has a loaded pistol with him, and the tipsy group decides it might be fun to fire off some shots. They begin to calculate which one of them would be likely to spend the least amount of time behind bars if he shot someone. A fourteen-year-old is chosen. The considerations as to where and at whom they ought to aim continue in a more muted tone, and soon these little sweeties make up their minds to shoot into my open window. Am I dreaming? They want to shoot into my window! I find that so unbelievable that I let out a chuckle. Maybe I misunderstood something?

But just to be sure, I crawl out of bed and creep on all fours

172

over the 1970s-style tile floor toward the garbage can. I feel very silly doing this, but it's better to get down on the floor of my own accord than to be put there by a bullet.

I can already see the reports on Spanish TV: Beaky exulting to reporters that I was a good person but . . . just not good enough, with me lying before the eyes of the world, covered in blood in my Mickey Mouse T-shirt on the mottled tile floor in this cheap hotel. If I'd known I was going to be shot, I would have chosen a better hotel and worn something nicer.

The boys have gotten so loud that if there should be a juvenile court judge anywhere in Sahagún, he's got to be hearing and recording every word. The only thing missing is the name of the victim. Thank heavens the little guy who is about to bump me off is a Castilian wimp whose resolve is wavering while the older kids

Sahagún is not always as safe as it looks!

cheer him on. I guess he'll soon fire a shot, then weepingly declare that he didn't mean to, and after being grounded for a week he'll go right back to drinking with his buddies. I get to the garbage can, grab it, and crawl off to the bathroom, where I fill it up with water as quietly as I can. Then I crawl to the window on all fours, pushing the full can in front of me. I jump up with the can to pour water onto the heads of the young idiots, picturing my own funeral.

I'll be buried anonymously in a shallow grave behind the Romanesque brick Church of San Lorenzo in Sahagún. David the masseur will say a few comforting words and tell a tearful Lara what a shame it is that this had to happen after I'd been on the Camino for just two days. Beaky will come up with some long-winded, high-handed stories, while Gerd props up his head on his walking stick and the Austrian woman rounds out the ceremony by solemnly tossing her Tyrolean hat onto my coffin and asking, "Is there a millinery store around here?" Yes, that's exactly how it'll be.

I whirl up quick as lightning and empty every last drop in the can. A split second later there's a loud splash on the asphalt. Now they really start yelling. Clearly I hit the group head-on!

I don't want to sit back and watch my fate unfold, so I run to the reception desk, awaken the snoring night porter, and force him to call the police. When the officers approach from the distance with their sirens wailing, the kids take to their heels, and I can only hope they abandon their quest for a victim.

There's that rage again. It is hard to maintain a Dalai Lama–like composure in a situation like this. Five minutes later, though, I see the funny side of the incident. Needless to say, I close my window and lower the shades. If there were fireworks tonight, I missed them once again!

~

I'm unable to fall asleep now, and as I lie in bed a long-repressed memory resurfaces. Years ago, when I suffered the near-fatal poisoning I described earlier, I had the dubious pleasure of hovering at death's door. In my mind's eye a mosaic of my feelings at the time starts coming together.

The panic was the worst part; it is consuming. But when you're really close to the end—a doctor brought me back just in the nick of time—it's quite a different matter.

You grow very peaceful and calmly sort out your own thoughts, including absolutely banal things that take on surprising significance as you lie dying. It all boils down to one question: What do I do unto others, and what do others do unto me? Animals included.

When you reach the point that you're barely conscious, it gets bizarre. You are keenly aware of everything but also dazed. You billow out, yet grow smaller and more compact from within. You slowly cave in on yourself and at the same time expand outward. Shortly before you collapse, a kind of gate opens up just a crack, but offering the capacity of a black hole. And then it's just a single step and you're there. It is the most banal moment of life, yet also the most solemn.

I can only attempt to describe it. It's as though you were to pop open a beer and play Beethoven's Ninth as recorded by the Berlin Symphony Orchestra with a double complement. Banal and solemn all in one.

I would not characterize what I went through as a "near-death experience." I was not on an alien "other side." I may have come close to a threshold, but I never stepped through a gate, and I did not see a light.

~

Last night I slept only fitfully, then stayed in bed until nine o'clock. I'm dog tired. There was no more trouble outside, but there was a bit of a racket. It's already so hot that hiking is out of the question. My practical solution is to skip over two segments again by taking the train to León. When I get there, I'll take two days off to discover what the last big city before Santiago is like.

I'm exasperated that I won't be hiking today, but my mental and physical fitness are not up to par, and I do want to complete the final sixty-two miles completely on foot so that I will be recognized officially as a pilgrim. Lara is probably already en route. My segment hopping means that I won't be seeing her anymore, but I have her e-mail address.

I'm rid of Beaky, Gerd, and the Austrian woman for good. Today is Sunday, which is a tough one for my Austrian woman, since all the shops are closed.

At the train station I find out that I have an hour and a half until the train leaves for León. I sit down on the deserted platform and stare at a mosaic labeled *Sahagún.* I photograph it out of sheer boredom. Sahagún! I wonder what this funny Arabic-sounding name means.

Then I unpack my diary and take notes. I wonder why I'm writing all these things down. For myself? Might someone else read these notes someday?

Maybe this is conceited of me, but I can't help feeling that I'm writing a book that feverishly awaits publication, although I've never had any ambition to write books. Even so, I'm meticulous about noting down everything, as though I absolutely have to, and my entries are getting more and more exhaustive. If people were to expect any book from me at all, it'd be a very different kind. But maybe that's the exciting part!

Most people who take this trek were inspired to do so by reading Shirley MacLaine or Paulo Coelho. Whatever we may think of their books, it is incredible how many people they brought onto this trail. They paved the way.

The most astonishing thing is that no one I have met so far on this journey has the least doubt about the power of the Camino de Santiago. All firmly believe in the presence of the one great being and His wondrous works in this world. Or maybe they *do* have doubts and just don't care to reveal them to a stranger. I express my doubts and entertain new doubts every day of the week.

Am I on the right track here, or am I just one among the multitude of crackpots? There are moments of inspiration that melt away my doubts, but with my weary feet positioned at some ticket counter, the world looks different. Or maybe I should say that my view of the world changes. Doubts? Perhaps I have to break the habit, the way you give up smoking.

Many years ago, two friends talked me into taking part in a reincarnation seminar. Five women were signed up, and a sixth person was needed to make the weekend course run. I was quite curious and let Carina and Christine talk me into going. The five women and I traveled to Frankfurt to meet the reincarnation therapist.

Carsten, the therapist, was a very pleasant man, well educated and open-minded. He explained some of the specifics and told us what it might be like to see something, but reminded us that we might not see anything at all. The best thing would be to relax and take things as they came.

The five women and he were firmly convinced that they had lived previous lives. I was open to the idea but didn't really buy it. The seminar leader assured us that at the end of the course we would find the common ground from our earlier lives that had brought the five women and me here. Before the course began, Carsten asked each of us to write down the places or countries to which we had an inexplicable aversion.

The first day of the seminar was quite interesting—a bit suspenseful and at times bizarre. We practiced meditation and contemplation techniques and saw a few wild images here and there, but we were more amused than overwhelmed. By the end of the second day we had all experienced life in the Middle Ages or in prehistoric times and registered our impressions without any emotional upheaval. Certain details seemed intriguing, but nothing was earth-shattering. Everyone got along beautifully, and there was lots of laughter.

On the third and last day, Carsten explained to us that he would now take each of us on an actual regression to our past lives. This process would be highly emotional, he said, and we should not be afraid. I was not frightened in the least, since I was sure it was going to continue as inconsequentially as it had thus far.

He talked to each of us individually to figure out what we found particularly vexing in this life. I knew right away what I wanted to reply, but I held my tongue. Carsten then asked me to choose someone from the group to stay by my side during my regression in case I needed help remaining calm. Huh? That sounded a little silly, but I went along with it. I asked Carina to come into the meditation room with me, figuring she was a good choice because she had a doctorate in psychology.

It was nice and warm in the room, which was illuminated

only by flickering candlelight. "OK, let's have a look at the life that preceded your current one," Carsten said solemnly. "Are you ready?" he asked, as though I were facing a double loop-the-loop on a roller coaster. I gave him a quick nod. All this fuss seemed unwarranted.

I closed my eyes and was able to complete the twenty minutes of contemplation by the book. Carsten did not maneuver the situation. He just got things rolling while pressing his hand gently on my solar plexus.

But this meditation differed markedly from the previous ones. The emerging images were crisp and distinct! Everything was incomparably more intense, and I had no influence whatsoever on the course of the story, which had a profound emotional impact on me. I felt a deep connection to the events that unfolded.

I was a young Franciscan monk, living in a monastery near the end of World War II. Breslau was visible in the distance. It was fall, and it must have been pouring, because the dark brown earth was muddy on the paths and fields all around the massive monastery. I could make out every detail of the dank gray monastery. Six other monks and an abbot lived there with me.

I clearly recognized myself, and the others' names came rushing into my head. I knew that they were virtuous people, but they remained vague and hazy to me, essentially faceless. The whole monastery complex was startlingly familiar, and I found my way around without any difficulty. A nun rode her rickety bicycle past a ravine to bring us leftovers from the local hospitals, as she did every day, so we would have enough food to get by. In the chapel I saw the other monks and myself during mass. I felt absolutely at home.

Suddenly I saw that I was in the abbot's study (while simultaneously lying on the carpet in the Frankfurt duplex), and I heard myself say aloud to the abbot—and to Carsten: "The coal merchant will be coming today. I'll go into the basement with him." An unspeakable fear, a feeling of utter annihilation gripped me. I went down a ramp and entered the chalky white basement with the coal merchant, who was pushing a wheelbarrow filled with coal.

My heart was pounding up in my throat, and on the carpet in Frankfurt I was gasping for breath.

While the man unloaded his coal in the basement, I didn't budge from his side. My job was to keep an eye on him and distract him. Behind a six-foot pile of turnips, we were hiding a Jewish family of four, a young couple with two small children—a boy and a girl. My eyes kept straying in their direction, and I prayed to God that the coal merchant didn't notice! An indescribable terror coursed through me.

He delivered the coal and left.

The hideout was dangerous, and we were all terribly afraid of making a false move.

Then I saw myself sitting in my cell at the open window, screaming in fear. It must have been early in the morning, and I heard two trucks rumbling across the ravine. Germans in uniform leaped out of the cars and stormed into the monastery. I was dragged out of my cell by two soldiers and placed in front of the rear outer monastery wall with the other monks, who were already lined up there.

The desperate family, dissolved into tears, was shoved onto a truck and taken away.

Someone in uniform read out our death sentences in German. The abbot and the other monks appeared calm, but a fear beyond words welled up in me.

I knew that I was lying on a carpet in Frankfurt at the beginning of the new millennium, but my whole body trembled, and even when I opened my eyes, I could not emerge from the story. Carsten and Carina reassured me, to no avail.

The abbot told the officer that we wished not to be blindfolded. This request was granted. Then the prior started singing a Latin hymn, "The Lord Is My Shepherd." Everyone joined in except me.

The rifles were loaded, the soldiers took aim at us, and I was quaking with fear. My knees were quivering, and my back was ice cold! I no longer believed in God! I had lost my faith! I shouted: "I don't want to die!" One of the other monks called over to me: "John, we are going the way of the Lord. Our path in life is at an end." I trembled like a leaf. My body was shaking, and I could not keep still. In Frankfurt, Carina pressed me onto the floor. I was inconsolable.

Shots rang out. I had been killed. It had all gone very quickly, and now I was dead. I'd been transformed into a flickering light somewhere. The seven other sparks spun faster and faster, pulled away from me, and disappeared. I couldn't do that. Three indescribable glowing apparitions came toward me to reassure me. One of them said, "You have had unconditional faith your entire life, why not in this one moment? Why not?"

On the slip of paper where I was asked to list the places I don't like, I had written just one word, *Poland,* although I'd never been there, at least back then. Someday I'll travel to Breslau and see what the deal is. But today I'm headed to León.

Did all those things really happen to me? I have no idea. I would never claim as much. But on the carpet in Frankfurt, something clearly did happen, and it affected me profoundly and enduringly. As for the common ground uniting our group during these individual regressions: apart from a single participant, we all saw ourselves as victims of fascism.

And now I'm sitting at the train station in Sahagún and giving free rein to my doubts. If I ever had an unshakeable faith, I want it back.

The train ride from Sahagún to León takes about an hour. I spend the entire time standing in the corridor, gazing stoically out the window at the Camino de Santiago as if I am hiking it in spirit. The segments I am now leaving behind would have been very strenuous. In my weakened physical condition, I would hardly have been able to make it in three days. Here and there I see individual pilgrims doing all they can to forge ahead through the hilly, heathlike countryside, which reminds me of the island of Sylt. So I won't be hiking this part of the trail, just skimming over it. I'll be spared some of the stress, but I'll miss out on much of the beauty.

The decision to go by train is the right one, and I don't feel guilty. I can make my peace with this situation. But the Camino has its own inexplicable momentum. It asks to be hiked.

My emotional seesaw ride on the Camino has been hard to take. I'm not like this at home. My morning grumpiness is a real problem here. In the mornings I sometimes feel like a deer hit by a car. Later, at noon, I'm cheery and at peace with the world. I'm focused on the trek, and I have my wits about me. Then later, as evening approaches, my thoughts get scattered, or I'm dead tired, or I'm all wound up *and* dead tired. Good thing I'm giving my body a break again. It's probably horrified by now, figuring that this hiking is going to go on forever.

While I'm still in the train, I broadcast an order to the universe, as I learned to do from Jose, to position a reasonably priced
superluxury hotel right in front of my eyes, smack in the middle
of León.

When I arrive at the León train station, I have to walk several
miles to get to the city, so I turn the walk into a sightseeing tour.
The gorgeous sandstone capital of Castile seems to be a cousin of
Madrid. It's a bit easier to get an overview of this city, and it's not
quite as elegant. It's more lighthearted, livelier and more inviting; there's none of that snootiness you find in capital cities. This
city begs to be conquered, and it restores your pep. I stand openmouthed in front of the splendid Parador de León and cannot
imagine how people thought up this architecture.

Over the rooftops of León

Right in the center of town, the elegant Hotel Alfonso V is offering a special promotion: a 40 percent discount if you stay two nights. That's the place for me; I am a passionate bargain hunter.

The first thing to greet you when you enter the hotel's modern stainless steel lobby and look up at the staircase is His deceased Majesty's coat of arms. I hope they'll give me a room even if I am wearing a stained denim shirt. It turns out to be a breeze—evidently they're used to far worse here when dealing with pilgrims. The wrinkle-free city shirt I bought in Carrión de los Condes, still in my backpack, is sure to wow them.

The room is sheer luxury. Not only does it offer a view of an enchanted little lane in the medieval town center—it even has a bathtub! After I take a bath and wash my clothes, I sit down at the desk, call home again, and write postcards to the people I've just called to tell them all the details about my near shooting in Sahagún. All of them want me to come home as quickly as possible, and while I mull over whether I ought to cut my trip short, the desk lamp starts hissing and sizzling, even though I haven't turned it on. There is a powerful flash of light through the entire room, then it goes dark. I'd better leave this room pronto.

The cathedral on the Plaza de la Regla is the undisputed highlight. Some people say it is the most beautiful cathedral in Spain. In any case, it is the purest example of early Gothic architecture in the country.

Suddenly I see my two Swedish friends Evi and Tina, standing under a wrought-iron chandelier in the aisle, grinning at me. They must have hiked at quite a pace to have arrived here today! I am absolutely delighted to see the two of them, and they feel the same way. We embrace with big smiles, and they want to treat me to dinner on the spot, but today I'd rather be alone. I don't know whether the two of them understand my decision, to judge from the disappointed looks on their faces. I hardly understand it myself, but since that's the way I feel today, I act accordingly.

Diffuse light in the cathedral of León

Later I meander around town and buy a ticket for a movie starring John Travolta. The Spanish title is *Combinación Gana-dora,* which means something like "the winning combination" (or maybe "the key to happiness"). The film is quite funny, although I didn't catch as much as I did the last time I went to the movies. In this one they speak very quickly. Perhaps I'm simply too tired.

I eventually settle in at a tapas bar, where the TV is blaring Spanish music. It's nice to hear loud music after all that silent hiking. On the Camino it tends to be—shall we say—quiet.

I am the only customer. It's much too hot right now, and no locals are going to show up at this hour. I'm sitting on a bar stool wearily lost in thought while sipping a *Spezi*.

While stuffing a date wrapped in ham into my mouth, I muse about where I might find God. My eyes survey the room. The bathroom doors have pictures of two nice chubby babies, a girl and a boy. On the sidewalk an elderly couple hobbles by on canes; the two of them have sad, hardened faces. The bartender is standing outside jiggling his foot nervously and keeping a lookout for something to happen.

The atmosphere in León is oppressive.

Finally there's some action on the *calle:* an ambulance picks up an elderly señora who has fainted, and rushes her to the hospital. And on the music channel, an incredibly good-looking Mexican man begins to sing a lovely sentimental song called *Imaginas me en ti.* I am glued to the TV. The text of the song goes something like this: "Imagine me in you," or "Visualize me in you." Whom? God? Is this song trying to tell me something yet again?

I try to imagine God in me, and feel good. Is that it? Do I simply need to imagine "it" in me? Perhaps I just have to imagine what I need at any given moment? I'll try that out over the next few days—that's what a pilgrimage is for.

Shortly before sundown, hundreds of locals start dancing a Spanish folk dance on the plaza. They look nice all grouped together. On the way back to the hotel, I walk past a savings bank with a poster encouraging me to "Close your eyes and wish for something!"

OK, OK; I'm already doing that.

Over the past few days, I've often thought that everything I'm doing here is wrong, that I'm going in the wrong direction. If only I'd thought that way when I was actually going in the wrong direction! I was often so sure I was doing exactly the right thing. Deep down inside I knew it was wrong, but it's easier to squelch your inner voice than to acknowledge it. Am I now on the right track because I'm listening to that voice? It is easier to drift away from the shortwave radio channel you're looking for than to get it just right.

Everything that has happened in my life up to this point seems to resurface here on the Camino, and the facets of my experiences come together. Again and again I reflect on long-suppressed memories of my direct encounters with death.

I used to sit at my favorite café on Königsallee in Düsseldorf with a cappuccino and cheesecake and, being the inquisitive guy that I am, listen in on the conversations of ladies of a certain age. This is how some of my sketches evolved.

One sunny afternoon, I was sitting there as usual, when an elderly woman, accompanied by a younger one, began making her way up a flight of stairs with a cane. Just before she reached the top stair, she cast a desperate searching glance around the café. The only people there were other elderly women—and me. When her eyes met mine, she gathered up all her strength and stumbled headlong in my direction, knocking over a table in the process and falling at my feet. Her younger companion stood frozen to the spot. I had taken a first aid course, but in the heat of the moment, I forgot everything I'd learned. The woman had fallen in such an unfortunate manner that I feared she had broken her leg, or worse.

I tore open her blouse, placed her head on my knee, and shouted: "Call a doctor!" It was deathly silent in the café; no one was moving a muscle. There were no cell phones back in 1985.

The busboy leaned over the woman and remarked offhandedly in a Polish accent: "She's dead anyway." I screamed at the waitress in a way I'd never screamed at anyone, and she dragged herself over to the telephone. I was beside myself. The dying woman was staring at me with eyes wide open while I monitored her breathing. She slowly turned blue. Not a sound, not a moan, nothing. She died, her head on my knees. It took the doctor forever to get there and pronounce her dead. The woman's companion was quite composed; she didn't appear to be a close friend.

In my despair, I asked the doctor what I ought to have done. He said, "Nothing. You couldn't have done anything!" For the next sixteen years I stayed away from that café. The first time I went back, I kept staring at the spot where the woman died.

The evening after her death, I got together with people I considered my friends. Now I know they were not. When I went to see them, I was quite distraught and told them the story. One of them laughed at me and made fun of the dying woman's choking fits in a loud reenactment that could be heard throughout the bar. I bawled out the merry group and stomped out of the bar. Two years later, the guy who so realistically re-created the death scene succumbed to death by choking.

My second encounter with death was equally bizarre. I was in Hamburg with my agent, at the office of a film producer, waiting to discuss a new project. We had just sat down with a cup of coffee when we heard an earsplitting bang outside. We rushed to the window. The conference room was on the ground floor, so we were able look up and down Hoheluftchaussee, one of Hamburg's busiest streets.

About ten feet away from us, a gaunt, elderly man armed with a kitchen knife was standing in front of a laundry. Thirty feet farther to the right, a policeman was holding out his pistol and yelling, "Toss the knife away!" The owner of the laundry was standing at the front window, in tears. The elderly man held up his arms in front of the laundry, looking dazed. The policeman had evidently fired a warning shot, but the man did not throw down his knife. The policeman shot him in the knee, and the man staggered.

We shouted out of the window, "Stop it! No shooting! Stop shooting!" The policeman fired off two more rounds, and a shot went into the man's stomach. He turned white as chalk, keeled over in slow motion, and died.

I will never forget the face of the dying man. He looked resigned to his fate, almost relieved. There was hardly any blood. Every time I drive by that spot, I make a brief stop there.

The next day the newspaper reported, "The young policeman was about to go on his noon break when he saw a man with a knife running into the laundry. The man threatened the owner and grabbed fifty marks. The woman was unharmed, but the young policeman saw red and fired." A few weeks later, the police asked me to make a statement.

I had completely repressed and forgotten these two experiences. I feel as though they didn't really happen, but on the trail they come right back to me.

My third encounter with death occurred when I was asked by the Make-A-Wish Foundation to visit a seventeen-year-old girl named Alexandra who was stricken with cancer. Her wish was to meet me, so I visited her in the hospital. Alexandra's condition was dire. I spent two hours with her; she didn't have the strength for any more than that. It took me all of five minutes to feel overwhelmed and overwrought. I was too nervous to be spontaneous, and didn't know what to say to the girl. When I asked her what she would do if she got out of the hospital, she said: "I would get my driver's license and race down the autobahn at a hundred seventy-five miles an hour." That's what she was dreaming of. When I'm driving my car, I often think of Alexandra, and get a kick out of flooring it. I think it gave her strength to see that I was just an ordinary human being. Her heroism certainly gave *me* strength.

On another occasion, I was asked to give a speech for the opening ceremony of the Frankfurt University Hospital's summer festival for the AIDS ward. Before I spoke I sought the advice of the hospital minister on how best to present my remarks. He said only, "Just do what you always do."

The patients who were able to leave their rooms were wheeled into the tastefully decorated lobby. It was a lovely summer's day, and the lobby offered a view of the lush green park outside. Before me were men and women in various stages of this insidious disease. Some of them had already developed an advanced state of dementia and had the complete clinical picture of Kaposi's sarcoma, a proliferating skin cancer. Their faces and bodies were scarred, ravaged by their illness.

I stood on the staircase, which had been turned into a stage, and looked out at the patients in their wheelchairs and beds. Some were accompanied by relatives and friends, but most were alone. The staff was doing its best to give everyone here a pleasant afternoon. One of the patients was sobbing loudly the whole time, and it tore me up inside. I stood there like an idiot.

Ought I to have said, "God, I hate you for what these people are going through"? I didn't. Instead, I somehow managed to come up with something humorous. At first I focused my eyes on the nurses and doctors, but at some point I felt able to meet the eyes of the patients, and eventually there was a reasonably cheery atmosphere, just on a subtler and more guarded scale than I'm accustomed to.

I still felt bad about my performance. Afterward I chatted with a few of the patients, who turned out to be quite happy that I was there. A very young man in a wheelchair consoled me with little joking remarks along the lines of: "Bet your audiences aren't usually this sick, huh?"

I was heartened to learn from two mothers that my open affirmation of my homosexuality had helped them reconcile with their sons, which is as it should be. I had suppressed the memory of this day as well, but today everything's welling up in me once again.

On a day when stories of this sort start circling through your head, you just want to be alone so you can understand why you went through them and how they ought to figure in your life.

Insight of the day: My weakness is also my strength.

July 1, 2001

León

On the hotel terrace I indulge in a breakfast fit for a king but long for the simple art of conversation. How do the other pilgrims take this isolation? If I don't meet a pilgrim to hike with soon, I'll get fed up and call the whole thing off. Never in my life have I been alone for such a long time, and the very things I liked about being alone just a few days ago are starting to get on my nerves. This diary is no longer enough. León is beautiful and brings out the joy of life, but I don't know a soul! Yesterday I should have gone out to eat with Tina and Evi, but I didn't feel like it; now I really do.

I hasten into the lively medieval center, driven by the desire for meaningful human contact. The weather is marvelous, and walking through the pedestrian area without a backpack is liberating, although I've grown accustomed to the weight. After making my way along a few short blocks on the main shopping street, I run into Evi, and we throw our arms around each other. Man, am I in luck! I make a formal apology for having turned down the dinner invitation for the previous evening, and I ask her to join me for coffee. No sooner have we sat down in the wicker chairs in the middle of the pedestrian area than we are joined by a pilgrim Evi met along the way. This pilgrim, a German named Tobias, is from

Mainz. He's over six feet tall, and his halting English is tinged with a charming Mainz drawl.

Evi tells us that she's stuck in León because her foot is acting up again and that Tina has gone ahead on her own. Evi's anger at the prospect of having to cut this trip short is written all over her face. To let off steam, she tells us about the ten years she worked as head purser on a Scandinavian luxury cruise liner and traveled around the world. Finally, when she'd had enough of all those rich people, she chucked it all and went to Brazil to work with street children. A year ago, on the Camino, she broke her leg, which made it impossible for her to return to Brazil and continue her work. So now she's studying social work in Stockholm, financing her studies by giving English lessons. She is drawn irresistibly to the Camino.

Evi is originally from Gällivare in Lapland, beyond the Arctic Circle. I went to Lapland at seventeen, traveling on an InterRail Pass. It was the farthest north I'd ever been and the first place I ever experienced a midsummer night.

When Evi asks me what exactly I do for a living (I'm such a "funny guy," she says), Tobias jumps in and supplies all the details. This guy has seen all my shows! When I was having dinner with Evi and Tina in Frómista, I gave them a vague description of my profession, calling myself a "cabarettist." Evi doesn't seem especially surprised: "I figured it was something like that."

To everyone's amusement, Tobias fishes several odd items out of the depths of his backpack. The things he lugs with him! Electroschockers, pepper spray, and ultrasound clubs—his mother gave him all this stuff as protection against wild dogs. If he actually needed these things in an emergency, there is no way he'd be able to grab them before the animals sank their teeth into him.

Tobias, a giant with the physique of an Olympic swimmer, is just as afraid of wild dogs as I am. Luckily, I rarely run into them, and when I do, they're the docile kind. But the pilgrim's pamphlet claims that the danger looms much larger on the second half of the Camino. A Canadian pilgrim, it reports, spent a night outdoors and was stalked by a wolf. I hope it wasn't Lara! This happened at the very spot where I saw the monstrously ugly dog. Maybe it was him! That fat little guy wouldn't do anything; he just wants to play! It was really stupid of me not to have taken a photograph of the dog; any zoologist would have gotten a kick out of it. But supposedly there really are wolves here, and I did see eagles. Nothing surprises me now.

Tobias has stowed away his stockpile and hobbled on. In the pedestrian area I hear someone call out my name. I turn around, and in the crowd I spot a red-and-blue FC Barcelona T-shirt sparkling in my direction. It's Anne, the woman I gave my camping mat to back in Santo Domingo de la Calzada. We kiss and hug as though we've been friends for centuries. Evi and Anne already know each other as well. As I said, nothing surprises me anymore!

Of course, the lady from Liverpool sits down with us and tells me my mat has helped her sleep better, although it took her a week to figure out how to roll it up properly and let the air out of it. I didn't know you had to blow it up.

Anne cracks one joke after another, but we get the feeling that she's down in the dumps. When we ask what's on her mind, she tells us that near Calzadilla de la Cueza, in the middle of nowhere, she was sexually molested by the director of the *refugio*. This bastard tried to force himself on Anne while she was sleeping alone in the dormitory. She told David, the masseur from Sahagún (whom

Evi visited as well, of course), and David saw to it that the guy lost his job. Nice to know that friends stick together.

It turns out that Evi had a similar experience. She and Tina were walking through the secluded pampas when a Jeep stopped and a guy made a grab for them. The two of them were terrified and ran away.

How can I keep whining? This trail is far more strenuous and perilous for a woman than for a man. As proof of this fact, Anne shows us her remarkably torn up feet. The damage was done by designer hiking sandals, and it set her back several days. Now she's stuck here as well, and has to change *refugios* today for the second time, as you're allowed to stay only one night.

We chat about everything under the sun while the sun itself blazes down on us. Evi informs me that the Swedish word for pastor—which is what she wants to become—is *sielsorger,* which is quite similar to the German *Seelsorger*. That's a surprise. Suddenly Jose from Amsterdam shows up, as though she'd been ordered from the universe. Both Anne and Evi already know her. She, too, needs a day of rest, and she joins our group.

These coincidences are getting downright astonishing! I should point out that León is no hole in the wall—it's substantially bigger than Heidelberg. The medieval center extends like a labyrinth for several miles, and I am near the outskirts of town, in a pilgrim-free zone. Jose and Evi happen to be staying at the same hotel, even though there are countless other inns, as well as hotels within the city walls.

We laugh up a storm, and it's like being with old friends. We agree to meet for an 8:30 dinner at the Plaza San Martín, the hot spot of León.

The Swedish-Dutch duo heads back to the hotel in the afternoon to primp for the evening, while Anne and I stay put. Anne says she knows me from somewhere. She recognizes my face, but she just can't figure out why. She's been wondering about that since Santo Domingo.

We come up with all kinds of theories until I finally hit upon the only possible reason. Some of my TV programs were broadcast on late-night TV on the BBC. "Exactly. Yes, you're the funny German guy! I loved that program!" Anne blurts out.

Although the shows were only subtitled in English, and not dubbed, she thought they were great. Anne finds it peculiar to meet me here, and I feel the same way. My sole British fan is sitting across from me drinking coffee in the pedestrian area of León, and I feel as though I have known this Ph.D. in biology from time immemorial. Just a couple of months ago, Anne finished her most recent research project, a six-month study of field mice in Nicaragua. I knew it—this woman is headed for the Nobel Prize!

Anne eventually hobbles back to the *refugio* to revive herself with a shower before dinner.

This afternoon has been fantastic, and tonight I'll do something with the friends I'd been longing to see. At breakfast this good fortune seemed impossible. I am sitting in my wicker chair ruminating happily with my eyes closed when a pudgy, helpless-looking young man whom I've run into a few times during the past week greets me in a broad Swabian accent. Our conversations are generally brief and trifling, which is why I have yet to mention him. But I have already dubbed him the Lake Constance Pilgrim; that's the part of Germany he comes from. He is now bending my ear with inane banter.

The Lake Constance Pilgrim asks me straight out whether I have put on weight along the pilgrims' route. What a bizarre question! The guy is ten years younger than I, but he must be fifty pounds heavier. I ask him whether he saw me at the beginning of my trek. He of course says no, so I ask him how he got the strange idea that I've gained weight. He just shrugs his shoulders and stands there eagerly waiting for me to elaborate. I nip the silly conversation in the bud by maintaining a stony silence.

Even so, this guy has touched a sore spot. It would be awful if I really have put on weight. With all the personal athletic performance records I am setting here, it's not possible for me to be adding pounds! Still, I feel an urgent need to weigh myself.

The Lake Constance Pilgrim doesn't budge from the spot, and claims, "I'm waiting for someone!" I wonder whom he managed to pick up! I soon find out that he has a big surprise in store for me: his new traveling companions are none other than Beaky and Gerd. She's tipsy, hysterically cheerful, and beet red. Gerd is as tanned as a Moroccan.

Beaky is surprised to see me, and wants to know how I got here so fast. "By train!" I openly confess, which causes her to holler in a voice that resounds throughout the pedestrian area: "No way! That doesn't count. You can't do that. That is absolutely unacceptable!"

The Lake Constance Pilgrim glares at me accusingly, and Gerd cradles his head on top of his walking stick, as usual.

Evidently her diatribe was supposed to be funny. But no one's laughing. She ought to sign up for humor lessons with Tina.

I tell her that I couldn't care less, and besides, you have to show proof only that the final sixty-two miles were covered on foot. She knows that, but she doesn't like it. The laws of the world should conform to her wishes. She draws herself up to her full height like Eva Perón.

Beaky wants to know whether I stayed at the hotel in Sahagún "where the teenagers raised such hell." I am happy to confirm that I did, and I inform her that those kids had absurd plans to commit murder, and that she and her husband could have wound up as victims.

Gerd and Beaky hang on my every word and laugh hysterically. These two people really suck the energy out of you. While I launch into the details of the story, a feeling of absolute exhaustion washes over me.

She is a truly problematic individual; so is he. How did they link up with the pudgy pilgrim from Lake Constance? Perhaps they're childless and are looking to take younger pilgrims under their wing. The Austrian woman is no longer with them. I wonder what they did with her. Her name is Ute—or it was, anyway. Evi told me so. Ute has been on a pilgrimage for an entire year! First she was in India, and her current destination is Santiago.

Maybe a good long talk with her would have been worthwhile after all. I missed my chance, although Ute gave me ample opportunity. Instead I'm being bombarded yet again with Beaky's oppressive hiking anecdotes.

I decide to take leave of my shadow for what I hope is the final time. I think I understand the lesson she has taught me; now I just have to internalize it.

At the nearest *farmacia,* I jump on the scale, and it's a load off my mind to find that there's a load off my body.

Back at the hotel, I see that it's started to rain, and the wonderful downpour cools the air. This is the first time it's rained on my trek since June 10. Jose told me that the heavy woman from Seattle who climbed up the meseta got dehydrated and wound up in the hospital.

This is the oddest trip I've ever been on.

On the dot of 8:30, I stand on the Plaza San Martín fresh from the shower in my nice bright wrinkle-free city shirt. It is a lovely, balmy summer's eve. Hundreds of pilgrims and locals are sitting on rustic wooden benches by torchlight in front of the colorful restaurants. The plaza is aglow in the red-and-orange Spanish dusk, and a flamenco trio completes the cliché.

While I draw a deep breath, someone taps me on the shoulder. It's Lara from Canada. All I needed was for her to come along— and I mean that in the best sense!

"I missed you on the trail! Where were you?" she wants to know, and I tell her about my sporadic episodes as a dropout from the pilgrimage, when I took the train or bus. I now know that she was not the Canadian woman who came close to being devoured by a wolf.

Jose, Evi, and Anne now join me on the plaza, also fresh from the shower. The Swedish and Dutch women are clad in colorful summer dresses, and Anne is celebrating this special occasion in her shiny FC Barcelona rayon T-shirt. The ladies are radiant, and Anne, refreshed from a nap, is positively pulsating with good cheer. It almost goes without saying that Evi and Jose already know Lara.

The five of us are in luck; we find outside seating at a fish restaurant, and we order a heavy red wine to start, followed by a substantial dinner. This beautifully relaxed evening lasts well into the Spanish night.

Evi solemnly announces to us that she has decided to stop her pilgrimage as of today, and will take the train to Santiago tomorrow. Her foot is simply not cooperating. "This is the end, my friends!" she declares with a tear in her eye, while raising her full glass of Rioja to us. I'm convinced that she has already found what the rest of us are still seeking, so there's nothing holding her back from taking the express train to Santiago tomorrow.

Evi says she'd like to pull an all-nighter, and asks whether any of us are up for it. I can't see any downside to her idea, and declare myself willing and able to be her platonic-pilgrim one-night-stand, a decision she rewards with a kiss on my forehead.

The food takes so long to come that when the big plate of fish is finally served, Anne and Lara are forced to eat like seals, choking down their food at lightning speed. Their sixty-bed dormitory closes at ten sharp! Too bad. Anne is a lot of fun, and things were just getting started. Her comments about the ultra-Catholic pilgrims are sidesplittingly funny. She really ought to host her own comedy show. Anne is a doubting Thomas herself, and she doesn't think much of the Camino and her fellow pilgrims. Her attitude is similar to mine, but harsher: "It's all just rubbish!" She doesn't reveal to us why she is on the pilgrimage in the first place.

Tomorrow Lara is joining up with the night-shift pilgrims so that she can be sure to find a bed for the night. The likelihood of meeting up with her again is remote, so we all give her a big send-off. Anne and Lara gallop back to the *refugio*.

Jose, who is less talkative by nature, now has the chance to tell us more about herself. She did her graduate work in political science, but after getting her doctorate, she soon came to regard her studies as pointless, so she decided to become a nurse instead. Now she's working at a hospital in Amsterdam on a ward for end-stage cancer patients, and she's happy there. She radiates happiness from every pore. When I tell her that her trick of ordering things from the universe has already worked for me twice, she rocks with laughter: "Did you doubt it for a second? I don't lie."

I have no choice but to bring Evi and Jose up to speed on my crazy experiences with Beaky and Gerd. "Are you writing that down as well?" Evi wants to know. She seems pleased when I reply that I make daily entries in my diary, and she presses me to tell her why. "I have no idea! Just for the heck of it!" is my honest reaction. "You'll figure out whom you're writing for," Evi replies, flashing me a big smile.

By now I'm used to the comings and goings in León, so it doesn't surprise me when Evi motions to a woman who has been on the lookout for a seat on the plaza (which is still overcrowded) to come join our group.

This striking woman in her mid-forties, with long red hair and wearing a stylish, khaki, vaguely military hiking outfit, strides over to us. Evi introduces Sheelagh as one of Anne's pilgrim friends. Sheelagh, who is from New Zealand, sits down with us. After a quick glance around at our little group, she asks, "Where's Anne?" My God, does this woman have a beautiful voice; it's full but soft. She's probably a news anchor on a New Zealand television program.

When she hears that Anne is already in bed, she sighs, "Poor Anne! She'll never learn!"

New Zealanders evidently enjoy a good sense of humor—and a good drink. Before we know it, the four of us are the last ones left on the Plaza San Martín, merrily drinking our wine. Here and there a pub is closing down for the night, and the flamenco trio has fallen silent.

Evi clears her throat resolutely and asks the group to respond to this question: "Has God spoken to you on the Camino?" We look searchingly at one another, and it takes a while for someone to reply. Sheelagh is the first to speak up. Her reply is short and sweet: "Sure He did!" Jose says, "Yes . . . He did." I hesitate and add, "I think so."

Evi beams at us. "When He speaks to you, you get such a rush of joy . . . but then the doubts creep in. 'Am I crazy, am I just imagining it, do I think I'm something special?' But then, if you just go with it, incredible things come to pass! Miracles!"

I am now feeling somewhat uneasy. I am definitely in the "Am I crazy?" phase. What are we really talking about here? Can you seriously claim that God is speaking to you? That would be a killer opening gag for my next show: "Good evening, ladies and gentlemen. I no longer plan out the contents of my shows with my TV station; I now take the shortcut and speak directly to God . . . and now to the show!"

But the matter-of-fact way these wonderful, intelligent women are talking about themselves and God is not crazy; it is infectious and impressive. Sheelagh seems to sense my skepticism and discomfort: "Trust. Trust yourself and trust God, because that is the only thing He wants from you. Your trust."

To defuse the tension, Sheelagh reaches into her pocket and pulls out a tacky miniature deck of cards decorated with angels. She bought it in a little shop in León this afternoon. She has decided that starting today, she will have everyone with whom she has a meaningful encounter along the Camino pick a card. On the day she arrives in Santiago, she will claim the final card for herself.

Sheelagh fans out the cards facedown on the table. We take a break from drinking our red wine for the first time this evening. Evi gets to pick the first card; after all, she's ending her pilgrimage tomorrow. Her angel card is Light. Nothing could be better suited to this flaxen-haired Swede from the Arctic Circle. This woman *is* light.

Jose picks Enthusiasm. I don't know what that means for her. Is she lacking in that area? But she's quite obviously moved. I pick my card with an unpleasant tingling sensation. I can hardly bring myself to choose one. When I do, it says: Courage. That is exactly what I'm lacking now, even in the very act of picking the card. Courage! I will need it for the rest of the way—all I have to do is think of the wild dogs of Foncebadón!

This evening has been wonderful. Sheelagh and Jose bid us a tipsy good night at a very late hour and go off to their hotels. Evi and I—a promise is a promise—make our way through the bars of León and pull an all-nighter. With a toast to the end of her trip, she and I polish off yet another bottle of Rioja. This woman truly is the embodiment of wisdom, and she doesn't strike me as the least bit crazy, even though she is firmly convinced that she speaks to God. Maybe that takes courage!

I should perhaps point out that Evi does not hear a "voice" in the true sense of the word. It is more like an ethereal inner presence that breathes the words into her.

Evi confides several additional things to me, but my lips are sealed. I promised her I wouldn't record them in my diary. She is utterly convinced that my pilgrimage will turn into a book. I ask her how she got that idea. Evi smiles—actually, there's always a smile on her face—and whispers in my ear, "*You* can't see it, but *I* can!"

This talk with Evi meant quite a lot to me, and I'm honored that she chose to celebrate the end of her pilgrimage with me.

As I lie contentedly in bed and try to sleep, a baby begins to scream, and it can soon be heard throughout the hotel. Since this screaming is sure to keep me awake, I use the time to think about the Camino de Santiago. It is wonderful, though it can also be ugly and loud. The towns are beautiful, impressive; the panoramas are restful and unrivaled. But nothing grips me so completely that it holds me back from moving ahead. Santo Domingo was worth a stay. The trail is beautiful enough to keep you going, but no place is so extraordinarily beautiful, no landscape so special that you would want to stay there forever. It is a pathway in the true sense.

Rome holds me in its grip for all time, and I'll never be free of it. Leaving the Canadian Rockies caused me nearly physical pain. I will miss the singing of the birds of Australia to the end of my days. It was like being in withdrawal when I left. It would probably just about do me in to hear the singing of the Australian birds in the Rocky Mountains set in Rome. Here everything is just pretty enough to make you feel good, but you're also happy to leave.

I hope I don't run into Beaky and Gerd anymore. If I meet up with them just one more time, I'm likely to explode.

Today I really feel loved.

Courage! What do I need courage for? Come to think of it: Rage is easy to turn into courage; just add three letters to the beginning of *rage,* and you have *courage!*

Insight of the day: A true path does not grab hold of you.

July 2, 2001

Somewhere in the Middle of Nowhere, Beyond León

After the farewell party for Evi, I find it very difficult to get out of bed. It takes me until eleven o'clock to leave the hotel and set out on the road leading straight through León. The signs are easy to follow. Shortly before I'm out of the center of town, I get a craving for one more delicious cup of coffee and a cigarette, so I make an impromptu stop in front of a small hotel on a shaded side street and plop myself down on a bright red plastic chair. Less than five minutes after my arrival, Evi comes out of the hotel! Turns out I'm sitting right in front of her hotel. If I'd gone one street farther, we wouldn't have seen each other again. After another five minutes go by—predictably, at this point—Jose shows up. We chat about the previous evening again and can now take the photographs we wanted to take when none of us had a camera on hand. We snap photos of each other, in group and individual poses, as if to prove that we really exist.

Evi is dying of curiosity, and asks me politely whether I might be willing to read something aloud from my diary. Performance as such doesn't faze me—that is my profession—but reciting this type of content takes some getting used to, even for me. Regardless, I gamely whip out my creased orange notebook and translate the "My Shadow Beaky" passage into English. Both women listen in amusement, and don't say a word about what they have just heard. Then Evi grows serious and tells me, "The craziest things will happen to you along the way. Be confident and have faith in yourself! But listen to your inner voice. Not everything will be good, or right. You are now primed for all kinds of weird experiences."

I confess to them that I'm expecting to have a confrontation with Beaky. I don't want to see her again for anything in the world, but I seem to have a bad karmic score to settle with her. Jose has met Beaky and Gerd too, and since then she's been running away from them. She thinks they have come over from the dark side to infiltrate the pilgrimage and spy on us. Evi and I find this notion absolutely hilarious.

While we drink another cup of coffee, Evi and Jose insist that I continue keeping a meticulous written record of my experiences. But if I'm to go on writing, I have to leave the two of them for good, whether I like it or not. With a heavy heart I bid them farewell after two and a half hours, and set out on the road leading out of León.

On this stretch, the Camino shows how very pitiless it can be. It is dreadful, pure and simple. The trail leads through industrial areas and straight across desolate expanses. Of course, it's hot again, and to make matters worse, every ten minutes a menacing tigerlike jumble of tattered billboards leaps out at me. The area gets even more difficult to navigate along parched yellow fields, where the houses are built, cavelike, into the earth. Soon there is absolutely nothing to see but unending overgrown patches and here and there the odd dilapidated, deserted hut.

On a gentle slope right in the middle of this science-fiction scenery, with the afternoon sun beating down on my skin, a middle-aged man, suntanned, bearded, and bespectacled, comes my way. He's a scruffy eccentric in a white shirt and black pants. He doesn't look like a homeless man but rather like someone with amnesia, roaming aimlessly through this deserted area. As he wobbles toward me, he strikes up an inane conversation in Spanish.

"*Hola, amigo,* where can I sleep here?" That is certainly a weird question, but he's not drunk. I look down at his sockless feet, which are so sore from walking that they are bleeding. The laces of his muddy designer shoes are hanging down loose. His lips are chapped and full of blisters. He has barely any teeth in his mouth.

"Where do you want to go?" I ask warily.

"Santiago" is his terse reply.

"But Santiago is in the other direction," I answer, puzzled, and point westward.

"I know," he says, looking as though he would like to plunge a knife into my body.

"And where are you coming from?" I ask. He tells me that he was staying at an awful hotel six miles away, and just wants to sleep somewhere now. A simple bed would do the trick.

I tell him that there are quite a few *albergues* and hotels right along the trail in León; he couldn't possibly miss them. Then he wants to know where I'm headed. Any idiot can tell by my outfit where I'm going! Even so, I tell him my destination, which is supposedly his as well: "Santiago." He gives me a penetrating glance, and I get the feeling he's cooking up a nutty idea. What he says next knocks me for a loop: "You know what? I'll go with you. Where are you headed today?"

I don't say anything at first. Once I've regained my composure, I explain to him that I will be hiking about twelve miles without a break today. I'm hoping to scare him off, but I don't. He just says OK. He wants to come with me!

But *I* don't want *him*. I take a closer look at the man. He seems down-at-the-heels, but his mud-caked shoes are new and expensive. His black designer jeans fit him perfectly. The stained and wrinkled shirt is hanging out of his pants, but it is not cheap, nor are his glasses. Who is this guy?

I think of Evi. Trust your inner voice! My intuition says, "This could turn out to be interesting." Then I hear myself say out loud, "That's OK with me," while a voice inside my head starts protesting, Are you trying to get yourself killed? This guy is off his rocker; he's going to rob and murder you.

Too late! We're already walking westward, side by side. He's clearly walking right back to where he came from. The two of us seem to be the only living beings ambling along in this unpleasant region. Not a single car drives by. Nothing. Just the two of us.

The man is huffing and puffing, and beads of sweat pour out of his skin. I ask his name. He's Americo Montinez de la Something-or-other, fifty-six years old, Peruvian. He doesn't look Peruvian. But his accent sounds South American.

"And what brings you here?" I ask.

"Vacation" is his startling answer.

"Vacation? With no suitcase, no backpack?" I ask. "I don't need those things," he says. "I have lots and lots of money with me. When I need something, I buy it."

No way is he fifty-six. He looks much older. I have to admit, though, that he's quite amiable. I ask him what else he wants to do in Spain. Americo's reply is really wacky. "I want to pull a leaf off a plant that is found only in Spain. This plant grows outside Madrid in the Sierras. But unfortunately it has been removed at the behest of Opus Dei, a secret organization of the Catholic Church. And now I'm hopping mad at those people!"

OK, thanks, I've heard enough! From now on I'll pay no attention to my intuition. He is absolutely crazy! As soon as an opportunity presents itself, I'll get away from him.

But I want to keep the conversation going to make sure that his thoughts don't drift too far, so I gently suggest that he can't have come to Europe just because of this one plant. He looks at me as though he wants to go straight for my throat. Now he's losing it completely! He grows quite agitated, and tells me that his wife and daughters have declared him insane for wanting to do this. I draw a deep breath. They're right. But, he says, he doesn't care.

I ask him where in Peru he is from, and what he does for a living. He doesn't want to know anything about me apart from my first name and where I come from, although I get the feeling that he is strangely interested in me.

Americo tells me that he is from Cuzco, and that he is the shaman of the *índios* who live there. They call him Ruco Urco. He works with plants, and this leaf from the Spanish plant is intended for a friend who is stricken with cancer. Now that the plant no longer exists, he will make a pilgrimage to Santiago instead.

That still sounds nuts, but not quite as nuts as it did before. Still, this guy seems loonier and loonier to me, particular because he was walking in the wrong direction earlier. Even Beaky made more sense! I point out to him that he's unlikely to make it all the way to Santiago in his fancy city shoes. He roars with laughter, gives me a kind glance, and says in an almost childlike tone of voice, "Oh, yes I can; I have soooo much time." The old man actually keeps up with me astonishingly well. For a while we walk together in silence. He doesn't ask me anything. If I say nothing, he remains quiet and inscrutable.

Along the way, a friendly young German shepherd suddenly approaches us and rubs against my legs. I pet the animal and say in German, in the inane singsong voice people use in speaking to children, "Well now, who are you, sweetheart?" Americo—or shall I call him Ruco Urco—now turns to face the young dog and repeats the sentence I said in German without a trace of an accent, using the exact same intonation, like a tape recorder, or an old parrot. Then he grins at me, as if waiting for a reaction. It gives me the creeps, and I shudder. That was eerie. "Do you speak German?" My voice croaks as I ask the question. "Yes," he replies. He says nothing further in German. Then we walk together in silence for a half hour. I am fearful and uneasy. How do I get away from him? I want to be rid of him—right away, if possible. Even though he is older than I, I would hardly be able to defend myself if he were to assault me. My bulky backpack would bring me down in an instant.

Suddenly he starts talking again, and tells me that his passport was stolen. I ask him why he isn't heading to the Peruvian embassy. He says, "What for?" I say, "Without a passport, you're not going to get back to Peru." Ruco Urco laughs again and says that shortly before he travels back, he'll get his passport.

At some point I ask him whether he believes in God. "Definitely not! Only in the earth, the air, the water, the plants, the animals, and the sun." He rattles off this list with a grin that makes all his nonexistent teeth sparkle.

I suddenly notice that Americo's neck muscles have begun to twitch quite noticeably. I sometimes have this exact symptom when

I overdo it or am overtired. My slight dystonia was triggered by a fall. But the twitching is not as clearly visible in my case as it is in his. This is a rare ailment, not a crippling one, but it can certainly become unpleasantly painful. You might say that the muscle tone is thrown off track.

I have never seen that in another human being. And the longer we walk, the more noticeable his muscle spasms become. I draw his attention to this, and tell him, "I have the same thing. Exactly what you have. When I overdo it, my muscles twitch." The chance of meeting someone with this rare symptom is remote. He says he can live with it quite well, and anyway it's worse than usual today because he is tired. But he's sometimes able to switch it off for months at a time.

So I figure that if he's a shaman, there's no harm in asking him what I can do for this condition. The worst that can happen is that he fills my head with more nonsense. He looks as though he's concentrating very hard, then he says to me, "You're breathing incorrectly. You breathe only into your lungs, so you sometimes have trouble getting enough air. You have to breathe through your nose into the place four inches under your navel. Then everything will relax. Little by little, very slowly."

Astonishing. That is exactly what a doctor who specializes in natural medicine told me two years ago—although it didn't work very well. I explain to Ruco Urco that I've been told that, but that it doesn't do the trick for me. He says, "Because you are not being consistent about breathing through your nose. You have to breathe in and out through your nose. And you are putting too much of a strain on your lungs. You just have to breathe through your nose into the point." I ask him what he means by "the point." It's simply the right one, he informs me.

He adds, "You have to pay careful attention to when your muscular spasms worsen and when they ease off. You have to be very patient and gradually extend the good periods in which the tension lets up."

He stares hard at me, and says, "You have to watch very carefully and pay attention to your teeth." With a big grin on his face, he presents his five yellow tusks. We laugh. "Actually," he adds, "you just have to watch the way your cat breathes. Breathe the way she does. She'll teach you."

Hold on! Who said anything about a cat? I didn't. For the past three weeks I haven't said a word about my cat so that I wouldn't start thinking about her and missing her too much. I want to know what made him say this, and act as though I was a stupid foreigner and didn't understand him. "I should watch cats?" He hastens to correct me: "No, no, watch *your* cat." I don't ask him how he has come upon this bit of wisdom. Maybe he figures every German household comes equipped with a dog and cat in addition to a television set and refrigerator?

After hiking for several miles, much of it in silence—he never initiates a conversation anyway—we arrive in a godforsaken dump known as Virgen del Camino, which is split through the middle by a four-lane highway.

It is as hot as can be. The man is huffing and puffing and sweating, and I am overjoyed to be back in something resembling civilization, even though there is not a soul around. Probably everyone has attempted to escape the brutal heat by retreating to their homes. I invite Americo to join me at the only bar in town.

Behind the counter of the Mexican-style bodega is a chubby woman in her mid-fifties, wearing a tight, bright red dress. We are the only customers. I ask him what he'd like to drink. He wants tap water. "Maybe some coffee?" I urge him. You can always expect an offbeat answer from Americo: "I drink coffee only when someone dies." Voilà!

I order coffee for myself nonetheless, because the heat has made me feel as though I am on the brink of death. The poker-faced barmaid, who has evidently seen just about everything in her life, brings us coffee and tap water with a weary look. Americo grins from ear to ear, and looks as happy as a baby. "This water is fantastic. Unbelievable!" I don't consider that especially noteworthy, and go on drinking my coffee.

"You know what the best thing is about Europe?" he wants to know. I ponder two possible replies—the Alps and the Mediterranean—but the shaman beats me to the punch: "The fact that you can drink water from the tap. That is unthinkable in Peru." He orders another glass of water from the sink and sips it like Champagne.

Then he starts jabbering away as though he'd just drunk a glass of truth serum. "I think the best books ever written come from Germany. *The Tin Drum,* by Günter Grass, and *Momo,* by Michael Ende." I start to warm up to this peculiar Indio shaman, until he finishes off the list of his favorite works of world literature with an astonishingly offensive addition: "And *Mein Kampf,* by Adolf Hitler."

It is all I can do not to spit out my coffee, and I hope against hope that the unbearable heat in the bar has confused me. If not, this Peruvian may just get the daylights beaten out of him! I've already taken off my backpack, and my walking stick is within easy reach at my chair.

To judge by the disgusted look on the barmaid's face, I've understood every word correctly. I'll take a deep breath, then I can beat him up if I'm still so inclined. I can tell from the way the barmaid is looking at us that she'll grab hold of him for me.

So I start by stating calmly that it's a matter of taste as to whether the two titles he named first are the best books in the world, and that I find *Momo* and *The Tin Drum* unquestionably good, each in its own way. But *Mein Kampf* . . . I rise from my seat and draw myself up to my full height in front of him—a trick I learned from Beaky. That is beyond the pale!

Now I really fly off the handle. I deliver a long, loud, snarling lecture. His grin grows wider and wider during my enraged diatribe, and I get madder and madder while informing him that it would be ridiculous to try to explain all this to him; any halfway intelligent human being should know better than to pick up garbage like that and waste his valuable time on such trashy ideas.

The old guy smiles at me serenely and makes the outrageous claim that Hitler had the right idea—didn't he? That is the last straw. I tell this Peruvian that I feel personally offended by the idiotic remarks he's spewing, and that any further discussion will bring us to blows. I am enraged, I tell him, and he simply has to shut up now!

I fall back onto my chair with a gasp, and fix my gaze on the circus poster plastered on the wall. It's a picture of a tiger leaping out at me. I'm still seething, so I rise up again with my index finger in the air and shout at Americo that with an attitude like his, he would wind up in jail if he were in Germany—and rightly so. The freedom of each and every individual is one of the greatest things on this planet, and I would lay down my life for it any time! The volume of my own voice startles me, and I stop talking. He takes all this in stride and continues to grin at me. He's pleased that I am so upset. My face, which is covered in sweat, must be as red as the barmaid's dress by now.

She brings me another *cortado* and says, "It's on the house." Ruco Urco is still on top of the world, and starts to rant, "Wouldn't it be delightful if the Germans marched into Peru and liberated it?" I am appalled. This man is seriously getting on my nerves! He goes right on raving, "Or the ETA? Wouldn't it be fantastic if the ETA were to blow up Peru? That's what we need in Peru."

The barmaid feels she's been called into action as a worthy representative of her country, and from the counter she shouts one curse after another at the crazy healer. "The ETA is a bunch of swine!" she yells.

The shaman acts as though he has a monopoly on casual cheerfulness. "What are you getting so worked up about?"

Then Encarnación—that is the name of the barmaid, as she now reveals to us—pours out her heart, telling us how her life has been changed forever by the horrors of the ETA. She has lost several family members to their attacks. I listen spellbound. The things she tells us would themselves fill a whole book, and are impossible to summarize here.

When I look at my watch, I realize that I've spent more than three hours with Americo. I stand up without a word, heave my backpack onto my shoulders, and walk to the door. Ruco Urco smiles toothlessly and says, "I'm staying here; all the best!" I'm free of him at last. Encarnación, the barmaid, hurries over to the door to give me a firm handshake and wish me the best. She whispers in my ear: "Hitler was not even a pig! He was nothing but shit!"

Once I have left the bar, I turn around for a second and see that Encarnación has taken my place with Ruco Urco at the table. The two of them are chatting with their heads together. They look like a brother and sister about to launch into a long discussion.

While I slowly forge ahead under the blazing sun, leaving this unpleasant place behind, I realize that the crazy Peruvian has made me aware of something. Four inches under the navel. Perhaps he picked a fight with me on purpose, deliberately provoking me by choosing the most hurtful argument he could think of. I'm open to many things, and willing to compromise and yield, but when it comes to fascism, I have a firm, unshakeable, unyielding attitude, and anyone who doesn't share it feels my wrath.

How can one possibly mention Hitler in the same breath as Michael Ende and Günter Grass? This idiotic comparison made the whole thing even worse. *Momo* and *The Tin Drum* were written from a perspective with which I can identify completely—and they are the diametrical opposite of the third, unspeakably sorry excuse for a book. Even a crazy person could not like these three books at the same time.

The result is clear: 2 to 1 for the good guys.

In the bar, my rage was transformed into courage. So it does work after all!

Now I'm almost disappointed that Americo has decided not to come along with me.

The more I acknowledge my rage, let it out, and recast it as courage, the fewer problems I'm likely to have with the occasional muscle spasms on my neck. During the entire trek, I have been enraged. No wonder I was suffering from bilious colic. If you hold in your rage, your gallbladder has to boil over. This odd Peruvian was deliberately trying to make me boil over. How did he do that?

My thoughts turn to Evi's parting words. "The craziest things will happen to you along the way. Be confident and have faith in yourself!" I am confident and have faith in myself, and I don't have the slightest idea how many miles I covered today, but it's a good number.

Insight of the day: Sometimes the most rational thing is simply to be wonderfully crazy!

July 3, 2001
Astorga

Somewhere in the middle of nowhere, I spent the night at a motel at the side of the road. Spain is starting to look like Mexico! It is much drier and some of the haciendas have bright green cacti that are a good six feet tall. After leaving the bar yesterday, I was glad to put another nine miles behind me.

This morning I didn't head downstairs for breakfast until ten o'clock. I needed quite a lot of sleep after yesterday, which really wore me out. As usual, I am the only customer in the restaurant. The waiter comes up to me and asks, "Are you Hans Peter from Germany?" Baffled, I reply, "Yes." And without a word, he hands me a tightly folded piece of paper, which says, in Spanish, "For Hans Peter from Germany. Many thanks, and long live *Momo*! Yours, Ruco Urco."

I ask the waiter, "Who gave this to you?"

"I have no idea. The man didn't even have a backpack, and his shoes were quite muddy. His shoelaces were untied."

Americo, my wacky Peruvian! I find out that he got to this hotel late last night, and stayed in the room right next to mine. And at about 6 A.M. he was off again, after dropping off this note. Ruco Urco. I read the name again and start to laugh. Sounds like a name straight out of a Michael Ende story.

Today I plan once again to push my sore feet and knees to their limit. The temperature has dropped quite a bit, thank heavens. It's 60 degrees outside, and there's a slight breeze. It's a bit like spring at the Baltic, and a fine day for hiking. I'm feeling bright-eyed and bushy-tailed, and up for a good long walk, so I decide once again to set an unusual record: I will sing aloud all the songs that won the Grand Prix award from 1973 to the present while I hike nine miles on the dirt road. When I return to the main road, I decide to keep going straight for another twelve miles until I hit Astorga. I'm having great fun singing and see no need to stop when I run into other pilgrims. It's my "vacation" too, and I can do what I like.

A merry group of women pilgrims from Ulm recognizes me and finds my offbeat singing funny. They figure I'm traveling with a hidden camera. I confirm that I am, and tell the women they can wait at an out-of-the-way scallop signpost for the television truck to pull up behind me. They look thoroughly baffled. I forge ahead with a song on my lips and a spring in my step, although I can't help wondering whether the point of a pilgrimage could possibly be to see if I can belt out the lyrics to "Save Your Kisses for Me!" by heart. It makes me feel great, but is there any other point to what I'm doing? Maybe it's just wonderful to be able to put yourself into such a good frame of mind?

What happened to my bad mood? Could it be that it came from ugly songs I cooked up in my head? Was twelve-tone music play-ing in my brain? If so, I was not playing it intentionally.

I decide to spend the remaining miles without speaking or thinking, following advice from Sheelagh, who said to me in León: "You don't feel the toll this trek is taking on your body when you walk without thinking and speaking. Just don't think about any-thing! It sounds easy, but it is quite difficult. And something won-derful will happen. Try it some time!" So here I am, trying it!

Shortly afterward, when I'm walking through a tiny hamlet, I see a child's scrawl on the wall of an old elementary school at the edge of town: *Yo y tu*.

Me and you. A schoolchild was clearly practicing penman-ship with colorful chalk. Now, there's a motto for me! So I will walk in silence, without thinking. I instantly forget my chosen motto, and attempt to move ahead devoid of thought on the dirt road, which seems to be heading slightly uphill toward nothing in particular.

These lonesome dogs are everywhere.

Silence is easy to maintain; I've gotten fairly used to that. I say nothing to the farmers on the field as I pass by, and they respond in kind. They seem to respect my silence. But it is nearly impossible to stop thinking. In my mind I keep breaking out into song, or my thoughts turn to disjointed drivel along the lines of "Where are my keys?" "Buy cigarettes!" "Aching feet!" "Could go for some potato salad!"

At some point I find I'm actually able to switch off my stream of thoughts and simply stop thinking. Incidentally, it is virtually impossible to describe a path after the fact when you are not thinking about it, since you see things without sorting them out or judging them. Dispassionate perception is hard to put into words.

Everything joins together: my breath, my steps, the wind, the singing of birds, the waving of grain fields, and the cool feeling on my skin. I walk in silence. Am I pressing my feet onto the ground while I walk, or is the ground pressing up onto my feet? Without my thoughts I lose my power of expression, and the landscape, the sounds, and the wind leave no impression on me. Even ugly sights like a dead cat on the path, or beautiful vistas like the snowcapped peaks of the Cantabrian Mountains, fail to leave an imprint. The complete absence of pressure is a merciful condition, bringing neither joy nor sorrow.

At the end of this journey, I discover that when I do not express myself in words and thoughts, nothing leaves an impression on me, not even wind or rain. If you don't take a break from expressing yourself in thoughts, actions, speech, song, and dance from time to time, the act of expression turns instead into unrelenting pressure.

The act of expression leaves an impression on others, who respond with their own expression, which in turn creates a new impression for the original speaker. People who constantly *ex*press themselves are thus always *im*pressed as a consequence. This is how marital discord and world wars come about. At some point this perpetual pressure becomes paralyzing. But there is no pressure in silence. When I am not thinking or expressing anything, I'm still there, after all. The only thing I'm really encountering and reencountering along the Camino is myself. In the future I plan to choose more carefully what I express.

Needless to say, I get hopelessly lost. With silence in my head and all this nonthinking for nine miles, I've lost track of the path's arrows and scallop signposts. And once I start to focus again, I am simply somewhere at some time. It is lovely here, but wrong. Later, though, it turns out that my meandering did not add up to more miles at all—in fact, I saved about two miles. A farmer sends me through a field with grain as tall as I am, which brings me back to the right path. How funny! I stop paying attention to the trail, lose my way, and still wind up taking a shortcut. Afterward I add on another twelve relatively thought-free miles, and I am far less exhausted than usual, which is of course due in part to the German-like temperatures.

As I approach Astorga, a gigantic stray dog—a beautiful mixed-breed St. Bernard—is there to greet me from afar with a hoarse bark. This dog is sitting sadly behind an iron gate and guarding an empty vacation home. The deserted, neglected house is bolted shut and barricaded. There is no water in the pool, nor is there food or shelter for the dog, who has barely enough strength to chase me away with a round of barking when I come up to the gate. He is trying desperately to open the gate with his bloody paw. This sad sight tugs at my heartstrings. I pet him through the gate, and spend twenty minutes talking to him. Then he lies back down on the lawn, heaves a sigh, and allows me to move ahead toward my destination.

I must have walked a total of twenty-one miles today. It's almost chilly outside when I arrive in Astorga.

I will write up my insight for the day tomorrow, because it is actually inexpressible. I have met God!

July 4, 2001

Astorga

Impressive stylistic mélange, seen through the drizzle:
the Bishop's Palace in Astorga

I seem to have walked exactly nine miles too many yesterday, and my body is longing for a rest. When I hike more than twelve miles a day, it kills the next day. But sometimes you have to overexert yourself to experience something truly consequential!

Today I'm in Astorga, staying at the Hotel Gaudí, across from the Bishop's Palace, which was designed by Antonio Gaudí and built between 1889 and 1913 in the neo-Gothic style. This Palacio Episcopal is a vision to behold. This castellated masterpiece looks different on each of its five sides, and seems like a cross between Neuschwanstein and Dracula's Castle. The drizzle accentuates the slightly creepy atmosphere. Inside, visitors are greeted by an extravagant orgy of light à la Gaudí, created by the colorful, cathedral-like windows.

At breakfast, where I enjoyed a view of this dark blue fortress, I briefly toyed with the idea of hiking on today after all. Then Stevie Wonder started singing "Gone Too Soon" on the radio! Well, how about that! It is of course a bit silly to base your decision on a song you happen to hear, but that is exactly what I did. There's nothing at stake; I have plenty of time. I trust I've made the right decision, and I spend an entire day in Astorga. I can keep my room for another night.

I can neither relate nor record what I experienced yesterday. It is inexpressible. I highly recommend hiking for seven miles without speaking or thinking. Larissa had told me something back in Grañon that I thought rather foolish at the time: "Everyone eventually gets to the point of bursting into tears somewhere along this route. You just stand there and cry. You'll see!"

Yesterday was the day it happened to me. I was standing right in the middle of the vineyards, and out of nowhere I began to cry. I cannot say why.

Exhaustion? Joy? Everything at once? Whining near the wine?! In spite of it all, I burst out laughing.

Then it happened! I had my very own encounter with God.

Yo y tu was the motto of yesterday's trek, and to me it sounds like a secret pact. What happened there is between Him and me. But the school wall bore three words: *me and you.* The bond between Him and me is an entity unto itself.

To encounter God, you first have to issue an invitation to Him; He does not come without being asked—a divine form of good manners. It's up to us. He establishes an individual relationship with us. Only a person who truly loves is capable of sustaining this relationship.

I am getting freer by the day. My emotional seesawing on the Camino has eased up, and I am seeing things clearly. After running the gamut of emotional frequencies, I have come to settle on a single frequency, and I get great reception. Emptying out the mind creates a vacuum that God can fill completely. So watch out! Those who feel empty can enjoy a once-in-a-lifetime opportunity! Yesterday it was as though a huge gong had rung in my head. And the sound will reverberate. Sooner or later the Camino shakes us to our very foundations. I know that the sound will gradually fade, but if I prick up my ears, I will hear the reverberation for a long time to come.

For all intents and purposes, my quest is at an end here, because I have found the answer to my question. From now on, this journey will be purely for pleasure.

When I walk around Astorga, where it's raining today, I keep smelling cinnamon. The humid air carries the sweet peppery aroma through the town. Cinnamon is my favorite scent, so I try to locate its source. I first assume that the aroma is coming from a bakery, but the local bakery smells quite different. The Bishop's Palace is emitting a faint whiff of cinnamon, and I imagine Gaudí cementing cinnamon sticks inside the joints of the Bishop's Palace.

On the square in front of the town hall I run into Seppi, a fellow from Finland. We've already met. Yesterday we had coffee together at the Hospital de Orbigo after my silent hike. Well, *I* had coffee, anyway. Seppi downed a half liter of beer. Seppi is an extremely good-natured, upbeat, bald athlete from Helsinki in his early forties. Yesterday he told me that he had left behind his Finnish friends six days ago, because he hikes about twenty-five miles a day, and no one can keep up with him. When I ask him how he manages to keep to that grueling pace, he tells me that he sings quite a bit and drinks beer, and in the hostels there are evening parties with even more singing. He's having the time of his life. After knocking back quite a few beers, Seppi staggers back to his hostel and belts out *"Hasta luego"* while his hat flies off his head. Once he's gone, I think: Is it right to tackle this pilgrims' trail the way he does? Just to look at the whole thing as one big whale of a time?

When I see Seppi today, he is soaked to the skin and down in the dumps, smoking a filterless cigarette on the steps to the seventeenth-century palace that serves as the town hall.

"Hi, Seppi! What's wrong? Why do you look so miserable?" I ask.

He points to his right foot, which has a thick bandage on it, and tells me, "I took a spill today, over a tiny rock that I didn't see. I wasn't paying attention. How could I be so stupid? But I was lucky! A German nurse was five minutes behind me on the trail. She had everything you could possibly need with her, from ointment to bandages. Isn't that incredible?"

This coincidence doesn't surprise me in the least. That's the way things work on the Camino! I would have been surprised if he *hadn't* been helped. God seems to have sent forth countless numbers of nurses with bandages and ointment. And, I realize, Jose is one of them!

Since I don't react the way he expects, he repeats the last sentence: "Isn't that incredible? Such luck. Days go by without my seeing anyone, then I fall down and a German nurse with first aid equipment is standing by."

"What are you going to do now?" I ask him, and he does what he does best: He pulls himself up by the bootstraps, saying: "I'll be able to go on tomorrow."

When I take a closer look at his swollen foot, my only thought is that it will be close to impossible. I pat his wet shoulder and move on.

For Seppi, the fun is over. He may have to drop out shortly before reaching his goal. It's like a game of Parcheesi: just when you're confident of victory and gloating because you think you've beat the others, you get knocked off your space. Do you keep playing, or do you quit? Whatever you decide, you have to change your approach the next time around so you won't lose. The rules of the game don't change. It is never the others who knock you off the board, but your own attitude. It shouldn't matter whether you win or lose. And if you win, you should just take note of the victory and not revel in it. I hope the Camino de Santiago doesn't kick me out of the game; my calves feel like two rock-hard lumps. Evi is out, but she was a good sport. Will Anne really make it to Santiago with her swollen foot? Will Tina finish on her own? A Spaniard I met in a bar yesterday was frustrated and on the verge of tears: "I'm dropping out. This isn't any fun. I can't do it anymore. I'm tired, and I'm stopping." I asked him: "Don't you like the Camino?" At first he didn't say anything, then he grumbled: "Yes, I do . . . but I just don't want to go on."

Later, as I continue my hike, I see him sitting in a bus. He waves to me wearily.

On the Camino I feel as though I'm back in school. I like learning certain subjects, and when I do, the process is effortless. If I'm lucky, I like the teacher as well. But I tune out subjects that are more complicated or that don't grab my attention because I don't understand them or because the teacher is obtuse.

Evi has been my favorite teacher, and I have learned quite a bit from her about trust. Tina's forte is humor. When I think about her, I can't help laughing. Anne's highly interesting issue is doubts. Americo showed me that moving ahead with my life will be difficult if I don't start to manage my anger. Antonio, the Andalusian with the cross, showed me how to be in the moment. The hat store owner taught me about sincerity. Gerd's dreary arena was resignation. Ute, the Austrian woman who hiked with Beaky and Billy Goat for a while, was constant. The three Frenchmen in the Peugeot heightened my attentiveness. The German woman in the blue underpants gave me a lesson in keeping calm. Larissa gave me a new perspective on devotion. Victor taught me consistency, Stefano vanity, and Lara letting go. Sheelagh's subject was courage. Jose was a master of change; Vitorio, the innkeeper, of detachment. Claudia, the Brazilian woman, specialized in pride, and Seppi, the fellow from Finland, taught me about high spirits. Yes, and Beaky, my shadow, was simply awful! I paid her so little attention that I don't even know exactly what she taught, apart from geography. In any case, she was in charge of all my weak subjects, and I have to concede that she was a stern school principal! The many animals along the way taught me how to care for others, and that nine-mile hike was a crash course in matters of love.

During my journey my thoughts keep returning to the question of suffering. Ultimately, suffering is a lack of comprehension. When you don't understand something, you have to have faith. Hence, it is sometimes our attitude that makes us suffer.

Tomorrow is the beginning of a harder lap. It is a slow ascent in the direction of Rabanal through the hills of the barren Maragatería, up to an altitude of 5,000 feet. Behind that, in the Montes León, there is unfortunately no way of bypassing Foncebadón! Whether I like it or not, I have to go through that nearly deserted mountain village, which people are always warning you about. Supposedly packs of wild dogs prowl around, looking to attack. It's best not to go through this area alone, and you shouldn't bring any food with you. Unfortunately, Seppi, that robust Finnish fellow, can't be my hiking buddy. We'll see what happens.

Insight of the day: The heart is always right.

July 5, 2001

Rabanal

When I go to breakfast in the hotel this morning, a very pleasant surprise awaits me: the only guests there are Anne and Sheelagh! The two of them had arranged to get together for coffee here in my hotel in Astorga. Now I think I know why Stevie Wonder was singing "Gone Too Soon" yesterday.

Sheelagh is distraught, however, and has obviously been crying. She tells me that two friends, colleagues at the New Zealand Red Cross, were decapitated by rebels on the Fiji Islands.

We race to the TV to catch the latest news on an American cable channel, which reports yet another horror story of a very different kind. Hannelore Kohl, the wife of our former chancellor, has committed suicide. Although she was only a passing acquaintance, this news item hits me like a bombshell. I stare agape at the TV screen.

Sheelagh is in no condition to continue on today, and decides to spend another day in Astorga so she can e-mail friends in Wellington, New Zealand. Since the hike tomorrow is so dangerous, though, I try to persuade Sheelagh to come with Anne and me. Sheelagh smiles and waves us aside. "Don't worry! I have trust!"

So Anne and I decide to continue on as a team and wait for

Sheelagh's arrival in one of the mountain villages ahead of us, Rabanal or El Acebo. We head off toward the mountains.

Anne and I hit it off beautifully right from the start. We hike at a very similar pace, so it is surprisingly easy for us to find a rhythm that works for both of us, and we fall into step automatically. At the beginning of the hike she is still a bit wary of me, and seems to be interpreting my friendliness as a tentative come-on, so after a few miles I ask her to stop for a minute. Then I give her the brief official explanation: "Listen, Anne. I don't want to have sex with you. I'm gay!" Now the ice is broken. Anne is taken aback at first, but then she breaks out into hearty and seemingly endless laughter. She grabs on to a rock at the side of the road, roaring with laughter and unable to keep her balance. She keeps shouting, "Oh, ooh, oh!" while holding her stomach and shaking with laughter. Once she has calmed down a bit, she exclaims: "Sorry, Hans! I thought you were being so friendly because you wanted something from me!"

"You can put that thought right out of your head," I announce with studied irony; "you're not my type!" That comment elicits more peals of laughter and does away with any last vestige of aloofness on her part.

Now that we can both breathe easier, Anne opens up like a book. She tells me that since beginning her pilgrimage, she has met only the most dreadful men, and in three instances, her friendliness was nearly her undoing. That is the only reason she has treated me so badly, although she liked me right from the start. She didn't want to be let down yet again.

The first guy—with whom she hiked for nearly a week, starting in Pamplona—was the self-designated "first official pilgrim of the

Camino." This guy, a Spaniard, even handed out unsolicited business cards listing *El peregrino del Camino* as his profession; there is a pile of them in nearly every *refugio*. So sick. He's the Mickey Mouse of the Camino, and races up and down the path in brown medieval monk's robes decorated with the traditional pilgrim insignias: slouch hat, scallop, cross, bocksbeutel, and self-carved walking stick. His goal is not to get to Santiago, however, but to lure women who are doing the pilgrimage alone into cheap hotels. Anne shook him off once he started forcing his attentions on her. The brown mascot considered it perfectly natural that she would jump into bed with him—as a little thank-you for the days they'd spent together.

I couldn't help blurting out, "How could you hike with a guy like that for even one day?"

Anne is furious at herself: "Gosh! I guess I am stupid!"

After that, Anne joined up with two gay men from London. That was great fun, she said, but the two of them were constantly on the prowl for sex, and this got on her nerves. So she was more than happy that they cut short their walk on the Camino when the pickings proved slim, and flew to Madrid "for some sex."

"Don't tell me you are looking for some sex," she asks me warily. My reply ("Not today!") puts her somewhat at ease.

During the past week, two much older Frenchmen from Reims named René and Jacques were breathing down her neck, running their hands over her short hair and her soccer T-shirt whenever they got the chance. They were always inviting her for coffee or tea, because those were the only words they knew how to say in English. Again and again they indicated with gestures that they wanted to invite the young lady from England to sleep over with them. The people you meet! But it stands to reason that the

Camino is not a sex-free zone, and some *refugios* get pretty lively.

As we continue walking, we share quite a few chuckles about night-shift pilgrims, counting nuns, my crazy Peruvian shaman, and other pilgrimage oddities. We are having a marvelous time spicing up our stories with surprising punch lines. Of course, we tell each other all kinds of things about our personal lives, with no holds barred, but since they really are personal, they will go unmentioned here. The lady from Liverpool is funny, kindly, sardonic, shrewd, a bit gullible, and very well educated.

She spent eight months teaching English to monks in Dharamsala in northern India, where the Dalai Lama was living in exile, and in return a Rinpoche instructed her in Buddhist teachings. Anything I've read about Buddhism is kids' stuff in comparison to the wealth of her experience she gained there, which she now generously shares with me. Her most significant lesson from the eight months is one simple sentence from the Dalai Lama: "Drop the thought! When something upsets you on the job or anywhere else, just drop the thought. Don't chew away at it, because dropping it is the only way of releasing it!"

My Liverpudlian friend also worked in Nepal, Afghanistan, Central America, Florida, and Canada. In 1989 she spent several months in East Berlin completing a research fellowship. She lived in Kleinmachnow, a few miles south of the city. When she pronounces the name of this town in her smoky voice and British accent, I laugh so hard I almost wet my pants. *Kläinmächkchgnou!*

Her halting German isn't bad. She has trouble understanding it after twelve years without any practice. But when I speak to her very slowly, she gets the general drift.

I tell Anne that I'm keeping a diary, that I got to page 357 today, and that she's in it. Anne is happy to hear this, and wants to know what I've written about her so far. When I tell her truthfully what it says, she shakes her head and complains: "It's always the same! When people meet me, they find me unfriendly at first! Am I that rude?"

I nod hesitantly, and she draws in her breath. She wants to write a book too, but she thinks she wouldn't be able to see it through to the end. That startles me, and I remind her, "You have trekked so far. If that isn't seeing something through to the end, I don't know what is! Just write as if you're talking to yourself." Anne's sense of humor and her take on the world are wonderful. I'd love to scoop her up and bring her home with me. Incidentally, her pilgrimage is for a good cause. Her sister suffers from Crohn's disease, a serious chronic gastrointestinal illness for which there is no effective treatment because it has yet to be thoroughly researched. To collect money to fund research, a newspaper in Birmingham is publishing a weekly update on Anne's pilgrimage and putting out a call for donations. Anne snaps a photo of us for the next week's edition.

Our hike is getting to be incredible fun. The higher we go, the more spectacular the views become, and Anne, who once worked at the University of British Columbia in Vancouver, feels as though she's in the Canadian mountains. I feel the same way. The summits may not be half as high here, but the Camino offers impressive vistas nonetheless.

When Anne and I get to Rabanal in the early evening, we are quite drained. Though I only know it from pictures, this place closely matches my vision of Tibet. Anne soon surprises me by remarking, independently, that it looks like Nepal here, and she's actually traveled through that country. So you might say that Rabanal looks almost like Nepal, except that the Spanish town is much, much lower!

I head for a country inn (which is practically full), while Anne opts for the pilgrims' hostel (also practically full) next to the small gray stone church.

Insight of the day: *It was good to hike alone, but enough's enough.*

July 6, 2001

Rabanal

Last night Anne and I had a good solid pilgrim's dinner at my rustic inn. The dark Tyrolean, arch-filled dining room was packed, and there was lots of red wine and good cheer. Of course, I've decided not to drink any alcohol until the end of the pilgrimage, much to Anne's chagrin. But a little teetotaling can't hurt.

At the next table, two young Swabian couples have been staring over at me the whole time in a friendly but obvious manner and giggling to themselves. Anne is rather put off by their behavior, and hesitantly asks me: "Am I imagining things or have they been staring at us? What's going on? What is it about us that makes them keep gawking at us with those goofy grins?" I shrug my shoulders, having no desire to explain that my program, which she happened to see one night in England on the late show, is seen on prime time in Germany by millions of people. She probably regards me as an ambitious German nobody from the sticks, and I'm happy to keep it that way. At some point she's bound to figure out what I do, but there's time for that, and until then the two of us can get to know each other better.

When Anne leaves me at the table to go to the bathroom the southern Germans seize their chance and approach me to ask politely for autographs. Naturally, I have nothing suitable in my backpack, so I sketch a couple of signed caricatures on beer coasters, hoping to finish up before Anne gets back. But just as I'm scribbling the last signature, Anne appears beside me with a look of surprise. The Swabians thank Anne and me with a handshake and begin an orderly retreat to their seats. Anne stares at them in fascination. "What did they want from you?" I come up with a white lie: "Nothing! Some directions!" Anne makes the same face she did back in Santo Domingo: "What kind of directions? You don't know your way around here! Or have you been here before?" Right—that was an unbelievably stupid answer, but I'm on a roll, so I keep right on lying: "No! I meant directions in Germany! They're Germans. But that doesn't really matter. They were very polite." Anne interjects: "Polite?! It is ridiculously polite to say good-bye with a handshake if you're just going to sit down again a few feet away. Or is everyone in Germany like that?" The subject is soon dropped, and I get off scot-free once again.

This morning, when we meet at my inn for breakfast, neither Anne nor I have any desire to leave Rabanal to continue our trek. Rabanal, perched on a 3,600-foot high mountain like a miniature copy of the Great Wall of China, is incredibly beautiful, and we're both glad not to be hiking. We have yet to reveal that to each other, though, so each of us makes sure to dawdle over breakfast, and tries to paint as dreary a picture as possible of the day ahead without so much as mentioning the word *stay*.

Anne strikes me as a busy bee who stoically does her daily stint, and my teetotaling yesterday makes Anne think I'm an ascetic who knows the value of sticking to the program.

We start talking at cross-purposes. I initiate this silly conversation by looking at the cloudless sky and declaring: "Uh-oh, it looks like rain today." There is not a soul in England who can make a face look more incredulous than Anne, who replies, "What? Rain? We'll probably die of the heat today on the trail. It's supposed to get hotter and hotter!"

This goes on for some time, until we finally order our fourth latte and blurt out at virtually the same time: "Please let's stay here!" Since Anne has to leave her *refugio* after one night, she quickly switches to a different one at the edge of town, and I book my room for an additional night. Today we while away the time in the beautiful weather by taking walks and visiting the sights. Maybe Sheelagh will get here today too; she will surely to be glad to see us.

Yesterday, on the way to Rabanal, I couldn't resist the urge to tell Anne the story of Ruco Urco, my mystifying shaman from Peru. Anne looks at me skeptically, and finally says, "Sorry, Hans! I like you, and the story is really quite interesting, but it is not the least bit plausible."

Since I know that the story is the truth, I insist, "Yes it is! Believe me—this guy really exists, and everything happened exactly as I described it to you!"

I know I sound totally naïve to Anne; when I listen to myself telling this story, even I think it sounds made up, and I wouldn't believe it if it hadn't happened to me! I'm also a little annoyed at my haste in relating this story. She probably thinks I'm nuts now. And I already knew she was a natural skeptic. I should have kept my mouth shut!

When we go for coffee in the afternoon, Anne brings up the subject again: "Do you really believe this Ruco Urco story?" Should

I deny it? I decide not to, and tell her the story again, but the more I say, the nuttier it sounds, so I tell Anne it'd be better just to leave it alone. Drop the thought! I wish the toothless fellow would turn up here so I'd have some living proof. The odd story hovers uneasily between us the whole day.

As evening falls, the little bell at the tiny village church summons the pilgrims to mass. Anne and I want to have the continuation of our pilgrimage blessed again, just to be sure, so we wearily enter the dark church. The pilgrims are pushing their way in, and by the time we enter, the only seats left are either way in the front or in the back row. Anne wants to sit up front. I opt for the back, since there are too many Germans up there, and I'd rather sit next to some of the old locals. So we part ways. The church fills up to the very last seat.

Just as the congregation begins a solemn hymn, the old wooden door behind us crashes open and slams shut. I turn around with a touch of annoyance—and have a vision, right there and then.

There is Ruco Urco, making his way through the nave to the altar on his chafed feet in those open designer shoes. This can't be happening! How did he get here?! With shivers coursing down my spine, I try like mad to get Anne's attention, pointing to the strange man and whispering loudly, "That's him!"

Anne doesn't seem to get it and motions for me to keep it down by placing her index finger on her mouth.

Americo is looking around for a seat but can't find one. To make sure he doesn't even think of leaving the church, I shout "yoo-hoo" to him in a ridiculously loud voice and force the elderly Spanish lady next to me to squeeze even closer to her neighbor. Ruco Urco recognizes me and beams like a little lost boy who has found his daddy. He clumsily makes his way to my row, and when the lady next to me sees the shady-looking character I've been waving over, she too has a vision, to judge by the way her jaw drops open.

Ruco Urco plunks down next to me, and I have no choice but to hug him, although he smells of both sweat and a great deal of alcohol. The lady next to us fans herself with her hand. Americo suddenly joins the congregation, singing the Spanish hymn in a fine bass voice. When the singing ends, the priest begins the sermon, and I can't help laughing at the inebriated, hiccuping Peruvian. I mockingly scold him in Spanish, "You can't go to mass drunk!"

He replies in perfect German, "I am tipsy."

"So you do speak German after all!" I say, trying to pin him down in my mother tongue. But his mind has already wandered off in a different direction, and he acts as though he's never uttered a word. He mumbles absentmindedly in Spanish, "No."

After mass, I rush out with him onto the coarsely paved square in front of the church and gently but firmly hang on to his greasy sleeve. He cannot escape until Anne has met him and he has told her every last detail of his story. We plant ourselves directly at the little entrance. Ruco Urco suddenly bursts into tears like a small child, and swears to me again and again, *"Mi ángel! Tu eres mi ángel!"* (My angel! You are my angel!) He finds it necessary to convey this same tipsy message to the churchgoers who pass him on their way home.

When Anne finally comes out, I call to her in English, "That's him! Ruco Urco!" I feel as though I've reeled in a nice, fat fish. Anne stands rooted to the spot, and I completely misinterpret her sudden dismay. She says coolly, "That is not Ruco Urco. That is Jorge from Ecuador." Interesting.

I quickly list the basics about him: "This is Americo from Peru, known as Ruco Urco. He is married and has two daughters!"

"That's wrong as well!" Anne smirks. "He has a son! That's what he told me, anyway!"

Americo, aka Ruco Urco, or Jorge, whoever this South American trinity is, tries to wriggle out of this somewhat embarrassing situation by claiming that all of these identities are essentially correct. He has two daughters in Peru, he explains, by his current wife, and a son in Ecuador by his ex-wife. He was born in Ecuador, but later went to Cuzco to live among the *índios*. Are we supposed to buy that?

"OK—who are you?" is the only suitable question here. Anne whispers to me in English that she had a big fight with Jorge about her FC Barcelona T-shirt. She doesn't want to tell me exactly what happened, since it's just as kooky a story as mine. That figures.

Meanwhile, the South American—his accent is a dead giveaway at least for that—is now bellyaching that they turned him away from the *refugio* because he does not have a backpack, so they pegged him for a homeless person, not a pilgrim. Proud as a firstgrader on the first day of school, he shows me his gold-colored pilgrim's passport, which he obtained on my advice and which bears the name Jorge and his country of origin: Ecuador.

I explain to him: "Anyone with a pilgrim's passport cannot be turned down by a *refugio* unless all the beds are filled!"

"That is absolutely right," Anne confirms in her brilliant Spanish. With a battle cry of "Let's go!" she herds us into the gray stone pilgrims' hostel. Anne marches straight to the manager of the hostel and raises a real Spanish ruckus. Barking directives like a corporal, she orders him to accommodate the South American in accordance with regulations. I've also gotten good at flying off the handle, so I too seize the opportunity to let off steam in Spanish. This language is wonderful for cursing; it bristles with hisses and forceful *r*s.

The hostel director quickly gives in and assigns Jorge a free bed. His face wet with tears, the South American soon shows up again on the church square and tries to give Anne a hug, which she ducks to avoid.

"How can I thank you?" he sobs.

"By going to dinner with us!" I blurt out, and Anne looks at me as though she'd love to give me a good solid smack. I appease her by saying, "My treat, of course."

Muttering under her breath, she follows me and Jorge into the little tavern down the street from the village church. As soon as we are settled at our table and have ordered our food, I ask my guest to tell his version of my Ruco Urco story. Jorge deftly changes the subject while sipping his red wine. I find that unacceptable, and push him to tell me why he made the stupid Hitler comparison. He has a good laugh, and claims that was merely a bad joke that I evidently didn't get, but it clearly did me good to let off steam, so I ought to be happy—that's all there is to it.

"And how did you know I have a cat? I guess you think everyone in Germany has a pet!"

"Oh?" He beams at me in his childlike way. "Is that the case in Germany?"

I mull it over and declare: "No, it's not, of course!" And he flashes me a quick smile and says, "Well, there you have it!"

I have to resolve one last issue regarding my mother tongue, and I cheerfully challenge him to say something in German. Jorge gives me a blank look and has the nerve to claim that he doesn't know any language other than Spanish. Anne whispers to me that he's nothing but a poor crackpot; we ought to finish up our meal and ditch him. That's fine with me! There's nothing more to be salvaged from this evening, so I wolf down my food.

Jorge wants to know whether Anne is an FC Barcelona fan,

since she's wearing the T-shirt with the team logo. Anne says, "No! You've already asked me that! It is the only short-sleeved piece of clothing I was able to find on the Camino with sleeves wide enough to keep me from getting sunburned. That is the only reason I'm wearing it!" Jorge calmly insists on knowing whether she's aware that her shirt is falsely broadcasting her love for this team. Anne is enjoying neither the food nor the conversation, and she is clearly on edge, but Jorge keeps at it. He is suddenly stone sober, and calmly steers Anne into a debate on the fine points of soccer. Both of them know everything there is to know about the Premier League in England. Anne is happy to admit that she is a fanatical fan of a team from Leeds. Once they start throwing around Spanish soccer lingo I zone out. Anne is growing more nervous by the minute. Their conversation strikes me as too silly to follow, so I treat myself to a quiet moment in the bathroom.

When I return to the table, the two of them have locked horns about some idiotic game results in England. Anne is bawling him out in Spanish, and during a brief pause in the heated discussion, she gives me a sidelong glance and remarks, "By the way, he speaks English too!"

Now, *that's* interesting! Since I wouldn't understand the details about the clubs and game results even in my native tongue, I find that it's almost easier for me to follow the course of their dispute by relying on their facial expressions and voices. Anne's nervous nature and lack of self-control are working against her. Ruco Urco is just pretending to be upset, but his face radiates equanimity. The lady from Liverpool is sorely tempted to toss her glass of wine into the South American's face.

Jorge has zeroed in on Anne's weak spot, and uses all the means at his disposal to pounce on it. Her reaction to the soccer conversation is all out of proportion. Her nerves are jangled and she can't keep her cool. One more sentence from him and she'll give him the slap she'd intended for me. She finds him overbearing—which the cheeky charlatan most certainly is—but perhaps that is his way of expressing his gratitude?! He knows just how to pick us apart and communicate his findings, all the while presenting himself as a screwball or a con man. He probably doesn't have a clear idea himself of the havoc he is causing. But whatever his motivation, he is helping Anne, and sooner or later she'll realize that.

The evening is becoming increasingly explosive, so I suggest skipping dessert, though I have a yen for the homemade *crema catalana*.

In front of the church, Anne and I say good-bye to Ruco Urco, and he replies assertively, "You're pretty glad to be rid of me, aren't you?" Laughing, he waddles off to bed, and Anne and I take our fifth stroll around the village. We don't say much, but Anne is quick to point out: "That guy is a horrid quack . . . but even so, I was definitely too nervous!"

Insight of the day: Sometimes even the most annoying people mean well.

July 7, 2001
Foncebadón and El Acebo

This morning my British travel companion and I are up quite early, and we set out in high spirits. It's remarkable that she and I have started to hike together on the very leg of the journey I've been dreading since the beginning of my pilgrimage: steep ascents in absolute isolation, coupled with the prospect of stray dogs in the ghost town of Foncebadón. Right from the start, I knew I didn't want to hike this part alone. I would have gone with anyone, but it's fantastic that I'll be with Anne!

As we approach Foncebadón, we keep our walking sticks ready for action. In our imaginations there are hundreds of wolflike dogs waiting to pounce, and we don't stand the slightest chance against them. In the old days there were packs of wolves and highwaymen here. The way I see it, that horrible wolf-hyena-bear in Calzadilla de la Cueza was their predecessor. It's intimidating to climb interminably up through a dense, secluded forest, straight toward a destination everyone's been warning you about. But it's bearable when you're with someone. Sure enough, when we reach a hill after about one and a half hours, we catch a first glimpse of the dark rocky ruins of Foncebadón.

Shortly thereafter, we are standing in the middle of this ghostly town. Suddenly a starving, ash-gray dog about the size of a terrier appears and slowly makes his way toward us. He is weak and ill and in desperate need of love and affection.

The few other stray dogs that creep nervously out to us from every which way turn out to be just as harmless, and they all crave attention. They seem more likely to protect us than to attack us. Nice little mutts with the best of intentions encircle us, happily barking and wagging their tails. The tale of the evil dogs of Foncebadón is nothing but a fable, at least for Anne and me. Of course, I have no idea how they react to a frightened night-shift pilgrim.

In one of the cavelike ruins, we are surprised to come upon an enchanting restaurant that had opened just a week earlier. Called La Taberna de Gaia, it specializes in medieval cuisine. All the ingredients are fresh; they even use water from their own well. The mother and the daughter, clad in medieval garments, stand in front of an old fireplace and cook good solid food. As we fall into conversation with these chatty ladies, I realize my everyday Spanish is nothing to speak of in comparison with Anne's cultivated college Spanish. She used her time in Nicaragua studying field mice to full advantage!

After lunch we trudge on toward El Acebo. It is a fabulous walk, and the weather is nice. Every once in a while, we stop to enjoy the majestic mountain panoramas. I'm fascinated by Anne's descriptions of Tibetan Buddhism, and I can picture what she's describing, because it fits right into this landscape.

The trail is quiet and deserted; a third of the way into today's route, we approach a homemade *albergue* on a hill. As soon as we arrive, bells start chiming. We later learn that this is the standard way to announce the approach of a pilgrim. The multicolored shack is inviting and covered with colorful hand-painted signs listing the distances to Berlin, Jerusalem, Rome, New York, Buenos Aires, and Sydney.

For pilgrims seeking a more comprehensive orientation: signposts indicating distances to cities around the world.

A young hippie couple inside gives us a friendly greeting, which includes a devout wish that our inner Jesus awakens along the path. Maybe they ought to tone down their phony piety, I think to myself, when I see behind the hut, in the blazing sun, a German shepherd puppy on a three-foot leash. The dog is nearly dying of thirst and hunger. In front of him is a rusty tin can that probably once contained something to eat, since he keeps licking away at it desperately. The inner Jesus really does well up in me, full of rage, and I ask the woman firmly but politely for a plastic bowl. She is puzzled, but she gives me one, and I fill it to the top with the water sitting in a cattle trough—looking as though it's waiting to be drunk up. I give it to the dog and he drinks gallons of it. When I ask whether the little fellow has had something to eat today, I get the terse answer, "No! We don't have anything to eat at the moment!" I try to find out why he's tied up on a leash, and I get the baffling response, "If we didn't tie him up, he'd run away!" Of course he would, if he's smart!

These hippies are hypocrites, pure and simple. How can people listen to the constant howling of an abused creature while wishing for pilgrims to find the Christ within them? These people have most certainly not discovered Him for themselves. Everywhere on their sanctimonious wooden hut are crosses and pictures of Mary. These people make me sick! Some Americans and Australians who later join up with us in front of this hovel are full of praise for the simple flower children. I ask my fellow pilgrims whether they've seen the little dog on the leash whining without water. "Oh yes—he's so cute." These shallow amateur pilgrims think he's sweet, the place is heavenly, and the people are absolutely wonderful. Idiots! I hope someone takes pity on this animal and takes him away from here. I would love to take him myself, but I can't go around stealing puppies.

When Anne and I leave an hour later, the dog is unhappy to see us go and whimpers after us. It takes me a while of walking in total silence to recover from the sight of that suffering creature, and I realize that I was wrong to leave the dog behind.

I should have given in to my strong impulse. The hippies, who have too much on their plates as it is, would have been happy to be rid of the howling animal, and I would have enjoyed an additional frisky little hiking companion. It weighs on my mind.

Anne tries to convince me that continuing the pilgrimage with the dog would have been out of the question, and that I did the right thing. I reply that I want to face the new challenges of each and every day on this trek, and that it would have been simple to take the dog with me. And if it meant that I had to break off the trip, then so be it.

The way I handled that situation was nothing but an outgrowth of my egotism, and I will not whitewash my behavior; there are enough pilgrims doing just that. So I say resolutely to Anne, "I'm taking the next dog with me, no matter what!"

"Bet you won't!" she dares me mischievously.

At the Cruz de Ferro, which stands nearly five thousand feet above sea level, Anne and I find the famous iron cross attached to a long stake cut from an oak tree. We comply with the traditional pilgrims' custom of adding a stone we've brought from home to the three-foot-high pile at the base of the tree. This tradition is said to be thousands of years old and is meant to symbolize the casting off of your sorrows. I offer up a lapis lazuli stone to the pile.

It gives you a feeling of exaltation to stand in front of this cross on the peak of Monte Irago and to know that you made it here on your own steam. As Anne and I gaze silently at the crucifix sparkling in the sun in the secluded mountains, a Volkswagen Passat with a German license plate from the town of Mettmann stops next to us on the narrow mountain road. A husband and wife get out and stand next to us. Once they recognize me, the woman asks me whether I actually hiked up here. I reply that I did but wonder for a split second whether I wasn't the one who got here with the Passat. The lady asks Anne to take a picture of me and herself, which Anne does with a good bit of annoyance. The couple quickly leaves, and Anne asks, "Why did they want a photo with you?" I tell her that the lady wanted to have a picture with a real pilgrim. Anne is too clever to accept that explanation at face value, and points out that the lady could just as well have been photographed with her instead. Anne remarks that my compatriots behave very strangely in my presence, and there must be some other explanation for that.

I don't feel like filling her in right now on what I really do, so I am as silent as the iron cross. I'll leave aside any discussion of my profession for the moment—even though I really and truly love what I do.

A silent spot with stones from around the world: Cruz de Ferro on Monte Irago

At times I really put my foot in my mouth when I'm with people who are not from German-speaking countries. Once, in Berlin, I was invited to a theater premiere, which was followed by a small banquet. For whatever reason, I was the only German to be seated with a group from the French ministry of cultural affairs. My French is reasonably fluent, though it can get a bit clunky during a full evening of conversation. But the French officials were speaking their mother tongue, of course, so I struggled valiantly to get by. The woman sitting next to me, who was an undersecretary—as far as I could gather from her long-winded explanation—wanted me to describe my line of work. I said, "Comedian!" She now deemed me too insignificant to deal with, and hissed, "Is that so! You're a comedian? But you can't be very famous; if you were, I'd know you!" The rest of the table also seemed to find that *très amusant*. I had a big fat meatball in my mouth, and didn't hesitate to speak around it; after all, the lady next to me had terrible manners too.

"What German comedians do you know?" I said into her ear while chewing loudly. The lady took a deep breath and exhaled slowly, then told me that she really knew just one German comedian. Unfortunately, she couldn't think of his name, but he was outstanding and imaginative and blah blah blah.

"What kinds of things has he done?" I inquired, almost incomprehensibly, with all my chomping.

"You ought to know!" she scolded. "He was even on the French news! He played the queen of Holland!"

Voilà—she was talking about me! Feeling somewhat flattered, I assured her that today was her lucky day. The comedian she was looking for was right in front of her, in the flesh. Whereupon she turned her back to me and treated me like a sleazy con man from the Westphalian hinterlands trying to pass himself off as someone far greater than himself. The evening was a waste of time, though it did provide me with a nice anecdote.

Anne and I stare reverently at the cross and maintain our silence. My God, here I am, still on this hike, and no longer thinking about cutting it short. We'll get through this quite easily. Anne and I discuss what we've learned so far.

I try to describe my thoughts to Anne: "You know, when I picture the light within me, and my heart focuses on it, I feel really good, and this cheerful compassion washes over me. But when my head reenters the picture, I think: For goodness' sake, that's crazy, stop it! You have to look at life in the cold light of day, so just do what needs to be done! I don't feel especially good when I reason this way, because my nagging doubts return." Anne replies simply, "Drop the thought!"

The key is to forge ahead. I realize that, along my trek, I've been learning primarily how to strike a balance between trust and distrust. What it boils down to is this: Trust is the way to go, but a bit of double-checking here and there can't hurt. From now on I'll treat myself like a new car. You can essentially trust it because it comes with a factory guarantee, but a checkup at the garage now and then guards against an eventual breakdown.

Do what you feel like doing, as long as it's not robbing the local bank and taking the branch manager hostage. If your thoughts run in that direction, it might be time for a vote of no-confidence. Trust yourself as long as you feel good about it and it's not causing harm to others. Anne's simple idea is just to let go—of everything!

OK—the stone is placed, symbolically, at least. I won't know whether it is really on the pile of stones under the cross until I come back someday. As I continue down the road, I get rid of a pair of socks, too. I simply cannot put them on anymore. I don't know how often I've worn and washed them. Along the way, in a little souvenir store, I buy wool socks in a lovely shade of sky blue.

El Acebo is without a doubt one of the highlights of this journey. A mountain village straight out of a fairy tale. Like a little swallow's nest, it sits atop a peak more than three thousand feet high, looking out over the legendary Celtic landscape.

I persuade Anne to take a room with me, and we share a very nice room with three beds in the oldest inn on the square. It has a view of a mountain range. She is clearly enjoying the small bit of personal space after nearly thirty nights spent in either an over-crowded dormitory or a cold tent. And I am enjoying the chance to share this gigantic room. I would have had to pay the full price for the only vacant room anyway, so I treat her to it. After all, we're something like friends by now. I feel as though I've known this woman for a hundred years. We'll see whether we are still hiking together when we reach the end.

Anne wants to head straight to bed when we get there, but I'm up for a cup of coffee. I settle in at a wobbly wooden table in the hotel's overgrown garden to complete my written notes. The neighbors on the other side of the lattice fence are not feigning Christian charity this time, but they also have an unhappy dog, a full-grown husky, who is chained up in a filthy, roofless pen in the blazing sun and panting helplessly. What's the point of chaining this animal up? The untended garden is huge, and is fenced in on all sides, so the dog would not be able to run away. I can't get any writing done, because the dog has been barking and whimpering for two solid hours. The owner keeps yelling out the window to him: "Inca, shut up!" The other neighbors seem to have grown accustomed to this pitiful spectacle; no one lifts a finger to help.

I just cannot fathom how people can treat a living being like that. These people would never think of putting a leash on a human being. How can they stand this desperate howling all day long? They're probably using it to drown out the desperate howling in their souls.

I try several times to reassure Inca from my side of the fence, but this weak display of affection drives Inca completely crazy, so I marshal my anger—and my Spanish—and shout with all my might to the neighbors, "What's going on here? Are there or aren't there Christians living here?"

In fewer than ten seconds, a man emerges sheepishly from the house. He opens the pen without a word, removes the leash, and lets Inca run around in the big garden. Inca is now as jolly as can be and romps around like crazy on the shady side of the garden. Then he rolls around on the lawn a few times and lies down. That was easy! I am so relieved. The dog looks bewildered and seems not to understand why suffering suddenly stopped. I feel better, and, more important, so does Inca!

Anne is exhausted all afternoon, so we don't do very much. Toward evening we take a stroll through this enchanted spot. At the place where the Camino again leads into the wilderness, there is a small, impressive monument into which a dented bicycle has been skillfully integrated. The bicycle belonged to a German bicyclist who had plunged to his death just beyond El Acebo, and the villagers came together to create a lasting memorial for him. Unfortunately, he is not the only one to have lost his life on the Camino. Again and again I see small crosses, like warning signs, adorned with flowers and engraved with names. Some died from exhaustion so overwhelming that their hearts gave out; others were hit by cars, or plunged to their deaths. These places to honor the dead highlight all the challenges the pilgrim faces here.

I have one hundred twenty-five miles left to go until I get to Santiago.

Insight of the day: I say what has to be said and nothing more.

July 8, 2001
El Acebo

Last night Anne made a racket with her snoring. It is impossible for me to sleep when someone snores. At my wits' end, I said to "the universe," "Listen! You have to stop that snoring within the next five minutes without giving the poor woman permanent brain damage!" After a few minutes, she grew silent, and slept quietly until the morning. Fantastic. My compliments to the universe!

It is much easier to walk the Camino with a friend. Anne is funny. I laugh a lot and the time passes more quickly. Astorga was exactly the right place for us to meet up again. Hiking alone was a very important experience, but hiking with a friend helps me to translate into practice the theories I've learned. The longer we walk together, the more we enjoy it.

Anne looks bleary-eyed when she gets up, and she's really worn out. I'm similarly disinclined to race ahead, so we decide to spend another night in El Acebo. We also want to wait for Sheelagh's arrival, otherwise we might lose track of her. If she does come, we even have an extra bed for her. Anne goes straight back to bed and instantly falls into comatose sleep.

Hunger drives me to the restaurant on the first floor, and while I'm there I sign up for an additional night. I'm lucky my room is still free, because the bull's-eye glass window now bears a sign saying *Completo*. The breakfast choices are limited to cookies, dry marble cake, and coffee, but I've gotten used to that by now.

While I happily gobble up my meager meal, I observe all kinds of comings and goings by pilgrims from every part of the globe. An Argentinian group is loudly celebrating someone's birthday. Then a chubby-cheeked pilgrim covered in sweat enters the bar. He looks familiar. The Lake Constance Pilgrim is standing in the doorway panting for breath. I can't believe it. I guess this means that Beaky and Gerd will show up momentarily.

Since there are no free tables in the room, I wave him over to my table and ask him in German what Gerd and Bea . . . his wife are up to. "Ingeborg; her name is Ingeborg," my fleeting acquaintance informs me. His name, by the way, is Thomas.

So Beaky's name is Ingeborg! I ask him where he left them. He shrugs his shoulders: "I have no idea! At some point all their fighting got on my nerves so much that I went off by myself."

True to form, the Lake Constance Pilgrim engages me in an exceptionally silly conversation. While we drink our coffee, he's anxious to find out what I'm doing with the little boy I've been walking with lately.

"What little boy?" I interject.

"You know—the little boy with the red crew cut and the soccer T-shirt!" He wants to know where on earth I dug him up. He can't be more than twelve years old!

Oh God—he means Anne! I guess Anne looks like a little boy from afar. That's just great! Now everyone thinks I'm traveling with a child. The Lake Constance Pilgrim gives me a skeptical look while I explain: "She's a good friend." A girl???? He insists that this child doesn't look like a girl.

"Yes, a girl," I repeat, feeling a bit annoyed, "and the girl is forty-three years old." He absolutely refuses to believe it—after all, he's not stupid. Luckily, Anne has a sixth sense, and in a short while she appears before us in her favorite shirt, thus enabling me to point to her and say: "There! That is the little boy!" Thomas blushes and takes to his heels. When I tell Anne the funny story, she goes into one of her endless laughing fits, complete with choking sounds. The whole time her head keep swaying forward again and again and seems about to smash against the rough tabletop. The morning ends well, and the next phase of the day starts on an equally high note, with one good joke after another. I know there is nothing more tedious than explaining a joke, but I'm going to try it here. To get this joke, it helps to know Spanish and English.

Pilgrim companions

Here we go: A young American woman with a flushed face enters the pilgrims' dining room in a state of exhaustion. The group of Argentineans is happy to see her, and one of the women jumps up and runs over to her. The American woman evidently speaks a little Spanish, and the Argentinean can get by in English. The following conversation is a blend of these two world languages. Let's take this slowly!

The Argentinean woman wastes no time in stroking the belly of the American woman, and asks in English: "How is the baby?"

The American is baffled, and replies with a question of her own: "Baby? What baby?"

The Argentinean says: "But you said to me in Spanish: *Estoy embarazada!*" (I'm pregnant.)

The American confirms that this is what she has said: "*Sí! He dicho: Estoy embarazada.*"

Then the Argentinean, who is mystified, makes sure by asking in English: "So you are embarrassed?" What she meant to ask in English was: So you are pregnant? But in English, of course, "embarrassed" means "painfully self-conscious."

The American grimaces, then finally gets it: "Oh! I thought *embarazada* means embarrassed!"

But the Argentinean interprets her statement as: "Oh! I thought pregnant means pregnant!" Now she considers the American a complete idiot—and has no idea that she herself has missed the point.

The two women are utterly exasperated, and part without a word. Anne and I spend hours doubled up with laughter, and our running gag is born. Wonderful! In the two original languages, it's a guaranteed hit. While Anne and I relate the funniest experiences we've ever had, to a steady stream of giggles, coughs, and shouts, Sheelagh shows up at the door looking flushed with exhaustion. We yell over to her, "Hi, Sheelagh, how is the baby?" When she answers "Baby?" in total confusion, our running-gag joy is complete.

Sheelagh has a hard day of hiking behind her. She's been on the road since 6 A.M. Even so, she is absolutely delighted to have found us again. She tells us a bit sheepishly that there is not a single bed left in the entire village, and wants to know where we're spending the night. Anne and I decide in silent agreement to pull poor Sheelagh's leg, and Anne claims that we were damned lucky to get the very last double room. Sheelagh's hope for a restful night seems to go out the window, so I quickly add: "Come, I'll show you our double room!"

When she enters the room and sees three beds, she does a double take. "Oh . . . three beds? But there are only two of you!"

I reply, "Not anymore!"

We idle away the rest of the day in the hotel garden, washing our clothes, drinking coffee, hanging up our wash, eating cookies, playing cards, and telling stories. In the garden next door, Inca the sled dog—who is no longer on a leash—is hanging on our every word, and gets to hear that Sheelagh is in charge of urban planning in Wellington, the capital of New Zealand, and that she has two smart teenage daughters of whom she is mightily proud.

Insight of the day: Long live the subtle differences between the world's languages.

July 9, 2001
Molinaseca, Ponferrada

When we first get up, Sheelagh insists on paying for the room. That doesn't sit well with me and I turn her down; after all, I've invited her to share it. Determined not to be outspent, she treats us to a fabulous breakfast in a top-notch bodega. Our feast runs up a bill nearly as high as the cost of the room, which delights Sheelagh no end. With four or five large lattes and just as many mineral waters under our belts, Anne and I leave a place that wasn't so bad after all.

When we don't hike, Anne feels as though she is not being challenged, and on those nights she is unable to fall asleep. Last night she wanted to chat about everything under the sun, which I didn't feel like doing—just washing my clothes was enough to wear me out. Sheelagh found a way of pleasing both of us: she told us an exciting ghost story, the way our mothers used to do. This story supposedly took place in the house where Sheelagh was born, in Wellington. Of course this detail made the story doubly exciting.

In 1860, in a Victorian country house at the bleak southwestern tip of the North Island in New Zealand, lived one of Sheelagh's Welsh ancestors, who worked as a horse breeder. The farmer had put a stableboy in charge of his favorite animal, a boisterous white stallion.

Behind the owner's back, however, the young fellow abused the wild animal by kicking and beating it into submission. Soon the animal was so frightened that all it took was the sound of the boy's heavy steps for the horse to neigh in fear and stamp his foot.

The owner was perplexed by the horse's unusual behavior but did not connect it with the young caretaker, who of course wouldn't hurt a fly in the presence of his employer. One night, when the stableboy again sneaked into the stable and abused the frightened animal, he forgot to close the gate. The proud but terrified steed was able to escape by galloping into the night on the cobblestone path, and soon died in a mysterious fall.

The estate owner confronted the stableboy that very night and fired him. The farmer could never sleep through the night again. He just paced back and forth on the floor in his room, as the creaking of his floor's wooden planks resounded through the house. The poor old man died of a broken heart after losing his beloved stallion.

And to this day, every night at the farmhouse in Wellington, you can hear the heavy steps of the stableboy, the terrified gallop of the stallion over the cobblestones (which are no longer there today), and the squeaking of the plank floor. No one in this country home gets a good night of sleep! It's even the subject of a New Zealand television documentary.

Wow! The way Sheelagh tells this story, with her remarkable voice and her knack for capturing the eerie sounds on the cobblestones and the wooden floor, fills you with fear.

Anne fell into a serene slumber partway through the story, but I lay awake in thought. I made Sheelagh promise to tell me more New Zealand ghost stories in the nights to come.

Today the three of us get going too late after our substantial breakfast, and it is already too hot when we set out. Sheelagh thinks that Anne and I are not her ideal travel companions because each of us brings out the easygoing, leisurely nature of the other, which may make for great fun but is highly contagious. She plans to do her best not to end up that way herself. That's our mommy for you!

The Camino is a sheer pleasure today as well. We walk along in perfect harmony. These two women are exactly the friends I've been wanting to find on the Camino—humorous, open-minded, and, most important of all, kind. We let one another in on our lives playfully, with few holds barred. Neither Sheelagh nor Anne pushes me too hard to talk about my profession, and for today I restrict my explanations to a handful of insignificant facts. Sheelagh is fine with that. Her only comment is, "Take your time. When you're ready, you'll surely tell me more, but the hints you're dropping certainly sound intriguing!"

The landscape is breathtaking. We spend hours hiking through a wild, dark green mountain region full of wild animals. I stop keeping such a careful record of my miles, which I guess was therapeutic for me. I realize now that it doesn't matter in the slightest how far we get in a given day, because unless something earth-shattering occurs, we'll all keep to our time frame.

Sheelagh wants me to tell her what Germany looks like, because she's never been there, and she can't really picture it aside from the Alps. And I realize that it is a tall order to awaken in someone's imagination something that is so familiar to me. Since I have never been to New Zealand, I cannot bring in any potential points of comparison, and Sheelagh has done most of her traveling in Southeast Asia. When I describe Berlin, Anne jumps in to help, and she provides a sensible overview. I try to project as lively and diverse a panorama as possible of my homeland by re-creating my images of North Rhine–Westphalia, Sylt, Rügen, Hamburg, Dresden, Munich, the Black Forest, and the Rhine valley near St. Goar, urging her to imagine bells ringing in the background, because anywhere in Germany there is sure to be a sound of bells around the clock.

Naturally I go into raptures about all the varieties of German bread! Evidently I've done more than simply whet Sheelagh's and Anne's appetite for a long trip to this small, exotic, eventful country. I also wind up feeling as though I've described a really lovely spot on our planet. I didn't realize how attached I was to it.

Isn't that nice of me? Here I am, taking out time on my pilgrimage to boost the sagging tourist economy of my cold, humid homeland. Sheelagh tries to return the favor by describing the pearl of Oceania with its hallucinatory background of twittering tropical birds, and her description is so compelling that it makes me want to book the next flight out there.

Later, as we make our long descent, we look out onto the village of Molinaseca, through which the clean little Río Meruelo flows in a big loop. From both sides of the river rise gentle slopes terraced by vineyards.

It happens that this place bears a strong resemblance to the northern part of the Rhineland-Palatinate, from the landscape to the architecture of the half-timbered slate roofs; the only thing missing is a little hilltop fortress. The closer we come, the more startling is its similarity to the romantic wine-producing villages in the Ahr river valley, and when the heavy church bells begin to toll, the illusion is complete. So I say: "Look, Sheelagh, you were eager to see what I was describing. Welcome to Germany!"

Sheelagh and Anne also pick up on the marked differences between this little town and the rest of northern Spain. Several children are swimming in the little river and singing all the while, so Anne decides to get into her bathing suit and jump in too. Since my swim gear is way at the bottom of my messy backpack, I skip the swim out of sheer laziness. After Anne is refreshed, the two women are in the mood for a little sightseeing tour.

Since we are not, in fact, by the Ahr River in Germany, it's far too warm for me in this boiling hot valley, and I decide to go on alone, but I walk slowly so they'll have no trouble catching up with me. Our relationship is uncomplicated, and we play it by ear, so this segment is not a problem for us. No one goes off in a huff. Ponferrada, our destination for today, must be about two hours away—or three, tops. After a quick good-bye, I move ahead at a leisurely pace under the afternoon sun. The path to Ponferrada leads steadily downhill.

Having friends on the Camino de Santiago is invaluable.

As I walk along, I sing an old, wonderfully schmaltzy Donna Summer song to myself—about feeling the magic and letting go of fear—and my spirits soar.

After a few miles, the trail passes through a little place called Campo, and from there no longer goes through wildlife but cuts directly across a boring gray hamlet and a heavily traveled, monotonous main road. After a few hundred yards, there's a place to turn left onto a quiet dirt road that seems to curve in the direction of Ponferrada after a little while. There are no arrows or scallop signposts pointing to this path, which means that it is definitely not the official trail, but fishing my little map out of my backpack is too much trouble. Normally I don't veer away from the trail—at least not intentionally—but since I can't make out the two women behind me yet, I have time, and if I should discover that this path is totally off-base, I can always walk back. This is another thing I wouldn't have done of my own accord two weeks ago, but now I'm up for a bit of experimentation. The secluded nature trail is certainly more inviting than the uneven pavement alongside the noisy asphalt street. So I take this route and merrily head off somewhere—just not on the Camino. I don't know why—maybe the devil's gotten into me.

I drift along with Donna Summer still in my head. Once I round the second curve, after about half a mile, I realize that the path leads straight back to the mountains where I started. While I stare into the void, about to turn around, I can just make out a dented street sign at a fork in the road, with a whimpering little ball of red fur below it. Surely no one would have tied a dog to a stake and abandoned it in this godforsaken pampa! It's too late; I can't act as though I haven't seen him. A little dog is sitting there,

yelping for my help—he has noticed me, too. The chance of anyone else walking this way today is virtually nil. I step up my pace
toward him, and when I get to the rusted stop sign, I come upon
the desperate little red dog, a very sweet mutt, some kind of cross
between a Pomeranian and a dachshund. His neck is chafed where
he's been tied up with an old rope. Never in my life has anyone,
with the possible exception of my mother—when I was born—
been so glad to see me.

He hasn't seen a living soul for days. None of the pilgrims goes
off the trail, but I, idiot that I am, have nothing better to do than to
slouch along off the beaten track, only to find this squealing dog!
The rope is easy to untie, so all we need to do is get out of the sun
and back to the official trail. Great—now I really am doing the
pilgrimage with a dog! Anne will be delighted; I can just picture
the expression on her face. *Bet you won't take a dog with you!*

It had to work out this way! I sure did tempt fate. The little dog
is very sweet, and he fixes his eyes on me the whole way back to
town. The dog and I hit it off remarkably well, although I get the
feeling that he is nearly as nervous and impulsive as Anne. Since
his fur is the color of red peppercorns, and he's probably Spanish,
I name him Pepe. Uh-oh! The second you give animals a name,
you form a bond with them, and it's hard to leave them. . . . After
the first few times I call him by his new name, he even starts to
respond to it. The clever Pomeranian in him comes through. By
contrast, he doesn't react to Spanish commands such as "Sit!" or
"Down!" That's the dopey dachshund part.

When we get back to town, I start grilling any locals I run into:
"Have you ever seen this dog?" and "Do you have any idea who
the owner might be?" No one has any helpful leads, and no one
even knows Pepe, let alone lays any claim to him. An elderly gen-

tleman actually suggests that I simply bring the dog back to where I found him and tie him up there again. No one at the bakery, the hairdresser's, or the flower shop has ever seen the dog either, and no one appears interested in him. Pepe is just as much of a stranger here as I am. When I stand still, he does too, and even if I drop his rope, he shows no desire to run away. I take him to a bar to get him something to drink. He slurps up a great quantity of water. At a butcher's shop I buy three fat pork sausages, which he polishes off with great gusto and still seems famished.

At the edge of town I find a small pet shop, and I inquire whether Pepe could be cared for here. The answer is no. But now that I'm in the store, I buy a dog leash and a bright red collar to match his fur. That's how we do things in upscale Düsseldorf!

There is clearly no point in making any further inquiries in this hick town, and I'm certainly not going to find a home for the little guy, so the two of us hurry along to Ponferrada. This town is bigger, and the people here are sure to lend a hand. Anne and Sheelagh must have caught up to me by now, and they are presumably well ahead of us. The dog is evidently enjoying my brisk pace. He would handle the Camino better than I do, but we would be forced to sleep outdoors, because it is unlikely that any *albergue, refugio,* or hotel would accommodate animals.

We reach the main square in Ponferrada in the searingly hot late afternoon. This square is certainly charming, but that is of no consequence here. Luckily, the town hall is open, so we go in. A helpful woman in thigh-high leather boots who works for the municipality explains to me that it would be out of the question to leave the dog at the town hall, and just in case I'm toying with the idea of simply tying him up outside, I should be aware that he would most likely be taken away by the town dogcatchers and euthanized. His only option would be a private animal shelter, where he could stay until a new home could be found. Or I could just keep him myself. "He seems to be a good match for you," she remarks, "and obviously he's gotten perfectly used to you."

She cannot provide an address of an animal shelter, however; shelters aren't under municipal supervision.

I'll look for Sheelagh and Anne later; my immediate concern is to find us a roof for tonight.

We canvass one hotel after the other, starting with the most luxurious and working our way down, with nothing to show for our efforts. No one wants us. They might have been willing to take me, even in my stained denim shirt, but not the dog. On a side street, a shabby inn in a run-down modern building is offering questionable one-room apartments for next to nothing. Since this establishment is probably our best bet, I reluctantly tie Pepe to a streetlight just down the block. Despite his harrowing experience, he doesn't make much of a fuss. He sits with a worried look on his face, his head slightly bowed. I have no idea whether a dog can build up trust so quickly, but Pepe appears to have done so.

I am offered an apartment in an adjacent building with a separate entrance. This is evidently where gentlemen go when they do not wish to be seen. Naturally I take it on the spot, and pay cash in advance, as required.

This is evidently Pepe's first time in an elevator, and he's quite frightened. I worry that he'll bark up a storm, but he bravely keeps it down.

It is beautifully simple to smuggle the dog under this little roof. When we enter the room, I feel as though I can read his thoughts. Oh, God! He thinks this miserable little room is my home, and now his as well. He casts a critical eye on these mini-digs, and curls up on the clean white bed. There's a big question mark over his fiery red furry forehead, and he doesn't seem to like the room any better than I do.

Even so, he claims the white bedspread as his property and, to seal the deal, gets it nice and dirty with his muddy paws. The chambermaid will probably never figure out what kind of frenzied play occurred on these delicate linens.

Once I've set down my backpack and given Pepe another round of culinary delights, I smuggle him out of the building again. Anne and Sheelagh are probably worried about me by now, since I'm several hours behind schedule. I ask where I can find the local *refugio,* the most likely place for them to be spending the night, and after a good half hour of walking, my new friend and I get to the *albergue.* It's in a modern neighborhood with what seem to be prefabricated buildings, in the otherwise medieval Ponferrada.

I can't enter the awful 1970s *refugio* with the dog, so I ask a friendly, heavyset Spanish pilgrim passing by whether she would be willing to look for Sheelagh and Anne in this huge building, and, if she finds them, to ask them to come out to see me on the concrete plaza. Meanwhile an international group of pilgrims has gathered around Pepe, oohing and aahing. When Anne and Sheelagh come rushing out of the *refugio,* they can't even see the dog at first; all they see is my head above the group of people crowding around the dog.

Anne calls out to me, "Oh, God! Hans, where were you? What happened?" Sheelagh figures that with all the people gathered around my legs, I must be injured. When they discover my little Spanish friend, their faces fall.

Anne is stunned. "Oh no! Where did you get him from?"

I tell them the whole story about going off-trail and finding this little ray of sunshine. I don't really care whether they get it. I get it, and that's what matters. As might be expected, both of them declare that I'm totally crazy—although they also fall in love with little Pepe in an instant, and hover over him. Anne is the first to pick up on the dog's nervousness; she has a good eye for that sort of thing. Then she asks the all-important question: "You *aren't* going to keep him, right?" I explain to them that I will give up the dog only if I can be sure that he's in good hands.

Our next stop is the police station in Ponferrada. Luckily, Anne's Spanish is more than good; it's perfect. And her shrewd crisis management skills prove outstanding at the precinct. The two officers are quite cooperative and applaud my spontaneous efforts on behalf of the dog. I raise the possibility of adopting Pepe, but one of them tells me that there is an endless amount of paperwork involved, as well as a long waiting period for me and a tormentingly long quarantine for the poor dog. He urges me to place Pepe in the care of a private animal shelter with a good placement rate. Over and over again, I ask the officer to give me his word that the dog will not be euthanized. I've heard the most awful stories about the way animals are treated in Spain, and I'm not about to rescue a dog just to lead it straight to a certain death! The officer persuades me that I can rely on his word, and so, after a good hour of discussion, I let him place the phone call.

It doesn't take long for the Spanish Society for the Prevention of Cruelty to Animals pickup truck to arrive at the station. The volunteer from this organization is a very pleasant man from the country who knows how to relate to dogs. Pepe is partial to him from the moment he arrives and doesn't budge from his side. I make this man assure me several times that he will treat the dog with kid gloves, and I insist on getting his business card before handing over little Pepe to be put in the truck. Once the dog is sitting expectantly on the open loading area, Sheelagh and Anne take a deep breath, then break out into a smile. The dog makes no attempt to get back to me, so I can say good-bye to him calmly. The loading area is shut, and the truck speeds off to parts unknown. I stand there like a little boy and burst into tears of relief and exhaustion and sadness. I hate to lose Pepe after such a brief time, but I realize it's better this way.

My culturally minded companions later head off to the world-famous Templar Castle (Castillo de los Templarios), which dates back to the late Middle Ages, while I, thoroughly tired, admire the sights from a bench once again. With my swollen feet propped up, I await the return of my damsels of the castle, who graciously wave to me now and then from the battlements. The three of us spend the rest of the evening unwinding in splendid Ponferrada at an exquisite restaurant selected by Sheelagh.

Insight of the day: Do what life demands of you.

July 10, 2001
Villafranca del Bierzo

I can hardly find the time to write now, although there is more to record than ever before. Anne, Sheelagh, and I have become fast friends, and in this brief time have formed something resembling a family. Sheelagh is the mommy who watches over us, and Anne and I are her mischievous children. Sheelagh takes care of absolutely everything. She keeps her eyes peeled for restaurants, stores, sights, and places to spend the night as we make our way along the Camino. My travel guide sits in my backpack—it doesn't measure up to Sheelagh's sense of direction and good instincts. Not that the big-hearted New Zealander is washing and ironing our clothing, but if things continue this way, it's just a matter of hours before she starts doing that, too. She looks so neat that she's got to have an iron in her backpack.

Last night on the square we met a stout, bearded Belgian man in his midforties named Eric. He is making a pilgrimage from Ghent to Santiago, and has been walking for the past three months. A car with his supplies drives ahead of him, and a broadcast van from the Flemish radio carries daily live reports about the Camino and Eric's experiences. So there really are pilgrims who travel with a broadcast van! Eric's feet are deformed in a way that I cannot begin to describe; let's just say that they're better suited to a pink hippopotamus than to a man.

Since we got up much later than Sheelagh today—about four hours later—and then hung around another two hours in Ponferrada to drink five or six cappuccinos, we didn't get going before noon again. Sheelagh has long since arrived at her goal for the day. "Mommy" is our role model. She zips along while we lag behind like wayward teenagers.

Anne doesn't feel well today. Last night she had a bit too much wine during our enjoyable meal on the square. Sheelagh and Anne really appreciate good wine. I do too, but I'm stoically sticking with water until we arrive in Santiago. Anne had barely any water to drink during yesterday's hike, and as a consequence she simply collapsed at Sheelagh's feet last night at the *albergue*. Sheelagh has only this to say: "Anne, you will never learn!" But today she's feeling up to the task of tackling the Camino. Our destination for the day is Villafranca del Bierzo.

We've become accustomed to hiking in the glaring Spanish sun and know how to use our hats, sunblock, and mineral water. Every once in a while I simply dunk my hat and my shirt straight into a cattle trough and put the soaking wet clothes back on. This cools my body down for a good long time, and keeps my clothing reasonably clean as well.

Every so often, I urge Anne to drink some water, and she does so. She's starting to realize that she feels much better when she drinks. It's about time!

This long, varied, and sometimes shaded dirt road is one of the simplest legs we've faced. It offers many lovely stop-off points, and we take advantage of nearly all of them. For six and a half hours, we move along slowly and all alone through Palatine-like vineyards on our way to the fertile town of Bierzo.

As we are roaming through the romantic little town of Cacabelos in the early evening, we come upon Sheelagh, who has just emerged from a shower, her wet hair ashimmer in the sun. She has been sitting on the curb in impatient anticipation of our arrival. "God! Where have you been? I was starting to think you hadn't left the last place at all!"

She ran out of steam earlier today, so she's not pushing on to Bierzo as planned. Instead she's staying here, at a very fancy motel-like *refugio* with single rooms. Sheer luxury! Sheelagh gives each of us a relaxing and skillful foot reflexology massage on her bed. This woman is unbelievably talented! She tells us another round of ghost stories from the New Zealand highlands, and we hang on her every word. Even so, I have to give Anne a sharp poke in the ribs to keep her from falling asleep again. Each of us takes a half-hour nap on Sheelagh's bed. Unfortunately, we can't spend the night in this dream *albergue,* because the little place has no vacancies, and you can't make reservations. The standard rule applies here: First come, first slept! So we go on without Sheelagh to Villafranca, which is about one and a half hours away. We arrange a meeting point for tomorrow night.

Villafranca del Bierzo is a romantic little town that looks as though it has been lifted straight from the Moselle River and plunked down here. We are thoroughly exhausted as we enter the town through the Puerta del Perdón (Portal of Pardon). Frail or ailing pilgrims unable to tackle the final arduous climb to Santiago can receive the indulgence they would otherwise get in Santiago de Compostela here in the local St. James Church. So it is also known as Little Compostela. The two of us briefly entertain the idea of simply forgetting the rest of the trip, getting the golden document here, and spending the coming week drinking fifty cappuccinos a day, eating greasy cookies in a cozy bar, and writing silly things, but our mommy would surely disapprove and be terribly disappointed in us.

Tomorrow begins the hardest segment, the *camino duro*. Before you hit the home stretch, St. James evidently tries to make your life as difficult as possible. Many a pilgrim has dropped out of the race just before getting to the finish line on the route that now awaits us. The pilgrims' cemetery reminds us how many Christians from every part of Europe have lost their lives here over the centuries.

We spend the night in a clean, reasonably priced little inn in the center of town.

Insight of the day: I've focused my attention on myself long enough. Now the others get their turn!

July 11, 2001

Trabadelo and Vega de Valcarce

The continuation of the trail offers hikers two separate routes at the outset. The longer one is a mercilessly steep nature trail over the mountains. That is known as the hard way, the *camino duro*. The other route takes you along the N6, a freeway with a good bit of traffic, to Vega de Valcarce. According to the pilgrims' guide, both routes are relentless in their own ways.

Full of foreboding, Anne and I get up quite early, in contrast to our usual habit, drink just a single cup of coffee, and intuitively opt for the steep mountain pass just behind the church. The path seems to lead straight uphill. After just five minutes, my knee begins to throb, and soon my whole leg is in terrible pain. I have no choice but to halt on this strenuous route, because the equally steep descent would do me in and put an end to my pilgrimage. With my knees, I have to settle for the alternative route, but Anne, who is terribly afraid of all the traffic on the freeway, stays on the nature trail.

A little more than a mile before Vega, the two routes merge in Trabadelo, so we say good-bye for now and arrange to meet there for a latte—or should I say, five! Each of us is now facing four hours of involuntary solitary pilgrimage.

When I get to the N6, a narrow two-lane freeway that crosses the mountains, I'm flabbergasted to find that there is no sidewalk or separate footpath for pilgrims. Instead I have to walk along the shoulder, which is about five feet wide, with hundreds of cars and trucks zooming along at top speed and making a deafening racket as they pass the poor hikers. In my humble opinion, pedestrians ought not to be allowed here under any circumstances, but I guess the fleet-footed Spanish see the matter differently!

To my right is the lane of traffic—so close you can almost touch the cars—and to my left, just under the dented guardrail, is a deep gorge with a powerful rushing river at its base, fifty feet below. Crossing over to the other side of the freeway so I could walk along the limestone rock face, with the traffic coming from the rear, would be even more perilous.

At times the space between me and the many big trucks amounts to a scant eight inches, and I squeeze my thighs against the waist-high metal guardrail and stare petrified into the roaring water. Without showing the slightest consideration for my plight, the trucks seem to take special pleasure in hounding me.

The many curves are horrifically hazardous, and running along them is the only way to avoid a collision. I move as fast as I can with twenty-two pounds of luggage on my back and the 95-degree heat. This is not doing my knees any good. It's like being inside a washing machine during the spin cycle, and it is a tremendous strain on my body. My mental grip on the situation is somewhat better, at least at first, since I sometimes encounter this kind of stress on the job—though never this concretely.

Because the road is so narrow here, every one of the truck drivers has now started to drive along the narrow shoulder I'm walking on. To top it off, I have to cope with a constant stream of reckless passing maneuvers on both lanes. After a mile on this highway of horrors, I've had about as much as I can take of the noise, the exhaust fumes, and the danger, and I yell at every single driver, "I've had enough! *Basta!* Piss off!"

To wrestle more room from the lane, I face the lane of traffic and stretch out my arm to the side, holding out my four-foot-long walking stick In this way I gain an additional six feet of space for myself. My stick forces the drivers, who are going way too fast, to veer away from me in order to avoid a collision. This does nothing to calm them down, nor does it make me safer. When I was a little kid just starting school I was taught never to run around on a street like this. I have always obeyed that rule—and why not? Being a pilgrim doesn't mean I should abandon good sense. They may permit pilgrims to use this route, but there is no rhyme or reason to it. So I decide to use my pilgrims' walking stick to make a daring high-jump to the other side of the freeway, to try hitchhiking. A hopeless pursuit. The Spanish don't pick up pilgrims. They just don't! Even if someone wanted to take me, there aren't any rest stops where they could do so. And stopping on this street full of blind curves would be an extremely dangerous decision for any driver.

I shout into my cell phone, over the rushing water and the traffic, in an attempt to get connected to the taxi dispatch center in Villafranca—only to learn that it doesn't exist. I pant along for five more miles, furious and cursing, through this scorching pilgrims' hell.

And in the curves, which now come at me in rapid succession, I execute a succession of lifesaving 650-foot sprints with my outstretched walking stick. I'm the epitome of heroism! This could become a new Olympic sport! Every muscle is engaged, and spectators would find it quite entertaining! Shortly before I get to the meeting point Anne and I have arranged, Eric's Belgian broadcast van passes me. Damn! I bet they were the only ones who would have agreed to take me along!

Dog tired, livid with anger, and limping, I get to Trabadelo, the first stopover, with no prospect of an Olympic medal. What kind of place is this, anyway? This town consists of a gigantic gas station with way more than twenty pumps and a medium-sized wood-working business with at least five circular saws whirring at once.

Ducking behind the trucker fueling paradise, I head out on the tranquil nature trail that Anne must be taking down the mountain in my direction. So serene! No motors, no honking, and no rushing water! Poor Anne; she has yet to find out that we have to continue our hike on the main road, and there's no way around it. I will have to break the news to her gently. That's just the kind of guy I am.

I find a place to sit down in front of a little bodega in the thicket, directly at the sandy fork in the road. I am the only customer. The slightly muddled, gray-haired owner, wearing a thin sweater covered with bits of straw, asks me three times in succession for my order, and each time I give him the identical reply. The man seems determined to forget. He's made a cozy little place for himself, decorating his mouse-gray house to the hilt with dozens of plastic gnomes, fairy-tale characters, mythical beasts, and cheesy fake deer. Over the years the sun has taken its toll on these little treasures, turning his tasteless but funny sculptures lemon yellow or pastel orange; they are as faded as the barkeeper's memory. What an absurd, unreal place this is.

A mere five minutes later, I see Anne in the distance, striding toward me. The firmness of her step tells me that she's livid as well.

Am I starting to hallucinate?

She throws down her blue cotton backpack and releases her pent-up frustration with a liberating shout, then her anger explodes.

This was by far the "most fucking" part of the entire Camino, she growls. Without any warning, she stumbled into a construction zone where workers were blasting a mountain and was scared half to death. Then she walked by a startled herd of young bulls, one of whom went galumphing after her. She escaped by the skin of her teeth.

I can't suppress the urge to laugh, and even Anne is happy to indulge in a cathartic case of the giggles. "You look awful! How was your route?" she wants to know, and my description turns her as pale as the fairy-tale characters surrounding us. And, like me, she doesn't get her coffee just because she's ordered it for the second time.

While we drink our coffee (which we nearly leave without paying for), we calm each other down, then I gently break the news to her that there are still five spine-chilling miles ahead of us on the main road, and that we'd better get them behind us as quickly as we can.

Without further ado, we leave the enchanted forest and head out to the two-lane highway of horrors on our way to Vega.

The street has a fresh surprise in store for us. It gets even narrower, and the trucks are speeding. That's how it seems to us, anyway. As though on a hysterical suicide mission, I run ahead, shouting and waving my long hiking stick back and forth, to keep the stampede of trucks at bay, while Anne, behind me, starts to go ballistic. She's in a state of desperation, cursing and bursting into tears.

Suddenly, out of the corner of my eye, I see her run straight into a lane of traffic, tears pouring down her cheeks and shouting like Tarzan to stop a truck that is honking its horn and flashing its lights at her. This is getting extremely dangerous! Grabbing her firmly by the neck, I yank the little lady back to the shoulder and manage to stop her just short of the guardrail. I'm trying to calm her down any way I can, and am tempted to slap her; losing our self-control could cost us our lives. Instead, I let out a series of primal screams that I didn't know I had in me, which give her such a scare that she falls into line, sobbing. I walk well ahead of her in an attempt to establish when the next surge of cars will be coming—no easy matter, since the deafening noise of the river makes it nearly impossible to hear approaching traffic.

At my command ("now!"), we start sprinting like mad every quarter of a mile when we reach the hairpin turns in the road, and, in place of a horn, scream our guts out to alert the cars to our presence.

In spite of our efforts, a truck nearly crashes into us while it rounds a curve! It comes within an inch of me. The driver doesn't notice me at first, so he doesn't react until the very last second. I guess he wasn't an FC Barcelona fan like Anne! Sheesh! I'm well aware that some of them are not altogether sober by this point. I wonder how much they drink all day!

Finally a little signpost behind a rock face points left to a narrow path heading to Vega, and the horror ends. My God, all this running around on the street! It was quite a shock to our nerves. But we were absolutely in the moment, and the only thought in our heads was "now"!

We have decided to lodge an official complaint with the king of Spain regarding this disgraceful treatment of pilgrims. If we should ever walk this trail again, we will rent a car for this segment, though that would be risky in its own way.

We arrive at the *refugio* in Vega a short while later. Our nerves are shot and we've had it for the day. Luckily, there are only four other pilgrims here. Oddly, Vega is not a popular place to spend the night, even though the *refugio,* a two-family house, is in an idyllic spot on a little river, directly at the foot of the Galician Mountains. A woman has remodeled her private apartment by setting up twenty tentlike bunk beds in her ballroom-sized living room. The señora herself lives in the kitchen! Pilgrims thus have the option of crawling inside their bunks for privacy whenever the need arises, although this will not give them full protection from the twenty other people in the room. Tonight there are only six of us, however, and outside, right next to the terrace, you can hear the sound of the crystal-clear Valcarce River. Anne and I waste no time changing into our bathing suits. We splash around in the river, then nap in the nearby meadow.

Tomorrow we'll get to Galicia, the last set of provinces we have to cross. The *camino duro* is said to justify its name here, as it's especially tough, but it can't be any worse than it was today!

Insight of the day: Even highways of horror can be places of pilgrimage.

July 12, 2001
La Faba and O Cebreiro

Today we are out and about quite early, because every pilgrim has to leave the *refugio* by eight. The route is said to be grueling, so we want to get it over with as quickly as possible. Sheelagh would be proud of us!

She did not show up at the meeting point yesterday, and she doesn't have a telephone with her, so we have no way of staying in contact. But we'll find her!

We head up to O Cebreiro in Galicia, which is about four thousand feet above sea level. Because it is the steepest and longest ascent on the Camino, a full seven miles long, pilgrims are advised to have their backpacks sent by taxi service. We searched up and down yesterday but were not able to find one. Our landlady didn't know how to handle this, and today we raced back and forth through town, but were not able to find anyone to transport our forty-four pounds of dead weight. It soon became clear to us that we were going to do our seven miles straight uphill in brutal temperatures, carrying our backpacks! Anne and I are so confounded that we procrastinate, waiting until ten o'clock to have a big breakfast in front of a bar in town. A Spanish woman, tense and rail-thin, hobbles over with one cup of coffee after another and chats nervously with us. She tells us that she's waiting for her taxi to take her backpack to the peak. She wants to know whether she should rely on it, and whether we think the guy will come—after all, she's already paid! Anne and I are all ears.

She was supposed to have brought her backpack to the bar at 6 A.M., and she had paid for the whole thing in advance on the previous evening, but this morning she overslept. The driver is willing to make a special exception for her and drive up with just her backpack, even though a single trip is not really worth his while, but because she's already paid, he'll agree to do it. Since she is barely able to walk at this point, she'll ride in the taxi as well. "My knees, you know, on account of the descents!"

A couple of minutes later, the driver shows up with his Jeep, and it goes without saying that he is more than happy to drive our backpacks up to the peak as well for a couple of marks per person. I use the occasion to ask him what kind of housing is available up there.

"Oh, God, oh, God; you have to make reservations. Hundreds of pilgrims are heading up there today, and there are only two small hostels. Most of the pilgrims will be forced to keep on going for another nine miles, and Alto do Poio is even higher than O Cebreiro." So we ask him to make a quick call to reserve a double room that can accommodate a third bed in one of the small *albergues*. He calls up, and it turns out that the nicer of the two *albergues* has exactly one room left. We're in luck—and he's taking up our backpacks too!

With a spring in our step and a palpable sense of relief, we start up the path, which is furrowed by deep footprints. "Very, very strenuous" doesn't begin to describe the steepness of this ascent. The burning heat and the increasingly thin air make the enterprise even more fraught, and though you're glad to be free of your back-pack, you have to readjust to the feeling of hiking this way.

The heavy soil is loamy, so it's hard to get a good foothold. Never in my life would I have made it with my backpack, and even with my stick it's difficult to climb up here. The loam sticks to your shoes, and the weight of your shoes seems to double every fifteen minutes. At every fork in the road, we run into pilgrims who are so thoroughly worn out that they've simply stretched out on the damp earth under the bushes to recover. After three miles on the *camino duro,* two elderly Danish women are sitting in a rift, red as lobsters and crying their eyes out. The two of them have decided that it is all over. They are not even able to get back up on their feet—and have no desire to do so.

This uphill trail is like a battlefield.

Anne offers to carry the older woman's backpack. I stare at her, speechless. I wouldn't be able to summon up this altruism even if I wanted to. I couldn't walk three blocks with the Danish woman's bulging backpack.

Wiping the tears and sweat from her brow with her loamy hand, the proud woman from Aalborg turns down my friend's unfathomably generous offer; she wants to make it on her own or not at all.

At three thousand feet, which we climb with legs of quivering Jell-O, Anne and I take a break in La Faba, a tiny hamlet, just before the *camino duro* becomes markedly more challenging. In the sole bodega, we grab nearly all the sugary soft drinks in the cooler and pour them down our throats.

A group of eight young Tyroleans, also on the verge of faint-ing, soon joins us and lunges at whatever beverages remain. While they are drinking, one of the Tyroleans recognizes me and sounds the alarm to his group. In the blink of an eye, the sweating Tyroleans are sitting at my table and giving me big bear hugs. What an absurd moment to be recognized. Even I wouldn't have recognized myself in my current state!

Once on a night flight, I was sitting diagonally behind the TV host Frank Elstner, whom I know very well. I didn't recognize him, though, until he spoke to me, which was very embarrassing, because Frank Elstner is one of those people who look the same in real life as they do on TV. I just wasn't expecting to see him there, so I didn't notice him. To get back to the subject at hand: Elstner is originally from Austria like these Tyroleans.

These people from Innsbruck are quite nice, uncomplicated, interesting, and on the ball. We take pictures of one another, and I sign their backpacks. I'll have to drop my act with Anne from here on in; she asks the Tyroleans to tell her exactly what it is that I do, and they are happy to provide full details in perfect English. Anne looks at me the whole time with a big grin on her face.

When we set off again, up the steepening trail, she runs ahead of me and maintains an almost reproachful silence. I assume she is also trying to save her breath. I don't feel I've done anything wrong. I never lied to her, just withheld some (admittedly crucial) information. She eventually comes to an abrupt halt, turns to face me with her hands on her hips, and scrunches up her face as hard as she can. "Hans! How famous are you in Germany?"

Since I can barely catch my breath and don't really feel like answering, I just stammer: "Oh, Anne! Come on! I don't know!"

"They treat you as if you were as famous as Lothar Matthäus, the soccer star. Are you as famous as Matthäus?" I feel as though my command of English has sunk right down to the level of Lothar's—and everyone makes fun of *his* English. I don't know whether I ought to say anything at all; I'm boiling hot, and this kind of talk seems ill suited to the Galician forest, so I say nothing and just scrunch up my face the way Anne always does. But she's a research scientist, and has no intention of letting up.

"Another question. Do you know Matthäus?"

My honest answer is, "Yes! Not too well, but . . . I do! Let's leave it at that for today!"

Anne shoots me a quick glance and gloats. "Then you must be very famous!"

She turns on her heel and hikes on without another word, as though nothing had happened. My trust in her grows with each passing step we take together. She does not wait for any reaction on my part. Brilliant scientist that she is, she is filling in the blanks on her own.

The route to O Cebreiro briefly opens out onto a magical view of the Galician Mountains, and I have the feeling of having hiked not seven miles but thousands. That's how much my feet hurt and how drastically the landscape has changed.

Magnificent northern European green stretches out as far as the eye can see, and the climate is becoming distinctly Atlantic. Galicia is quite different from Castile, and the cooler temperature makes the *camino duro* much more bearable.

O Cebreiro is glorious. It reminds me of the village the comic strip characters Asterix and Obelix come from, although everything here is originally Celtic, of course. And the unending panorama of green is staggeringly beautiful.

Our little room in one of the oval-shaped thatched houses, called *pallozas,* is absolutely adorable. Anne and I are sorry that we're not here to celebrate a honeymoon.

When we take a little stroll to look for Troubadix, the village bard in the Asterix comic books, we come across Sheelagh, who is once again on a desperate and futile search for a room. She didn't get very far yesterday and didn't make it to the meeting point we'd arranged. Today she managed to cover a superhuman amount of ground to catch up with us. In contrast to my disgruntled British companion and my whiny self, she got the N6 freeway and the mountains out of the way in one go, with her pack plastered to her back. Of course, this was a strain on her nerves, and she is totally drained. So we refrain from asking her, "How's the baby?" and steer her into our honeymoon suite à trois. Sheelagh almost cries with relief. For now she is out of action, pure and simple.

Low-slung oval stone houses in the ancient town of O Cebreiro, where you might sooner expect Asterix and Obelix than throngs of pilgrims

Anne and Sheelagh claim that Galicia resembles Wales. I think it's more like Ireland. Not that I've ever been there, but this is how it looks in my imagination. In that sense I'm just like Beaky. People here speak the earthy Galician language known locally as *galego*. This language sounds a bit like Portuguese, and in some aspects it seems quite familiar, like Italian. You don't get very far with Spanish when speaking to older locals who have been here for generations.

The town's pre-Romanesque church houses the Galician national treasure, the Holy Grail of O Cebreiro. According to legend, the following occurred here in the fourteenth century.

The priest was preparing Christmas mass one snowy winter's night. Mass was soon to begin, but not a single resident of the area had braved the storm, so the priest decided to close up the church. Just then, a peasant from the valley appeared at the door. He had struggled up the *camino duro* all alone on this icy night to receive Holy Communion. The priest was reluctant to hold mass for one dumb peasant and tried to get rid of him, but the peasant insisted on his rights and took a seat in one of the pews. The priest had no choice but to conduct mass, and offered the host to the peasant, whereupon the wine turned into blood and the host into flesh. The chalice (Grail) and the paten (host plate) are still on display in the church.

It goes without saying that Anne and I cast an extremely critical eye on the two venerable objects, and Anne, ever the skeptical researcher, peers through the bulletproof glass and hunts in vain for particles of the remaining blood in the chalice. But the church itself is a jewel; once you're inside it, you don't want to leave.

Anne walks through the nave and stops short in front of a

beautiful wooden statue of Mary and the infant Jesus. Suddenly she starts screaming hysterically: "Hans, come quickly!"

I race through the pews to get to her, fearing that she is about to collapse, but she grins at me and points to the infant Jesus, who is bestowing blessings with his hand: "You see? Baby Jesus is waving at me!"

The international pilgrims' mass that follows is wonderfully un-Catholic and freewheeling; it's geared toward skeptical pilgrims like Anne. The young priest from Lugo wants to establish contact with the people, so he finds out where all of us are from, then suggests that we might like to recite a short prayer in our native languages. No one feels like going first, and most stare down at their loamy hiking shoes. Anne, who is thoroughly exhausted, is nodding off again when the priest points to her and asks whether she wishes to say a prayer. I poke her, and she shoots up like a rocket, declaring in Spanish: *"Qué? Soy inglesa."*—I'm English!

The priest is delighted at his apparent success at having found a volunteer to lead them in prayer and asks Anne to say the intercessions in English. She scrunches her face into a pillow again, and turns beet red. Stammering something incomprehensible, she sits down again, having failed to grasp what is going on. So she nudges me in confusion, asking me to fill her in on what she's missed, but I'm unable to oblige, since I'm laughing so hard I can barely stay seated on the hard wooden bench. I always seem to be laughing in churches here. Good thing this institution has not figured out a way of driving me away altogether.

Toward the end of mass, I see the two Danish women with the bulging backpacks standing at the church door, covered in mud. So they made it too.

At dinner Sheelagh asks me again about my job, and I fill her in on whatever details she wants to know. We have a nice long night again. And Anne keeps her wine consumption at a level she can handle.

Insight of the day: It is good to know who you are!

July 13, 2001

Triacastela

One thing I know: Had I not met my two red-haired good fairies back in León, I might well have turned around and gone home. I was feeling quite wretched in León. I was sick and tired of not talking to anyone, and now Anne and I are acting like an old married couple. "Did you remember to put the room keys in your pocket?" "Your socks are still hanging in the bathtub; don't forget them again!" "Did you take your vitamins?"

But there's no stress, because neither of us bosses or pesters the other. We don't sacrifice our individuality. And if one of us feels like walking alone, the other doesn't dissolve in a fit of jealousy. We'll be back together in the evening, by dinnertime at the latest. Today the weather is Galician, that is, rainy, cold, and foggy. Finally! I couldn't bear the heat anymore. Sheelagh took off at the crack of dawn again so she could snag a three-bed room at the end of our next segment.

We have a thirteen-mile mountain hike before we reach Triacastela. Anne is not in great shape today, for reasons that shall remain hers alone. She has little interest in talking, but I don't get the feeling that she's enjoying her grumpy, silent hike, so I bombard her with questions. She did, after all, spend eight months in a Buddhist monastery, and there is surely a great deal more to tell.

I keep at her until she relents and volunteers information. She then gives me five enthusiastic hours of instruction in Buddhism—which is great! We launch into a lively discussion, and she soon stops being annoyed by my stupid questions. I have read a good deal about Buddhism, but debating these issues with Anne, who was taught by a Rinpoche, gives me a different perspective. It's wonderful that these teachings always encourage you to express criticism and doubts about specifics, which are then subjected to careful analysis.

But Buddhism doesn't seem to have an answer to my all-important question. Why does everything happen? For the sake of simplicity, Buddhists don't ask this question. Perhaps it is typically German to want to get to the bottom of everything, and not simply to accept things as they are.

There is surely an answer! But by and large, Tibetan Buddhism harmonizes with my way of thinking, and it provides a straightforward explanation for things I have discovered to be true.

The theory of reincarnation also has to be given serious consideration. It is certainly conceivable that each of us has lived a thousand times, even though we have no memory of having done so. I don't have the slightest recollection of what I was doing during Christmas in 1978, or on my thirteenth birthday, not to mention at the moment of my birth. Maybe in each of our lives, we are someone altogether different, while retaining an immanent essence.

When I was a schoolboy, I was always the same person, yet I was different in each class. In English, where I was the top student, I was self-confident and cheerful, because it all came to me so easily. In math, I was the "logarithm dummy," the dope who didn't understand a single word and resorted to scribbling his friends' telephone numbers on the board when called up to solve problems. To my math teacher's horror, I was suddenly very different in geometry class, which I found easy as pie. In gym, I played the comedian for thirteen years straight. I was thoroughly intimidated in biology class, where the teacher put me and my friends Britta and Trixi through the mill for two long years. In religion and psychology, I was the talkative, eloquent one. If we can be so different within one and the same life, why shouldn't that continue over several lives?

Maybe life is like a steeplechase. The jockey is the soul, the horse is the body, and the course is life. Every one of us has to jump over ten hurdles, but we get to determine the sequence and the time frame. In this analogy, we would always have freedom of choice, but the hurdles themselves are governed by fate.

Our ability to surmount the ten hurdles is then judged by a celestial jury. Anything we do before and after the crucial hurdles is not factored in, and constitutes a kind of time off from the central purpose in life.

Nearly every life can ultimately be reduced to a dozen key hurdles; otherwise, obituaries would run to millions of pages. Few things in life are truly significant, and if you take a good hard look at yourself, you realize that the number of strong desires in your life is really quite small.

We walk up a path to the top of the San Roque pass, where there is a ten-foot-high bronze statue of a pilgrim battling storms and rain. Anne and I take pictures of it. In good weather, the monument would look a bit silly, but today the wind and rain are lashing against the poor guy from just the right direction.

A little later, in a shelter, we meet up with Anne's "tea and coffee" French friends René and Jacques. She is, of course, "delighted" to see them. They jealously give me the once-over but run their hands over her short hair again anyway, which I quickly put a stop to by pushing René's hand away. Poor Anne freezes up when someone treats her like that. When the two Frenchmen ask me if we are a couple, I say yes, and nonchalantly add that we got engaged in O Cebreiro. They seem offended that the woman of their pilgrim dreams would choose an uncouth German over two Frenchmen well versed in the art of love, and they soon slink away. So much for them!

The stream of pilgrims has picked up considerably. Just before the Galician border, you saw about eight pilgrims a day, or in some instances as many as ten; now they are coming by the hundreds. And any space to sleep is hotly contested.

Disaster awaits us upon our rainy arrival in Triacastela. In front of the gray school's run-down gymnasium is an endless line of wet pilgrims hoping to be admitted. Through the fogged-up glass façade we are able to make out hundreds of people inside— where it seems to be ice cold—setting up places to sleep on a floor, caked with mud from everyone's shoes. There is not an inch of space left for those still in line. Anne and I feel like Albanian refugees searching for a humble little spot to spend the night, and we decide to keep on going.

It occurs to me that Triacastela is the only place on the trail with a pilgrims' prison. So either some people go ballistic here because they can't find a place to stay, or they run riot because they have the hardest part of the Camino behind them. Who knows? In the small center of Triacastela, which is just as gray as the rest, Shee-lagh is sitting in the only café—garish and cheerless, of course—drinking tea and looking around for us. She catches sight of us instantly and dashes happily out into the street.

She actually managed to get a three-bed room in a lovely inn at the edge of town, while hundreds of others had to hike on in frustration. Sheelagh, our night-shift pilgrim, is a godsend; without her, Anne and I, inveterate slowpokes that we are, wouldn't get even a spot in the old gym. We just don't have the grim determination the other pilgrims share.

Insight of the day: The fundamental hurdles in the steeplechase of life make all the difference.

July 14, 2001

Triacastela

The three of us have been damned lucky so far. We've been able to find a three-bed room every time, since very few people look for one. I can't imagine bedtime without Sheelagh's unbeatable ghost stories. Our Kiwi mama is the greatest! She has a velvety voice, perfect for storytelling, and my German ear has no trouble following her New Zealand accent. When she is telling her tales, I rarely interrupt her to ask the meaning of a word. Whatever she says sounds soft and rich and very, very meaningful.

Sheelagh has told us that she aspires to a high place in New Zealand politics. She already belongs to a national movement that in the Oceanic political spectrum is roughly equivalent to the Green Party in Germany. I'm certain that New Zealand will be glued to her every word!

We are a funny trio. Short, high-spirited, down-to-earth Dr. Anne with an impish sense of humor and a red bristle hairdo, and Sheelagh, ethereal and intelligent with flowing red hair—and then there's chubby me, towering over the two of them by a good foot.

Today, bright and early, a grumpy Anne and an exhausted Sheelagh braved the English-style rain and dense fog to head off to the Samos Monastery. Samos, which was founded in the fifth century and is thus one of the oldest monasteries in the Western world, is said to be a must for pilgrims, although it does not lie along the official path. This monastery can be reached only by way of a complicated detour, and I decide to forgo the hassle. Instead I sit out this round and devote myself to washing clothes, sleeping, reading, and relaxing. Sheelagh left me one of her books, an exciting history of the colonization of New Zealand. In return, I sent her off with my new ersatz pilgrims' rain jacket.

I don't know how we'll be able to say good-bye to one another at the end. The three of us have become so attached, and we can rely on one another implicitly.

Tomorrow I have to walk thirteen miles, and in the evening I'll meet the two of them in Rente, a small town past the county seat of Sarria.

Insight of the day: You don't have to take every detour.

July 15, 2001
Sarria and Rente

The Camino from Triacastela to Rente is very romantic. For the most part it is a country road with very little traffic that winds through hilly forests of oak. Bagpipe music would suit this landscape, and sure enough, Galicia's national instrument is a kind of sheep's-udder shawm that produces squawking sounds!

A cloying smell of cow dung pervades this place and occasionally overpowers me, making me gag. I'm lucky not to throw up, as the sun, which has unexpectedly returned today, heightens the aroma of the greenish brown manure. To make matters worse, I start daydreaming, get lost again, and have to take a much longer route. At least this way I get to see the jewel of Samos that is off the pilgrims' route. Nice! Nice and strenuous, that is! All this hiking on asphalt is grueling even when the weather is ideal. And even after all these days on my feet, I still don't enjoy the act of walking per se. Each and every day, I have to force myself all over again, and once I start walking, it takes me about an hour to find my rhythm.

When I hit my rhythm and stop thinking about the process of walking, I still don't like it, but it's not as taxing. Any break that allows me to take off my backpack is still a real blessing. Starting near Sarria, you have to hike the Camino all the way to Santiago without interruption if you want to be accepted as a true pilgrim. Luckily, it doesn't matter how long it takes you to cover this segment, but of course you ought to get through at least a couple of miles a day. I merrily accept this final challenge and spend the whole time wondering what's making me so happy.

Nothingness is making me happy! Because I'm thinking about nothing, nothing is weighing on my mind, and nothing is really pushing me along.

When I reach the foul-smelling town of Rente in the afternoon, I find Anne and Sheelagh seated and dangling their feet from a rough stone wall in front of a lovingly renovated farm. They have already reserved a pretty room with three beds.

While we enjoy the tasty dinner that the hale and hearty farmer serves us (and her old German shepherd) in her rustic kitchen, we decide that starting tomorrow we'll speak an hour of German a day. Both women know a little bit of my language already, and this way I'll be able to tutor them.

Insight of the day: Nothingness is the key to absolute happiness.

July 16, 2001

Portomarín

We have our first German lesson over breakfast in the farmhouse kitchen. Even the farmer picks up key words like *Ei* (egg), *Brot* (bread), *Milch* (milk), and *Schinken* (ham) pretty quickly. But the old German shepherd evidently can't stand this language. When, at the urging of the farmer, I try to teach him some commands from his ancestral homeland, he barks loudly and refuses to obey. Anne thinks that when I use my mother tongue, I seem very stern, and she—like the dog—is not at all sure whether she likes that.

Here's what I thought of the first lesson: the students, right down to the German shepherd, are highly gifted, but, apart from the farmer, they need to put in a little more effort.

After the class, Sheelagh takes to the road at once, informing us in broken German that she's off to reserve a clean three-person room with shower in Portomarín. All the more reason for Anne and me—now that we're unchaperoned again—to get a nice relaxed start to the day with one latte after another. The farmer, who is clattering up a storm while she washes the dishes, makes it abundantly clear that she has no intention of cooking us a hot lunch.

When we finally get going—in some miraculous way—Anne is exceedingly chipper and up for a good long walk. Her injured ankle has stopped bothering her, and I can barely keep pace. Although the path is flat, it is very uneven, and I'm afraid of twisting my ankle again, so after a couple of miles I tell my supersonic rocket of a hiking partner to go ahead without me, that I'll catch up later. Toward the end of each leg, Anne is generally slower than I am, so I'll be able to make up for lost time automatically. She needs to walk at her own sprightly pace or else she won't have the strength to get through today's hike. I'm more inclined to a leisurely stroll, so each of us stays true to form.

Anne sprints ahead and even steps up her pace, which she had kept down for my sake, and I trudge along behind her in waltz time, whistling a tune.

The trail goes through wonderfully flat fields redolent of liquid manure, past meadows and oak groves. And since Anne and I started out so late in the day, I'm alone on the Camino. At least I think I am. As I step gingerly through a virtually impassable, mud-filled riverbed, I hear a woman's voice behind me, and she eventually catches up to me.

This attractive dark-haired pilgrim with a batik scarf and capri-length lederhosen just started her trek yesterday, so she's still quite eager to find new acquaintances. I am relieved to discover that she is not Brazilian. Rita is from Holland, and when I reveal that I'm a long-term pilgrim, she wants to know everything about my experiences on the Camino. She slows down her pace considerably so that she can walk with me for a few miles, and I am happy to give this woman, who seems quite reasonable, all the information she likes. I'm even thinking of introducing her to my best pilgrim friends this evening.

Suddenly Rita stands stock-still and the color drains from her face. "Do you hear that?" she asks, with a look of terror.

I prick up my ears but don't hear anything other than the twittering of birds—and I smell the liquid manure, which is so strong that it ought to count as noise pollution.

"What should I be hearing?" I ask Rita, somewhat baffled. She is still all ears and wide-eyed. Then she throws me for a loop. "The spirits! Don't you hear them?"

Why do I keep running into the loony ones? Why are they drawn to me and why do they stick to me like flies? I decide to be as cold and aloof as possible.

Here I am, right smack in the middle of a Karl May novel, pondering how to get rid of this poor madwoman from Utrecht. I probably never will—she's so happy to keep company with me. I'm almost tempted to tell her, "Yes, I hear the spirits, and they're telling you to disappear this instant!"

But Rita doesn't let me get a word in edgewise and happily offers me a full account of what the utterly dreadful spirits are supposedly telling her. By comparison, Sheelagh's ghost stories ought to be rated PG. Rita has wild fantasies of restless spirits and haunted souls out to prey on poor pilgrims. Someone like me, she warns, so close to my destination and to achieving purity, should be particularly careful. I'm just what these dastardly demons are waiting to pounce on!

Don't make me laugh. Dumb! I'm flat-out dumb. Where were my instincts? Now that she's spewing all this garbage, she clearly looks crazy. But how was I supposed to know? When she was still behind me on the trail, she said some friendly things that sounded reasonable enough.

When I was eight years old, my grandma said to me, "Anyone

who speaks to you from behind or is otherwise hidden from view is up to no good!" So true!

To top it all off, Rita makes the ridiculous claim that my dead grandmother sends her best regards and urgently needs to tell me that she is incredibly proud of me! If my dead grandma wanted to communicate with me, she would hardly do it through Rita. First of all, she'd know it would scare me to death, and second, she never took to people like this crackpot from Utrecht.

Rita doesn't make me angry—she's too weird for that—but she does start to get on my nerves, so I say in Dutch, "Listen, you can unload that garbage on someone else, but not on me! Adieu!"

Evidently she had not counted on such a gruff reaction from me. In a huff, and without saying a word—exactly like my Brazilian ex-fiancée Claudia, come to think of it—she dashes off.

I hope I catch up to Anne soon. The other pilgrims are turning out to be real kooks again today. Next up is a wizened lady from Madrid with a screechy voice who also tries to strike up a conversation with me. But my thirst for communication with complete strangers has been quenched for now, and so, for no reason at all, I give her the cold shoulder to guard against any further contact.

One hour later, something strange happens. Right in the middle of a thick forest of ugly, stunted pine trees, I run into Sheelagh! I can't believe it! Single-minded Sheelagh, who always starts out so early in the morning, is standing at a fork in the road, totally baffled.

"Oh, Hans, I am lost!" she calls over to me helplessly, with arms upstretched. She is hopelessly adrift, and on the hunt for trail markers. You really have to focus on the pale yellow arrows to find your way through this labyrinthine forest of stunted trees, but I still don't see how she could have gotten so utterly off course.

Sheelagh is very happy to see me and throws her arms around me. She has been quite distraught and close to tears. She cannot figure out how she lost her sense of direction. This dark bit of woods is downright eerie. When I ask her whether she's seen Anne she says no. Sheelagh's need to hike alone is taken care of for today, so she links arms with me and we continue on together.

I'll wait for dinner tonight to tell Sheelagh about my encounter with the strange Dutch woman; this *Hansel and Gretel* backdrop is not the place. My friend is gradually getting back to her old self and is no longer clutching my arm. She's now a few steps ahead of me, in fact, walking alone. She loves independence. While we walk, I hear the sound of a siren somewhere in the forest, and I say to Sheelagh, "Listen! It's an ambulance."

Sheelagh stands still and listens but doesn't hear anything. Now I'm sounding like that nutty Rita. But I'm certain that I heard a siren. We continue on in silence and pass through an even more desolate area. Even the clear sky suddenly clouds over. Once again we wade through a stony damp riverbed.

What happens next goes so swiftly that I don't really see it. Sheelagh tumbles to the muddy ground with a thud. Oh, God—I hope she hasn't broken anything! She hits her head against a big boulder, and now she's lying with her face in the mud, covered in sludge from head to toe. I freeze up for a moment, then bend over her carefully. "Sheelagh, what's wrong? Are you hurt?" She is in a state of shock, and after a few excruciating seconds she cautiously shakes her head. How could this happen to Sheelagh, of all people, who always takes such good care of others and herself? She tries to stand up even though she lacks the strength to do so, and refuses my support with helpless gestures. Handicapped by her heavy backpack, she can't get back onto her feet, so I pull her up to a vertical position.

Now I can see the extent of her injuries. Her forehead is cut open under her hairline, as is the bridge of her nose. Her cuts are bleeding. Her knees and forearms are also in bad shape and are bleeding heavily from various scrapes, which could use a good cleaning. Suddenly Sheelagh turns white as a sheet and seems about to topple over again. I gently lower her down onto a big rock in the road and put my arm around her.

Next thing we know, a Jeep appears out of nowhere, stops right in front of us, and honks as hard as if we were on the N6 heading to Vega de Valcarce. The man behind the wheel cannot drive around us and grows impatient, keeping his hand on the horn and insisting that Sheelagh get up so that he can drive off through the mud in the opposite direction.

I ask him what he could possibly be thinking—doesn't he see that this woman took a bad spill? He doesn't care. In the heat of the moment, I don't even think of asking him for help, especially since he is so impatient to be off. He's guilty of failure to render assistance! He doesn't reply to anything I say; he just keeps honking his horn. Eventually I lift Sheelagh up to allow this jerk to drive by. He steps on the gas, and the spinning wheels of his Jeep cover us with a good deal more sludge. We sit down in the bushes under a tree, where I tend to her wounds the best I can by cleaning them gently with disinfectant spray and sterile wipes. Her knees are seriously injured, and cleaning these wounds, which I do quite vigorously, at Sheelagh's request, must be excruciating. Sheelagh is too proud to cry out in pain; instead she digs her fingers into my forearm.

I try to stanch the bleeding with bandages from my little first aid kit. After all this patching up, Sheelagh stands up bravely on her own and hobbles along, holding on to me for support. Suddenly she bursts out laughing and tells me again and again what a jinxed day this has been and that she doesn't understand how any of this could have happened.

After several miles, which seem never-ending to Sheelagh, we get to a little bar in a clearing at the edge of the forest. In front of the crooked little house, on the terrace, a little witch doll is fluttering in the wind, clad in black and sitting astride a broomstick. In the sunroom adjoining the dining area, I lift Sheelagh onto a chair and ask the young waitress to bring us two lattes, a hot meal, and a double brandy for Sheelagh.

The waitress, who is terribly upset, runs into the kitchen, and reemerges with the manager, an elderly woman from Argentina. Holding her hands over her head, she runs up to Sheelagh, and shouts: "Oh, God, has something happened again? What is it now?"

I explain, "My friend took a spill, but it's not so bad. She's already feeling better."

The manager breathlessly fills us in on the situation: "People keep falling down. You know, the valley you've just come from is jinxed. Things of that sort are constantly happening here. People fall, get panic attacks, or spend hours wandering around through the forest."

Sheelagh is almost back to her old self, and sips her brandy with a little smile on her face.

Several miles before we get to Portomarín, we meet up with Anne again, who's dozing under a tree. When Anne sees that Sheelagh has been hurt, she turns pale and exclaims, "Oh, no, Sheelagh! Who beat you up?" Sheelagh really does look as though she got mixed up in a barroom brawl. Her big sunglasses can't conceal her bruises.

During a brief break we all take under the oak tree, we tell

Anne about the bewitched valley, and after a moment of hesitation she confesses that she also was terribly nervous and on edge the whole time she was in that ugly little forest, and very glad to be out of it.

Toward evening we reach the fabulous town of Portomarín, which is situated at the edge of a reservoir. Nearly fifty years ago, the town, including its late Romanesque cathedral, was relocated from its original home in the valley to this mountain and lovingly reconstructed in the aftermath of a flood.

The windy little village, which looks like a street festival, is overrun with pilgrims, and it takes us two solid hours to find a clean three-person room with a shower. Our room even has a balcony overlooking the lake. Since this is a four-star hotel, it goes over the financial limit we'd set, but we pool our resources and enjoy this special treat today.

In the evening we economize on dinner by opting for a low-priced pilgrims' meal with French fries and dessert included, and we talk over the events of the day. I don't bother telling my Dutch ghost story, but at some point, nutty Rita appears before us in the flesh on this little square.

"So, how are the spirits doing?" I inquire, and she has nothing better to do than to recount each and every detail of her day to Anne and Sheelagh. Anne again scrunches up her face until it resembles a brocade pillow, while Sheelagh stares openmouthed at the Dutch woman's ugly batik scarf.

Once our wacky Rita has gotten these stories off her chest, she sets off again without saying a word about Sheelagh's injuries. Anne declares that I simply can't be left on my own without dragging in the most peculiar people.

A nice Irish fellow named Dave joins us and cozies up to our injured Sheelagh. Anne and I decide to make a graceful retreat, since Sheelagh seems receptive to his advances. Dave, who can put away quite a bit of liquor, probably considers Sheelagh a good sport who might enjoy a nice free-for-all.

When Sheelagh comes back to our hotel a little while later, and we ask her to tell us an exciting bedtime ghost story again, she bursts into tears, and can't stop weeping. The evening with the Irish guy was quite nice, she tells us, but she has not gotten over the fall earlier in the day. She is feeling so humiliated, and the Camino has become so daunting. Does all of this make any sense? Our conversation becomes quite tough and emotional, and we bare our souls. We talk well into the morning hours, first from our beds and then out on the balcony. Eventually sheer exhaustion takes over, and we doze off. It is somewhat scary to see Sheelagh so helpless. Up to now she was our mainstay, and now it's time for Anne and me to take over.

Insight of the day: One for all, and all for one!

July 17, 2001
Palas de Rei

We have four days of hiking left before we reach Santiago de Compostela. We have decided to walk together for these final days to keep an eye on each other and to enter the sanctuary together. We are getting cheerier and sillier by the minute. There are now throngs of pilgrims on the Camino, and hundreds are on their way to Santiago.

When people talk to us, we pose as Albanian refugees who happened onto the pilgrims' route by accident. With Sheelagh's face looking so beaten up, it sounds plausible. I speak to total strangers in the guise of a kooky interviewer from Polish TV. The three of us are flat-out crazy and having a great time. You can hear us laughing from far away in the eucalyptus forests. Other pilgrims turn around in aggravation, and when we get closer, they find us so annoying that they can't wait to get away.

Finding a free bed is a matter of pure luck. Even the night-shift pilgrims are not faring well by this point. At one point, we stride through a forest with six-foot-tall ferns. Sheelagh is elated, and declares: "Look Hans! Here we are in New Zealand!" She says that New Zealand looks just like this.

Of course, Sheelagh and Anne are also diligently learning German, though they still find that my speaking German to them takes some getting used to. Even so, we learn the German times of day and the compass points quite nicely. We chatter away the whole day, keenly aware that we have to enjoy to the full our few remaining days together, since we may never again have the chance to share such an intense experience and to feel so carefree.

Although today's hike was certainly strenuous, it went by almost too quickly. In the evening we reach Palas de Rei, where we have no problem finding a room and a massage therapist, who kneads us into shape again for our final days.

My feet are still blisterless!

Insight of the day: Lots of talking can also be golden.

July 18, 2001

Castañeda

Our boisterous mood continues, and we devote another hike to enjoying one another's company to the fullest. The route to Santiago is not as difficult now, and the busy stream of pilgrims gives us the opportunity to move away from our self-imposed solitude and dip into real life again. We're now going through lots of little villages, all smelling horribly of liquid manure and cow pies. At times I hold my sopping wet bandanna in front of my mouth so I won't succumb to my constant queasiness. Our German lesson focuses on the vocabulary of liquid manure, cow pies, and organic farming.

To distract us from the stench, Sheelagh, who is now quite cheerful, tells us about her long-standing platonic love for a coworker. She gets along with him beautifully but he's never made a single romantic overture toward her. She spends all her spare time with him anyway. She wants our advice. Since Anne just reacts by scrunching up her face, I take the initiative and break the news to Sheelagh that judging by her description, I'd say this friend is gay. I ask her whether she's ever broached that subject with him. Sheelagh looks confused, and asks: "Do you really think so?" Anne steps in to confirm my impression, and advises Sheelagh to be frank with him. "It seems quite clear to me that he's gay, and just wants to toy with your affections," I add.

Suddenly Anne gets the urge to buy a house! (I did mention that we are now nuts, didn't I?) As we hike through a farming community that bears a striking resemblance to England, we pass by a small dilapidated farmhouse up for sale and priced at the equivalent of twenty thousand marks. Anne is madly in love with the ramshackle cottage and is absolutely determined to buy it. So we comb through every corner of the little town to track down the owner. Anne is serious about her odd plan and cannot be talked out of it. She wants to drop out of the rat race, move here, open an *albergue,* and stay here. Forever!

"Anne, you don't want to buy a house. You just don't want to get to Santiago! You're afraid!" I tell her bluntly. Anne's silence speaks volumes, and Sheelagh squeals, "Me too!"

All three of us are dreading our arrival. We are now pilgrims through and through, and we could go on indefinitely. When we reach our destination, it's all over; the essence of a pilgrimage is of course the journey itself.

Anne just as abruptly loses all interest in buying the house. "Let's get to Santiago!" she urges us. None of us dares to admit openly how tight our bonds have become, and that it will be quite painful to tear them apart. The three of us feel as though we are facing our deaths in Santiago, and the manure heap surrounded by thousands of flies lends the place the sweet stink of decay.

We don't start looking for a room until just before sundown. It's a romantic area, and rooms are hard to come by. Every place is full. We go to a telephone booth in the little town of Castañeda and frantically leaf through the telephone book in search of a bed-and-breakfast. Then we see the magic words: *Casa Millia!* Sheelagh and Anne urge me to call up, and I am happy to oblige, but when a loud woman's voice at the other end of the line answers in *galego,* the language of Galicia, I'm in over my head after just a few words. I ask the woman repeatedly to speak slowly in Spanish, but she keeps chattering away in this regional dialect. The only thing I catch is that she rents out rooms, which I already knew. Now I'm really on edge. I pull Anne back into the telephone booth, put the phone into her hand, and say: "Here! I don't understand a single word! You do it!" Anne then does her best to negotiate this matter, all the while rolling her eyes. But this experienced British troubleshooter emerges from the telephone booth with a big smile on her face—and a room reservation! Unfortunately, Anne did not understand the crucial piece of information, namely the directions to the place, so we wander around for another good hour.

When we finally find the beautiful cottage on the mountain slope, the chubby owner, squeezed into a colorful dress, stands in front of the door with her hair freshly coiffed. Business matters are evidently dealt with by men in Galicia, so she addresses her remarks exclusively to me in her incomprehensible dialect. The only function she will allow Anne is that of interpreter. She wants to know which of the two women is my wife, and since Anne has her face all scrunched up again, I point to battered Sheelagh. The woman seems pleased with that information. I guess she assumes that I call the shots in our relationship, as is right and proper.

She offers us a room in her private residence for a ridiculously low price—that's how I understand the situation, at least. Then she decides to give us a grand tour of the house, showing us each of the lovingly restored rooms on both floors, which are all furnished with rustic antiques.

The house looks like the stage set for an American sitcom. On the lovingly polished wood floors there are valuable patchwork rugs. Large vases filled with fresh flowers complete this picture of tasteful kitsch. When we enter the spacious, luxurious kitchen, she explains the functions of the individual appliances to the women.

After the house tour, we give her the sum of money we've agreed on and, to our amazement, she hands us the house keys, says good-bye, and goes out the front door with a wave of her hand. Finally we realize that this bargain price was not for a single room but for the entire house! Fabulous. Each of us has a separate room, and there are two big bathtubs and three toilets at our disposal.

Sheelagh takes a shower, then goes to the kitchen to bake a cake and make us cocoa. Good thing the señora showed the women where to find everything! I could stay here for months; this place is heavenly. All three of us have always dreamed of a house like this! We become a "family" once again.

The bedroom windows offer a dramatic view of the Galician Mountains.

We never want to leave this place. It is just like an American sitcom with one of those inevitable happy endings. "Oh Happy Day!" would be the perfect title. Sheelagh tells us that this house looks like New Zealand.

We drink cocoa, eat cake, play parlor games, and talk, talk, talk until well into the night.

Insight of the day: Every now and then you find paradise on earth.

July 19, 2001

A Rúa

The next-to-last day! I'm barely finding any time to write. We take advantage of every minute we have together, and that takes precedence over everything else.

It was very hard for us to leave the house this morning, because this was the highlight of our time together. We lived there for one night and made the most of the few hours we had. I've felt less torn leaving apartments I've lived in for years.

The señora came by right on time to give us a proper good-bye.

While we walk along the Camino, we're rather subdued, and we take lots of pictures of one another, as though we're afraid we might soon forget our time together. We're painfully aware that we're about to say good-bye, and we keep consoling ourselves with the fact that we'll still have several days together in Santiago.

We dawdle along aimlessly on our last day before Santiago. Even Sheelagh's usual single-minded determination has given way to a certain leisureliness.

Today Sheelagh and Anne want to learn the names of German household appliances.

Toward evening we reach A Rúa, where we find a room at a beautiful farm. While we are eating dinner with a Dutch family

The end is in sight.

of five completing the pilgrimage by bicycle, I share my thoughts with the group in English. "I don't know what it is! I just don't like walking, even though I've just done nearly three hundred seventy-five miles on foot. I think the trail is great, and I'm glad to have met you, but the act of walking does not give me the slightest pleasure. And it always hurts!"

The Dutch family finds what I'm saying hilarious, and they all have a good long laugh. When the father finally quiets down, he says, "What? You've walked nearly three hundred seventy-five miles, and you still don't enjoy it?"

I say, "Yes, I'm leveling with you! I simply want to get to Santiago! That was my goal!"

The Dutchman looks at me skeptically and says, "I wonder what kind of reception Santiago will offer you. I've hiked the Camino twice, and one thing I've learned is that in Santiago, everyone gets the reception he deserves. I hope you will be well received there!"

The three of us look at one another in silence. What kind of reception could possibly await us? Surely they won't shoot at us! I've already been through that!

Insight of the day: Time is not what determines the feeling of being home.

July 20, 2001

Santiago de Compostela

The final day!

When we left A Rúa, I took a stunning picture with my disposable camera. *Bäckerblume* magazine will just have to choose my "Camino at Sunrise" as the pilgrims' photo of the year. It captures and reflects my state of mind. I can only hope that the cheap camera was able to convey some sense of the atmosphere. Up to now, every third photo has been overexposed, underexposed, or not exposed at all. Or my fat thumb has blocked the essence of the shot.

We are in high spirits. If only we could find some way to stretch out the remaining fifteen miles. The trail is almost at an end. Today! The three of us have made it. Well . . . apart from the fact that I cheated a bit at the beginning.

Today every mile is solemnly marked by a stone. People are streaming toward Santiago en masse, and many of them (including the three of us) are singing the famous French pilgrims' song, which Sheelagh learned back in elementary school:

> *Tous les matins nous prenons le chemin,*
> *Tous les matins nous allons plus loin,*
> *Jour après jour la route nous appelle,*
> *C'est la voix de Compostelle.*

Every day we take to the road,
Every day we forge ahead,
Day after day, the route calls to us,
It is the voice of Compostela.

Since it is otherwise quiet in the forest, we can even sing this song in rounds with pilgrim groups that are far ahead of and behind us. It is an absurd feeling to sing in unison with people you can't even see and will never meet. We are chiming in a mystical chorus with people who aren't there!

We keep on singing as we hike along the runway of the international airport and climb the last steep mountain, the Monte do Gozo, which looks out onto Santiago de Compostela from its summit. It lies before us, gleaming majestically in the sunshine. Our final destination manages to look both cheerful and solemn, dark and bright, and seems to comprise all kinds of unlikely contrasts.

Anne is wiped out by the hike and buys a bottle of beer at a kiosk. When she enters the church, she's still holding the beer in her hand, and I'm tempted to light up a cigarette. We've certainly gone to the dogs! What's happened to our manners?

As we near our destination from the east, I think about what the Dutch man said in A Rúa: In Santiago, everyone gets the reception he deserves.

Shortly before we reach the medieval center of town, I make out a young woman coming toward me, waving her hand. The glare of the sun makes it hard for me to recognize Lara until she is standing right in front of me. The stunning lady from Vancouver arrived here yesterday. She is proudly sporting a new dress. We celebrate with a big hug and arrange to meet the next day on the square in front of the cathedral (a place I have yet to see).

With a grand gesture, Lara points out the direction to us. "At the end of this street you'll see the way to the square!"

The three of us zoom ahead to the archway that leads to the cathedral square. Our emergence from the archway will signal the death of our status as pilgrims.

From the dark tunnel of the pilgrims' gate, we step out into the cathedral square, which is bathed in sunlight. Standing on the Plaza del Obradoiro our journey has come to an end, yet something new is about to begin, something we don't understand in the slightest. What have we gotten ourselves in for? Is this pilgrims' heaven?

A huge crowd in a festive mood awaits us. The square is cordoned off and soldiers are lined up to form an honor guard. The flags of Galicia, Spain, and Europe are waving on countless poles—the square is a veritable sea of flags. In front of the Parador, the finest hotel on the square, a long red carpet has been rolled out. A police motorcade is accompanying a big black car to the hotel's entrance. The Spanish national hymn is playing. Prime Minister José María Aznar steps out of the limousine, waves to the crowd, and walks along the carpet into the palace. *Everyone gets the reception he deserves.*

Well, it doesn't get any better than this!

Of course this parade is not meant for us, but our euphoria makes us feel as though it is. To come upon this ceremony unawares after several weeks of quiet is thrilling and bewildering all at once.

Now we want proof that we made it. Our certificates! We head straight for the pilgrims' office next to the shrine.

Hundreds of people are waiting to get their *compostelas*. In a

At our destination!

high-ceilinged, wood-paneled hall, we join the line in front of the magnificent set of windows. It feels like a Renaissance post office.

Anne is in front of me in line, and a solemn-looking gentle-man asks her, "Did you ever take a bus; was there a time when you did not hike, or when you hitchhiked?" Anne is able to say no truthfully. This whole thing is like a paperback edition of the Last Judgment. The young man casts a critical glance at her pilgrim's passport. It contains all the necessary stamps, so the man solemnly hands her the *compostela* parchment scroll after adding to it the Latin version of her name and the date.

What am I going to say when I'm asked? I will tell the truth about when and where I took a bus and the train. And I hitch-hiked, too!

It's my turn. A young woman with long black hair combed straight back thoroughly inspects the stamps for the last ninety miles in my *credencial,* and then, without so much as a single question, hands me my *compostela* with a smile. It carries this all-important statement at the end:

Dominum Joannem Petrum Kerkeling hoc sacratissimum Templum pietatis causa devote visitasse. In quorum fidem praesentes litteras, sigillo ejusdem Sanctae Ecclesiae muni-tas, ei confero. Datum Compostellae die 20 mensis Julii anno Domini 2001.

The church bells are ringing. Sweaty as we are, we run from the office straight into the mass. At the entrance to this house of worship, we kiss the foot of the stone statue of St. James. This foot has been kissed so many times over the course of centuries that it has shrunk by several sizes. After my shower, I'm going to kiss my own feet for having hiked so well and so valiantly!

The gigantic cathedral is jam-packed, and the spectacle begins. The famous Botafumeiro, an enormous censer hanging from the ceiling, dispenses thick clouds of incense that befuddle your senses. It's fastened to the ceiling by a long rope and swings through the entire nave, accompanied by dramatic organ music.

During the glorious mass, as many as a hundred newcomers are greeted: " . . . and we welcome a woman from Wellington,

CAPITULUM hujus Almae Apostolicae et Metropolitanae
Ecclesiae Compostellanae sigilli Altaris Beati Jacobi Apostoli
custos, ut omnibus Fidelibus et Peregrinis ex toto terrarum
Orbe, devotionis affectu vel voti causa, ad limina Apostoli
Nostri Hispaniarum Patroni ac Tutelaris **SANCTI JACOBI**
convenientibus, authenticas visitationis litteras expediat, omni-
bus et singulis praesentes inspecturis, notum facit. Dnum.
Joannem Petrum Kerkeling
hoc sacratissimum Templum pietatis causa devote visitasse.
In quorum fidem praesentes litteras, sigillo ejusdem Sanctae
Ecclesiae munitas, ei confero.
Datum Compostellae die _20_ mensis _Julii_
anno Dni _2001_.

Secretarius Capitularis

The *compostela*—proof that I made it

New Zealand, a woman from Liverpool, England, and a man from Düsseldorf, Germany. All three walked here from Saint Jean-Pied-de-Port in France, and have ended their pilgrimage today!"

We feel as if we're in the hereafter and are looking in on our own solemn funerals.

We stand there with flushed cheeks and heavy backpacks, tired but happy. And of course, after the ceremony we adhere to the ritual of embracing the statue of St. James that stands over his grave.

In front of the most luxurious hotel—the one that Prime Minister Aznar is staying at—we spring for a bottle of champagne. We couldn't be happier! Sheelagh surprises Anne and me by digging her deck of tacky angel cards out of her backpack. She places three cards facedown on the white tablecloth: "I've saved these for today! One for Anne, one for Hans, and one for me. I have no idea what's on them! Each of us gets to pick a card."

Anne goes first. She picks a card, gazes at it, smiles, and puts it into her pants pocket without a word. Sheelagh picks Balance. She seems to have found that! I take the remaining card. Joy! *The Joy of the Camino de Santiago.*

I have come full circle.

Anne and Sheelagh have a craving for French fries, and I slip away for some time on my own. On a side street I come across a cluttered souvenir shop, where I look for suitable gifts for my friends. When I find what I'm looking for, the saleswoman wraps the three little silver souvenirs in gift paper.

When I get back to the table on the square, I give each of them one of the packages, and keep the third. "So," I tell them, "now let's open our presents at the same time!"

They can hardly wait to find out what's inside. The gifts are silver bells with handles that are the statue of St. James. The apostle is portrayed as a pilgrim with a walking stick, scallop shell, and wide-brimmed hat. Sheelagh and Anne are clearly moved by this gesture. I tell them, "Every time one of us rings the bell, the others will sense it. We will think of one another, and picture ourselves back on the Camino."

We try out the little instruments, ringing them at the same time in the street café.

Arriving in Santiago feels like entering the Pearly Gates. Every pilgrim arrives at the same wonderful place at the end of the journey, but the reception is different for each one. Perhaps the welcome also takes its cue from mood of the newcomer?

Getting here in the winter, during a blizzard, with a cold wind whistling on your neck and facing the empty square is probably hellish. And in the foggy rain, the ornate red cathedral must seem like a forbidding haunted castle.

Still, the place remains the same.

My pilgrimage can be interpreted as a parable of my path through life. It was a difficult birth—which is literally true in my case. At the beginning of the route—and in my childhood—I had trouble hitting my stride. Until the middle of my path through life, no matter how many positive experiences I enjoyed, I experienced many twists and turns that sometimes threw me off-course. But at about the midpoint of my journey, I started moving cheerfully toward my destination. It almost seems as though the Camino has seen fit to grant me a little peek into my future. Serenity might be a goal worth pursuing!

Each individual day of hiking was structured like a microcosm of the Camino as a whole. Every detail mirrored the whole, and the whole reflected the details. Just as I found it difficult to start the pilgrimage, I typically find it difficult to get going in the morning. In the afternoon I find my rhythm, and as evening falls, I walk toward my destination feeling exhausted but tranquil and steadfast, my strength renewed.

In our Western world, which is practically devoid of spirituality, we suffer from a lack of ritual. The Camino is a ritual that offers a genuine opportunity to take up a challenge. Every one of us needs something to hold on to, but the only stability comes from letting go.

The trail is both demanding and delightful. It is a challenge and an invitation. It wears you out and drains you, then it builds you back up again completely.

It takes all your strength away, and restores it three times over. You have to walk it alone or it will not reveal its mysteries.

Those who cannot take this pilgrimage should rest assured that it is only one of an infinite number of possibilities. The Camino is not one single path but thousands, and it poses only one question to each of us: "Who are you?"

The three of us sit together on the bustling square and celebrate well into the night, savoring our own funeral feast. When the day has come to an end, Anne turns wistful, and I ask her, "So— what did the Camino de Santiago mean to you? Are you now a believer?"

She pauses for a moment, then admits with a smile, "The Camino had just one meaning for me: I have made friends with you and Sheelagh. That is what I believe in, and that is what made the whole journey worth it."

The weeklong celebration of St. James kicks off with midnight fireworks. The high point of this week is July 25, Galicia's national holiday, the *Día de Santiago*! We spend five all too brief days together in Santiago, and enjoy the hustle and bustle of the festival. We go to concerts, dance, and enjoy a crazy celebration together. I throw my worn-out hiking boots away, after taking a photograph of them.

A mere two hours after I start walking in a beautiful new pair of shoes, big blisters form on my heel. Shortly before I fly home, I get to use my blister bandages after all.

July 25 is our departure date. Ever the early riser, Sheelagh sets off at dawn to catch her flight to Madrid. We say nothing, just embrace.

In the afternoon, Anne drives me to Vigo, which is about forty miles away, in her SEAT rental car. Sitting in a car seems strange and unnatural, and it will take a few days for us to get used to life with technology. After drinking our standard five lattes in a bar, we keep our farewell as simple as possible. When Anne finally drives off, honking loudly, I feel more lonesome than I ever did at even the most strenuous part of the Camino.

I hike through the town of Vigo to get to the train station with my pack on my back and my walking stick in hand. I just need to walk a few final miles. I look quite normal for someone on the Camino, but I stand out now that I'm far from the pilgrims' path.

Tomorrow I fly home. Sitting in the train to Porto, I try to collect my thoughts about God and sum them up.

The way I see it, "God" is a unique liberating spark that fans out infinitely to foster and embrace self-realization. By contrast, those who get swept up in any group aimed at robbing us of our individuality and dousing the liberating spark wind up crushing themselves in the process.

The creator tosses us into the air and then, to our happy amazement, catches us again at just the right moment. It is like the spirited game parents play with their children. The message is: Have faith in the one who's tossing you, because he loves you and will quite unexpectedly be the one to catch you too.

And when I think back on all that has happened along the way, I realize that God kept tossing me into the air and catching me again. We encountered each other every single day.

Epilogue

I put my silver bell on my desk at home and didn't touch it for over a year. When I was a guest on a TV talk show hosted by Sandra Maischberger, one of the topics we discussed was my pilgrimage, and I had my bell with me. Sandra Maischberger asked me to ring this bell for the first time since I completed my journey.

I did so, and thought of Sheelagh and Anne, as I'd promised them. Right after the program, I listened to my voice mail, and I heard a bell ringing and Sheelagh's voice saying, "I heard the bell!"

Sheelagh's daughter Phoebe had fallen head over heels in love with a German man in Hamburg during her trip through Europe, and stayed there with him. The two of them watch TV occasionally, and she recognized her mother's bell. Her German boyfriend translated my story for her, and Phoebe went straight to the phone and called up her mother in New Zealand, and I heard Sheelagh's voice two minutes later.

The next call on my voice mail was Anne's ringing bell. "I heard the bell too! Baby Jesus is waving at you!" Sheelagh had called her up in England and roused her out of her sleep with the ringing bell. I would have loved to see Anne's scrunched-up face when she answered the phone!

to Angelo, the love of my life

About the Author

Hape Kerkeling, one of Europe's most popular comedic enter-
tainers, is the winner of the Karl Valentin Prize for Humor, the
Chatwin Award for Best Travel Book of the Year, and numerous
other prizes. *I'm Off Then,* his first book, has become a bestselling
sensation in Germany. He lives in Berlin.

About the Translator

Shelley Frisch is author of *The Lure of the Linguistic* and transla-
tor of numerous books from the German, including biographies
of Nietzsche, Einstein, and Kafka, for which she was awarded the
2007 Modern Language Association Translation Prize for a Schol-
arly Study of Literature. She lives in Princeton, New Jersey.

Camino de Santiago

La parroquia de: _Parroquia de Santa María A Real_
Obispado de: _____
Abadía de: _____
Cofradía de: _____
Asociación de: _____

Presenta a:

Hans Peter Keleng
(Nombre y apellidos)

D.N.I. _50 086 089 79_

Dirección: _____
Alemania

De la Cofradía (o Asociación) de: _____

que ha salido el día: _00_ de _Julio_ de 20_01_

de: _St Jean Pied de Port_

En peregrinación, hacia Santiago de Compostela.

a pie ☒   en bicicleta ☐   a caballo ☐

Y ha recibido, en el día de hoy, la presente Credencial de Peregrino, en la que se ruega se estampe el sello de la localidad que corresponda, para acreditar su paso. Que el Apóstol Santiago, proteja a los peregrinos en su Camino.

Cumplió la Peregrinación.

Santiago, a ___ de ___ de 20 ___

20 JUL. 2001

Certifica

FIRMA

Fecha: _15.7.01_

Fecha: _____

Teléfono y Fax 982 54 52 3
PORTOMARÍN (Lugo)   Fecha:

PARROQUIA DE S. TIRSO
PALAS DE REI (LUGO)

_17-7-0_

SELLOS

KM 88.0
CASERON

Fecha:

Taberna
la Luz
ONDE   Buen
              camino

Fecha:

PARROQUIA DE STO. TIRSO DE
DIOCESIS   DE LUGO
PALAS DE REI
OBISPO

echa:

CASA DE LOS SOMOZA
TURISMO RURAL
Tfno.: 981 50 73 72
Coto - Leboreiro
15800 MELIDE
(A Coruña)

MINISTERIO PARROQUIAL DE
SANTIAGO DE ORENTE

Fecha:

En el Camino de Santiago
O'Pino
HOTEL-RESTAURANTE
Telf. 981 511 035
RUA DE ARCA - O PINO

Fecha:

PARROQUIA DE SANTIAGO DE ARZÚA Y UNIDO LEMA

Fecha:

Fecha:

Fecha:

Fecha: